T0302149

The Circular Economy in Europe

The Circular Economy in Europe presents an overview and a critical discussion on how circularity is conceived, imagined, and enacted in current EU policy-making.

In 2013, the idea of a circular economy entered the stage of European policy-making in the efforts to reconcile environmental and economic policy objectives. In 2019 the European Commission declared in a press release that the Circular Economy Action Plan has been delivered. The level of circularity in the European economy, however, has remained the same.

Bringing together perspectives from social sciences, environmental economics and policy analysis, *The Circular Economy in Europe* provides a critical analysis of policies and promises of the next panacea for growth and sustainability. The authors provide a theoretical and empirical basis to discuss how contemporary societies conceive their need to re-organise production and consumption and explores the messy assemblage of institutions, actors, waste streams, biophysical flows, policy objectives, scientific disciplines, values, expectations, promises and aspirations involved.

This book is essential reading for all those interested in understanding how ideas about the circular economy emerged historically, how they gained traction and are used in policy processes, and what the practical challenges in implementing this policy are.

Zora Kovacic is a post-doctoral research fellow at the Centre for the Study of the Sciences and the Humanities, at the University of Bergen, Norway. Kovacic was trained in the social sciences, with a Bachelor of Arts in Economics and Development Studies from the School of Oriental and African Studies (UK) and a Masters of Science in Environmental Studies from the Autonomous University of Barcelona (Spain) and the Technical University of Hamburg-Harburg (Germany), which included ecological economics and environmental engineering. Kovacic obtained her PhD in 2015 from the Institute of Environmental Science and Technology (ICTA) of the Autonomous University of Barcelona. Guided by post-normal science, her research focuses on the challenges of uncertainty and complexity that emerge when scientific knowledge is used in policy-making. She analyses and theorizes how quantitative evidence and uncertainty are mobilised in sustainability and development policies.

Roger Strand is Professor of Philosophy of Science at the University of Bergen, Norway, originally trained in the natural sciences with additional studies in philosophy and Classical Latin. Since 1993, he has been affiliated with the Centre for the Study of the Sciences and the Humanities (Senter for vitenskapsteori, SVT), University of Bergen, where he also served as the Director in the years 2005–2011. Throughout his research career, Strand has worked on issues of methodological underdetermination in science, scientific uncertainty and complexity. This has gradually led his research into broader strands of philosophy, ethics and social research and broader issues of policy, decision-making and governance at the science-society interface. He has led numerous research projects on the ethical and societal aspects of biotechnology emerging sciences and technologies, addressing the need for more dynamic governance of science in society.

Thomas Völker is a science and technology studies (STS) scholar currently working as a policy analyst in the research department of the Austrian Science Fund. Völker is initially trained in sociology, obtaining a Bachelor's and Master's degree from the University of Vienna. In his PhD thesis he studied "futuring" practices in transdisciplinary sustainability research from an STS perspective. After finishing his PhD at the University of Vienna in 2015, Völker joined the European Commission's Joint Research Centre (JRC), where he developed his research interests towards questions about participatory decision-making at the multiple interfaces between science, policy and society. Völker has been working both in academia and policy with his research focusing on practices of knowledge production and circulation in environmental governance as well as on collective experiments with participatory democracy in policy making.

Routledge Explorations in Sustainability and Governance

Resource Accounting for Sustainability Assessment
The Nexus Between Energy, Food, Water and Land Use
Mario Giampietro, Richard J. Aspinall, Jesus Ramos-Martin, and Sandra G.F. Bukkens

Science, Philosophy and Sustainability
The End of the Cartesian Dream
Ângela Guimarães Pereira and Silvio Funtowicz

The Circular Economy in Europe

Critical Perspectives on Policies and Imaginaries

Zora Kovacic, Roger Strand and Thomas Völker

Routledge
Taylor & Francis Group
LONDON AND NEW YORK

earthscan
from Routledge

First published 2020
by Routledge
2 Park Square, Milton Park, Abingdon, Oxon OX14 4RN

and by Routledge
52 Vanderbilt Avenue, New York, NY 10017

Routledge is an imprint of the Taylor & Francis Group, an informa business

First issued in paperback 2021

British Library Cataloguing-in-Publication Data
A catalogue record for this book is available from the British Library

Library of Congress Cataloging-in-Publication Data
Names: Strand, Roger, author. | Kovacic, Zora, author. |
Völker, Thomas, author.
Title: The circular economy in Europe : critical perspectives on policies and
imaginaries / Roger Strand, Zora Kovacic and Thomas Völker.
Description: New York : Routledge, 2020. |
Series: Routledge explorations in sustainability and governance |
Includes bibliographical references and index. | Identifiers: LCCN
2019033724 (print) | LCCN 2019033725 (ebook) |
ISBN 9780367183585 (hardback) | ISBN 9780429061028 (ebook)
Subjects: LCSH: Sustainable development--Europe. |
Environmental policy--Europe.
Classification: LCC HC240.9.E5 S767 2020 (print) |
LCC HC240.9.E5 (ebook) | DDC 338.94/07--dc23
LC record available at https://lccn.loc.gov/2019033724
LC ebook record available at https://lccn.loc.gov/2019033725

ISBN: 978-0-367-18358-5 (hbk)
ISBN: 978-1-03-208535-7 (pbk)
ISBN: 978-0-429-06102-8 (ebk)

Typeset in Bembo
by Taylor & Francis Books

Contents

Illustrations

Figures

Tables

Contributors

Zora Kovacic (born 1985) holds Italian and Brazilian citizenship. She is currently a post-doctoral research fellow at the Centre for the Study of the Sciences and the Humanities, at the University of Bergen, Norway. She has previously held research positions at Stellenbosch University (2018–2019) and at the Autonomous University of Barcelona (2012–2018). Zora was trained mostly in the social sciences, with a Bachelor of Arts in Economics and Development Studies from the School of Oriental and African Studies (UK) and a Masters of Science in Environmental Studies from the Autonomous University of Barcelona (Spain) and the Technical University of Hamburg-Harburg (Germany), which included ecological economics and environmental engineering. Zora obtained her PhD in 2015 from the Institute of Environmental Science and Technology (ICTA) of the Autonomous University of Barcelona.

Guided by post-normal science, her research focuses on the challenges of uncertainty and complexity that emerge when scientific knowledge is used in policy-making. She analyses and theorizes how quantitative evidence and uncertainty are mobilised in sustainability and development policies. Zora has contributed to science advice mechanisms, including a Scoping Workshop devoted to the European Commission Group of Chief Scientific Advisors on "Making sense of science under conditions of complexity and uncertainty" in 2018, training courses directed at policy officers of the National Secretariat for Planning and Development of Ecuador in 2014 and 2015, and policy advice to the municipal government of Stellenbosch in South Africa. Zora has also been part of the scientific committee of the bi-annual post-normal science symposia since 2015. She has collaborated in the research projects EPINET (FP7), MAGIC (H2020), NETEP (Marie Curie IRSES), PARTICIPIA (ACP-EU EDULINK II), and Co-Dec (LIRA2020).

Zora's main research interest is in the development of the study of complexity and science for policy. Complexity matters for informing policy because in the context of complexity, science cannot give one representation, advice, or option. Zora encountered this challenge in the first case study she worked on for her PhD: she was studying water governance, and the different representations of water used to inform policy seemed to talk past each other. On the one hand, she encountered the narrative of water efficiency, which referred to water use in agriculture, and on the other hand, she encountered the water scarcity narrative through which conservation policies were formulated for the main water bodies. These two representations were used both to promote and restrict the use of water, albeit in very different policy areas. Zora has thus used complexity theory as a means to think through scientific controversies, policy inconsistencies and uncertainty in governance. Her doctoral dissertation, supervised by Mario Giampietro, developed a method of quality assessment of quantitative evidence based on complexity theory. She applied this approach to the study of indicators used in financial and economic policy, water governance, and to the assessment of new and emerging technology in energy policy. Her work has been greatly inspired by collaborations with Mario Giampietro, Louisa Jane Di Felice and Timothy Allen on complexity and social metabolism, Roger Strand on governance and reflexivity, Silvio Funtowicz and Jerome Ravetz on post-normal science, Violeta Cabello on deliberative governance mechanisms and transdisciplinary practices, Josephine Musango and Suzanne Smit on development and the informal economy.

Interest in complexity led to the work of Charles Pierce on semiotics. Semiotics shows that the knowledge needed for governance must be validated by experience. This insight has important implications for the use of science for governance. It means that what matters is not only different types of knowledge, but also how knowledge is acquired. Zora has worked with public policy both in the European context and in the Global South, especially in Brazil, Ecuador and South Africa. These diverse experiences have created an awareness of the importance of validating knowledge through practice in the science-policy interface. In a consortium meeting of the MAGIC project, the coordinator Mario Giampietro talked about cyborg salmons – that is, salmons bred from aquaculture, as opposed to salmons that evolved from natural selection, through a semiotic process of millions of years. Cyborg salmons are created out of abstract ideals, not of validated practices. The meeting produced a yearning not to be a cyborg, or an automaton, as individuals and as researchers, who use ready-made thoughts and give quick-fix advice to policy-makers. This means overcoming the urge to speak not only scientific "truths," but also of giving solutions, of letting a naïve wish to do good overtake common sense.

In this book, some of these ideas are taken up with the aim or arriving at a conciliation through humble criticism. Conciliation and care are not to be confused with the oppression of one's perspective in the name of the common good. In this book we will try to express our concerns, doubts and uncertainties with humility and respect. The yearning not to be an automaton resonates with Zora's interest and practice of Logosophy, which offers teachings that lead oneself to self-knowledge and self-improvement through a process of conscious evolution. A basic insight in Logosophy is that in order to become who one wants to be, one must let go of what one is. It is impossible to go somewhere, while at the same time expecting to stay in the same place. Applied to the circular economy, this means that becoming something else, sustainable for example, requires letting go of what is now unsustainable. Rather than making current practices circular, a reflection is needed about the identity, practices and culture that may need to be renewed.

Roger Strand is a Norwegian citizen (born 1968) and Professor of Philosophy of Science at the University of Bergen, Norway. Roger was trained in the natural sciences (obtaining the degrees of *cand. scient.* in 1992 and *dr. scient.* in 1998) with additional studies in philosophy and Classical Latin. Since 1993, he has been affiliated with the Centre for the Study of the Sciences and the Humanities *(Senter for vitenskapsteori,* SVT), University of Bergen, where he also served as the Director in the years 2005–11. Since 2013, he has also been associated with the Centre for Cancer Biomarkers at the same university, leading a research programme on the ethical and societal aspects of cancer research. Roger has been a Visiting Professor at the Autonomous University of Barcelona and is currently Adjunct Professor at the Norwegian University of Science and Technology in Trondheim with a special mandate of implementing the principle of Responsible Research and Innovation within the Centre for Digital Life Norway, a virtual research centre for systems biology and computational biotechnology.

Throughout his research career, Roger has worked on issues of methodological underdetermination in science, scientific uncertainty and complexity. This has gradually led his research into broader strands of philosophy, ethics and social research and broader issues of policy, decision-making and governance at the science-society interface. He has led numerous research projects on the ethical and societal aspects of biotechnology, nanotechnology and emerging science and technology, including the two EU-funded projects TECHNOLIFE and EPINET that both addressed the need for more dynamic governance of science in society. These projects were coordinated in close collaboration with his colleague Kjetil Rommetveit. Within higher education, Roger has called for interdisciplinarity, reflexivity and responsibility, including in his work as member of the Norwegian *Bildung* Committee that initiated a broad public debate about the role of education and academia in contemporary Norwegian society. In Norwegian and European research policy, he is mainly known for his contributions to the development of the policy concept of Responsible Research and Innovation, RRI. In the EU's 8th framework programme for research and innovation, the so-called Horizon 2020, Roger leads the contributions by the University of Bergen in the projects MAGIC, HEIRRI, SUPERMoRRI and TRANSFORM, the three latter being projects that work to develop RRI in education, research, innovation and policy. In 2014, Roger chaired a European Commission Expert Group on Indicators for RRI. In 2015, he and his colleague Matthias Kaiser were commissioned by the bioethics committee of the Council of Europe for a report on the ethical issues raised by emerging sciences and technologies. Strand served as a member of the National Research Ethics Committee for Science and Technology in Norway (2006–2013).

For more than 20 years, Roger has been interested in the development of complexity theory and the concept of post-normal science, discussing and working with internationally leading researchers in the field, notably Silvio Funtowicz, Jerome Ravetz, Ragnar Fjelland, Dominique Chu, Ângela Guimarães Pereira, Zora Kovacic, Mario Giampietro and Andrea Saltelli. Most of this work has involved the close collaboration between Strand's home institution SVT, the Institute of Environmental Science and Technology at the Autonomous University of Barcelona and the European Commission-Joint Research Centre at Ispra in Italy. Zora Kovacic, Silvio Funtowicz and Roger Strand form the Board of Directors of the European Centre for Governance in Complexity, a micro-NGO dedicated to develop research and public debate on such issues. Roger's original point of departure was epistemological. His doctoral dissertation in biochemistry studied the so-called "in vivo-in vitro" problem, that is, that almost all of biomedicine tries to develop our understanding of living, intact, unperturbed organisms by use of methods that invariably kill, dissect, partition or at least perturb the organisms. How can knowledge about the living – in vivo – be constructed out of laboratory experiments in vitro –that is "in glass"? The epistemological studies led into science and technology studies (STS) and research on the social and political character of scientific knowledge while also sparking an interest in complexity in the tradition of Robert Rosen and relational biology. Out of all of this, an image of scientific knowledge emerged that showed the complex relationships between model and system, knowledge and action, facts and values, science and politics, and ultimately nature and culture. Science does so much more than creating maps of the world. Fundamentally it also changes the terrain, through technology but also by changing how humans think, speak and act. While this insight has been developed and consolidated within STS since at least the 1970s, it is almost absent still in research policy or any other field of policy or governance as the third decade of the twenty-first century is approaching. Especially under the heading of post-normal science, a lot of Roger's policy-related efforts have been dedicated to find ways of introducing such post-empiricist insights and norms and practices of reflexivity into the world of policy and governance.

It seems fair to say that these efforts have not been crowned with considerable success, notwithstanding a few notable exceptions. The present book will introduce concepts such as uncomfortable knowledge and socially constructed ignorance. Since 2018, Roger has directed his interest into why the task of introducing thoughts of reflexivity and complexity is so hard. In part, there is a need to better understand how the institutions of governance work and what assumptions they make and need to make. The EU research project MAGIC, www.magic-nexus.eu, of which the present volume is a part, has advanced this understanding and paved a way forward through the approach of quantitative story-telling. In part, however, the reflexive curiosity also needs to be directed back to the complexity theorists and post-normal science activists such as the author himself. Roger is currently working with renewed inspiration from ancient Chinese philosophy in

Daoist tradition as well as the later Zen Buddhist writings, as well as from oriental practices such as kundalini yoga and kyokushin karate, in which he holds a black (Shodan) belt. In the practices of yoga and martial arts, as well as in their philosophical counterparts, there is the understanding that change for the better calls for a balance between push and pull, between giving and receiving, and between intention and the willingness to let go of one's own plans and one's own ego. When STS and post-normal science have been relegated to the dead position of uncomfortable knowledge, it may be that Roger and his colleagues have been unaware of their own Western action bias. Roger's contributions to this volume are his first attempts towards a theory of policy and governance that incorporates a higher degree of spiritual awareness; a theory of governance in the Dao.

Thomas Völker (born 1982) is an Austrian science and technology studies (STS) scholar currently working as a policy analyst in the research department of the Austrian Science Fund. Thomas previously held positions at the European Commission's Joint Research Centre in Ispra (2016–2018), the University of Klagenfurt (2015) and the University of Vienna (2009–2014). He was a visiting scholar at the RWTH Aachen's VDI Chair of Futures Studies from 2013 to 2014, finishing his PhD thesis after being awarded a Marietta-Blau grant. Since 2018 he is also associated with the Centre for the Study of the Sciences and the Humanities (SVT) of the University of Bergen.

Thomas' research circles around three broader topics: the ongoing co-production of technoscientific and societal orderings, new ways of governing technoscience in more participatory ways and practices of technoscientific future-making together with the ongoing negotiation of collectively shared ideas about desirable futures. He has been developing these broader interests within two main areas during the last years: one is the analysis of engagement initiatives designed and conducted at the science-policy interfaces of the European Commission. The other involves research on environmental governance, indicator politics and the role of collective imagination in Circular Economy policies.

Initially, Thomas set out to become a world-renowned bass player, but switched to a career in sociology very soon due to an unfortunate lack of musical talent. He is trained as a sociologist and in his Masters thesis applied a cultural studies approach to look into practices of valuation, asking how ideas about "quality" are formed in evaluative discourses of music magazines. Finally leaving music behind, Thomas was then confronted with STS and decided to dive deeper into that field. This decision led him to the Department of Science and Technology Studies of the University of Vienna. At this department he held a position as PhD candidate in a project called "Transdisciplinarity as Culture and Practice". In close collaboration with Ulrike Felt he wrote a thesis on practices of "futuring" in transdisciplinary sustainability research. The thesis explores collectively held imaginations of science-society relations in sustainability research in Austria. It was during the time of writing this dissertation when Thomas' research started to focus more on questions of collective imagination and the governance of science and technology as well as on issues related to sustainability policy. This interest was deepened at the RWTH Aachen, where Thomas worked with the group of Daniel Barben that focused more on the technology and innovation side of STS. After his time in Aachen, Thomas worked with Martina Merz at the Department of Science Communication and Higher Education Research in Vienna, focusing on issues of quality again. This time around it was about how "quality" as a category is constructed and applied in academia. This work focused on the interplay between practices and cultures of the humanities, natural and social sciences from a perspective interested in the formation and stabilisation of epistemic cultures.

Finally, at the Joint Research Centre Thomas gained experience in working in policy-oriented research at an institution that understands itself as situated at the "science-policy interface". In his time at the JRC Thomas worked with Ângela Guimarães Pereira in interdisciplinary project teams and focused on policy analysis, on modes of engagement and participation and on questions about the role quantification in policy-making. Importantly, Thomas has been involved in work that aims at fostering more engagement-oriented and participatory processes within EU institutions. This has been done through a number of collaborations with both colleagues from other JRC departments and with policy makers from European Commission policy DGs. Additionally, Thomas has contributed to a number of workshops and designed and organized citizen engagement trainings for the European Commission. It was especially in these workshops and trainings that Thomas realized how important it is to go beyond academic rigour (which he enjoys immensely) and to "translate" (in the sense of John Law) ideas and concepts to various different situations.

Working at the JRC, Thomas also joined the H2020-funded research project MAGIC. In this project he worked with Zora Kovacic, Roger Strand and Mario Giampietro on Circular Economy policy, asking for the multiple meanings and futures of 'circularity'. This research about the ongoing assemblage and stabilization of imaginations of circularity and the materialities that are co-emergent with them led to the idea of writing the book your reading at this moment. A particular focus of this work is to understand indicator development at the EC as a site of collective imagination.

A second project Thomas worked on with Ângela Guimarães Pereira addresses practices and models of engagement and participation at the Joint Research Centre, using a co-productionist approach to participation and what Chilvers and Kearnes call 'ecologies of participation'. This research takes an initiative of the JRC called ENGAGE, which is an attempt to bring together and consolidate various ongoing initiatives on citizen engagement, as a case for studying institutional understandings and negotiations of participatory governance in a European policy context. This is particularly fascinating since the JRC provides a unique site for conducting and studying engagement experiments at the science-policy interface.

This work ties into Thomas' intellectual trajectory in that it allows him to focus on practices of knowledge production and circulation in environmental governance as well as on collective experiments with participatory democracy at the European Commission.

While Thomas has been working on these questions for quite some time now, there is still some residual interest in pop-cultural pleasures left. He recently co-wrote a paper on the role of science fiction novels in Big Data discussions. And, just so this story can come full circle, he is still playing the bass.

Acknowledgements

This book would not have been possible without the continued help and support from our colleagues as well as the European institutions that we write about in this book. The work leading to this book was performed as part of the project MAGIC. This project has received funding from the European Union's Horizon2020 Research and Innovation Programme under grant agreement No 689669. We are obliged to clarify that the present work reflects only the authors' view and the Funding Agency cannot be held responsible for any use that may be made of the information it contains. Furthermore, numerous civil servants and policy-makers, within as outside of European Union institutions, have made themselves available for research interviews and other inquiries. Without their time and generosity, this book would have been impossible. The University of Bergen is acknowledged for its generous financial support in the publication of this book. We are also deeply grateful to all our colleagues in the MAGIC project for their valuable inputs and support throughout. We cannot name all but would like to mention some of them: First of all, our project coordinator, collaborator and mentor Mario Giampietro, for teaching us what we know about ecological economics, giving us the opportunity to undertake this case study and finally, as the Series Editor, welcoming our contribution to the Routledge book series "Explorations on Sustainability and Governance". We would also like to thank MAGIC colleagues Sandra Bukkens, Maddalena Ripa, Silvio Funtowicz and Kirsty Blackstock for all their help and support with this book, and our colleague Irmelin W. Nilsen who prepared the artwork and sorted out hundreds if not thousands of small and big issues in the final hectic phase of preparing the manuscript. Lorenzo Benini and Gernot Rieder were so immensely kind to read and comment drafts. And finally, we thank the publisher and above all Julia Pollacco at Routledge who provided invaluable support and encouragement throughout this project.

Preface

This book is different and a pleasure to read. It uses the wisdom of oriental philosophy to stimulate a reflection on the surge of the concept of circular economy in the sustainability debate. According to the proposed frame, "circular economy" is a *name* that is used by us to deal with the TAO. To bring this point home, in Chapter 4 the authors use a different version of this name "*dflkjdrl haqwnmz*" (the translation of "circular economy" into a fictitious language). This helps the reader focus on the meaning and on the purposes associated with the use of such a term. It is a worthwhile strategy: in oriental philosophy, in fact, there is always a yin-yang tension associated with the meaning of every new name. This tension is generated by the combined consideration of *who* introduced it, *why* it was introduced, *how* it is used and *what* the consequences of its use are. As such, the introduction of the term "circular economy" in the sustainability discussion cannot be considered to be either "good" or bad". Rather, this name can be used as a clue to better understand not only the "external world" that western science and technology want to fix, but also *us* – i.e. the *who*, the *why* and the *how* of those that use the name "circular economy". Importantly, the name "us" refers to an object of study that western science and technology tend to neglect.

What is the novelty of the term "circular economy" and what type of yin-yang tension does it generate? The term "circular economy" represents a good novelty, because for the first time both orthodox neo-classical economists and the establishment officially acknowledge that the economic process needs physical inputs, such as energy and materials, and generates wastes and emissions – represented by the flows that have to be circularized. On the other hand, the name "circular economy" is used to indicate a mission. It suggests that the current need of interacting with and depending on nature is an inconvenient aspect of the existing economy. That is, the circular economy admits the existence of a nature with which we are still, temporarily, forced to interact, but the adjective "circular" affirms the total conviction that very soon technical innovations, human ingenuity and the invisible hands of the market, in the form of a new business model, will finally get us out of this inconvenient situation. Put in another way, if the concept of circular economy is a welcome novelty because it shows the understanding that the actual linear economic model is not sustainable (it is not compatible with the work of nature required to stabilize our life support system), on the other hand it is a worrisome novelty because it shows a serious lack of understanding of the biophysical roots of the economic process. It shows good will, but good will can become dangerous if accompanied by ignorance.

The complexity of the process associated with the generation and use of names guarantees that the story to be told about this fascinating name does not end here. Assuming that the name "circular economy" can be considered by some critics as a new edition of the new invisible clothes of EU sustainability policies, the book questions whether crying that "the Emperor has no clothes" is a good thing to do. This question points at the delicate relationship between science and society. Those worried by the fact that "circular economy" represents the last outfit of cornucopians trying once again to sell a perpetual growth machine would definitely go for the cry. However, this criticism does not consider that this name charged of hubris – i.e. the Cartesian dream of prediction and control given by the combination of science, technology and the market – may represent a powerful Trojan horse forcing institutions to finally include biophysical aspects into the discussion of sustainability. When moving from the description of a socio-technical imaginary based on economic narratives generated by a combination of ingenuity and invisible hands to the actual measurement of visible plastic bags floating in the sea or tons of CO_2 emissions flying into the atmosphere, we will be forced to add feedback received by experience in the framing of sustainability issues. After giving legitimacy to the use of other names such as "plastic bags", "soil", "biodiversity", and "emissions" in circular economy narratives, we will have a new source of legitimized information to be included in the master narratives about economic growth that will allow us to check the plausibility of the proposed socio-technical imaginaries.

But the book provides a deeper reflection with respect to this point. What if the need of a common ideal, a shared illusion – the invisible clothes of EU sustainability – is essential for the unity of the social fabric of a fragile construction such as the EU, especially when going through difficult times? By providing hope – i.e. the simple denial of pending troubles – we can allow society to remain functional while finding solutions. This reflection is essential for discussions of sustainability: it is about the meaning that should be given to the name "us". Who is us? How much do we want to change our identity in order to become more sustainable? This question brings us back to the wisdom of oriental philosophy. In the relation between the TAO and the names, names have to be continuously changed. For example, from the use of the name *circular economy* (a new business model) we could move to the use of the name *sustainable production and consumption* (a new combination of social practices). This is a different name in which it is easier to include *us* in the analysis. Personally, I am sceptical of the strategy of continuing to praise the invisible clothes of the EU emperor. In the existing situation, this will translate in endorsing a policy of doing "more of the same" – i.e. investing more of the scarcer resources in socio-technical imaginaries, whose plausibility is dubious. But I have to admit that the willingness to take part in the emperor's illusion depends a lot on whether you are living at court.

If you want to reflect on the issue of sustainability through a new, informed and thought-provoking lens, this is a book worth reading.

Mario Giampietro

Part I

Circular economy as a policy concept

1 Introduction

The sixteenth century map

The first chapter introduces the reader to the policy concept of the circular economy and provides them with a first understanding of the structure of the argument in the book. Both for stylistic and methodological reasons, we do so by introducing the metaphor of "the sixteenth century map". Sixteenth century maps were intended to be accurate representations of the world but not from "the view from nowhere". The ideas, dreams and fears of the authors of these maps were ubiquitously present in the maps, for instance in the shapes of monsters and unicorns. What is known and thought about the circular economy so far indeed resembles a sixteenth century map, in which ad hoc detailed information is combined with imprecise notions of circularity. Repeatedly, the book will return to this metaphor, critically discussing the implications of navigating by such a map. Chapter 1 takes up the question "What is the circular economy?" and shows that it might actually be a lot of things at the same time while also being different things in different places. The chapter also introduces the structure of the book and briefly describes each chapter that follows.

Has the circular economy been delivered?

On the 2nd December 2015, the European Commission – the executive power of the European Union – issued a press release with the title "Closing the loop: Commission adopts ambitious new Circular Economy Package to boost competitiveness, create jobs and generate sustainable growth" (European Commission, 2015b). The press release emphasised the high ambitions and broad scope of this new policy initiative: "The Package has broken down silos in the Commission and contributes to broad political priorities by tackling climate change and the environment while boosting job creation, economic growth, investment and social fairness".

Three and a half years later, on the 4 March 2019, the European Commission released news on the results of the 2015 initiative:

> Three years after adoption, the Circular Economy Action Plan can be considered fully completed. Its 54 actions have now been delivered or are being implemented. According to the findings of the report, implementing

the Circular Economy Action Plan has accelerated the transition towards a circular economy in Europe, which in turn has helped putting the EU back on a path of job creation.

(European Commission, 2019)

Figure 1.1 is a facsimile of the news release, with its title "Commission delivers on Circular Economy Action Plan".

This book was written during the period January–July 2019, by Zora Kovacic, Thomas Völker and Roger Strand, three researchers who worked and lived in Europe. Did we experience that we now lived within a circular economy, as indicated by the news from the European Commission? Not at all. Europe of 2019 was quite similar to Europe of 2010 or 2000, namely a modern society characterised by very high and clearly unsustainable levels of consumption of natural resources. During the following chapters, the readers of this

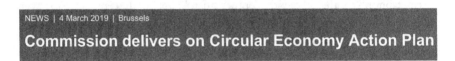

Commission delivers on Circular Economy Action Plan

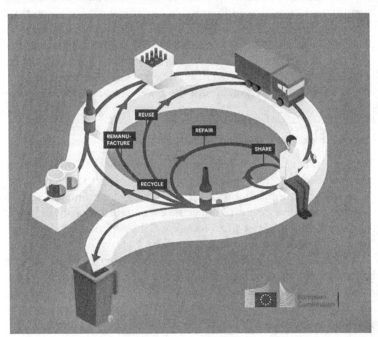

All 54 actions under the Circular Economy Action Plan launched in 2015 have now been delivered

Figure 1.1 Facsimile of European Commission press release on the Circular Economy Action Plan, dated 4 March, 2019

book will have ample opportunities to learn that the economic system of modern industrial societies is not circular, cannot be circular and is not on the way of becoming circular in the sense that natural resources are used again and again and there is no need for extraction from Nature anymore. We shall see later that it is by no means trivial to define or measure the degree of circularity of the economy. By the relevant EU institutions' own measures, however, the increase has been measured in decimals – from 11.0% to 11.7% and perhaps 12%. Later chapters will enter into the details.

How should one understand, then, statements such as those above, from the European Commission? Cynics in the world of social science as well as in the real world outside of academia would tend to explain the statements rather than understanding them. They might explain them in terms of the interests of the actors who delivered the statements. Press officers might feel the need to please and comply with the civil servants and politicians responsible for the policies, and the latter might feel the need to boast about good results in order to strengthen their position in institutional logics and hierarchies and towards the electorate. While such explanations may be informative, the problem with them is that we still do not understand the statements, that is, unless we dismiss them as being expressions of bad faith. In our work with the circular economy, however, we never observed bad faith. Most of the time, the very opposite was the case. In numerous conversations and discussion about the policies related to the circular economy we encountered highly committed and intelligent individuals who were sincerely devoted to developing a more sustainable future Europe. Accordingly, our research challenge became one of not only elucidating the social structures that enabled and shaped the policy discourse of the circular economy in Europe. It also involved a hermeneutic task of getting a sense of what a reasonable, knowledgeable, well-intended European civil servant might mean if he claimed that the circular economy had been delivered. As an author team, the three of us are a highly interdisciplinary crowd both between ourselves and within each individual, having been trained in and worked in and with fields as different as economics, environmental social science, science and technology studies (STS), biomedicine, philosophy of science, ethics, environmental philosophy and more, fields that have very different approaches to research and the investigation of statements and states of affairs. To us and our academic curiosity, the circular economy has been a gold mine, a Pandora's box of strong and contradictory claims about the economy and the environment and what ought to be done with the two. Part of our hermeneutic approach has been to ask a question that we learned from our mentor and colleague, Silvio Funtowicz, one of the founders of post-normal science (to be explained in later chapters): In what kind of world would this statement make perfect sense? What can we learn about the meanings, policies and imaginaries of the circular economy by regarding them as being uttered in meaning-making contexts? In this book, we shall pay visits to several such contexts, political as well as scientific ones, contemporary as well as historical, and on different sides of the political spectrum and the various cultures in the world of science. At the same time, within the multiplicities of systems, meanings and voices, we have come to regard the topic of the circular economy as important if not key to understand what many would regard as the central challenge of our time: How do we (Europeans) care for our human needs and our social and economic systems without destroying or degrading the natural environment that ultimately provides us with the basis for our life and our social and economic activities?

The sixteenth century map

What is the circular economy, then? The answer is anything but straightforward. The book will revolve around three main ideas: the circular economy is a policy in the making, it is an imaginary about the future, and it is far removed from what is known about the economic process in biophysical terms. Throughout the book, we will analyse many definitions, and focus on how the concept has evolved in the European policy context. As a starting definition, the circular economy is an alternative to the linear economy, in which natural resources are extracted, used and discarded. Circularity involves recycling, increasing product durability, creating repair and restore cultures, sharing economies, and many more ideas. Natural resources enter the economy and then are re-used for as long as possible, reducing both the need for resources, and waste and emissions. This general definition, however, refers to a blurred picture: many of the concepts and ideas that compose the circular economy are not well defined, and some are in contradiction with each other. The circular economy is best understood as an assembly of many different ideas and initiatives.

The difficulty of generating a well-defined picture of the circular economy can be partially explained by the fact that the process of defining the circular economy is still on going and partially by the complexity of what is to be governed. One of the main ideas of the circular economy is to reduce waste. Yet, there are many different ways of accounting for waste that make it hard to know how much waste is produced in Europe and how much is, and could be, recycled. Waste is accounted both by source, that is, classified as municipal waste, industrial waste, construction waste, agricultural waste, and by stream, that is, plastic waste, metal waste, food waste, wastewater, etc. These two accounting methods overlap, as for example, municipal waste includes part of plastic waste. Overlaps make it difficult to identify double accounting and gaps. The difficulty in accounting for waste is well recognised, and the European Commission has increased its effort to close some data gaps, as for example regarding food waste. Policy, however, does not stand still waiting for data to be produced. Metaphorically, we may say that the European Commission is navigating with a sixteenth century map as its reference.

The sixteenth century map is a metaphor used by the Ellen MacArthur Foundation in its 2013 report, in which the Foundation estimates the economic benefits of the circular economy for the European Union. The report, however, cautiously remarks that "What came out clearly resembles a 16th century map more than an exact account of the complete economic benefits" (Ellen MacArthur Foundation, 2013: 6). This is a fascinating metaphor to be used in such a report. Maps, as they are usually understood, are intended to be representations of the world, aiming to be as accurate as possible. As such they give information about the relative position of things, distances between different points and are thus useful tools for navigation. Furthermore, they define spatial boundaries, delimit particular areas and demarcate them from others. In doing so maps also create spatial classifications as for example in maps depicting waste production or maps about circular economy initiatives. On the other hand, maps can contribute to a shared sense of belonging as for instance maps depicting the boundaries of sovereign nation states do. This kind of map is closely tied to censuses and both cultural technologies co-emerged with bureaucratic modes of governance. In addition, maps can show historical changes over times. All of these different features of maps make them ideal instruments to lend authority and legitimacy to decision makers. Consequentially, maps as sources of authoritative state power can be and have been contested. This is happening for example recently in DIY mapping activities, in which public maps depicting for example oil spill after disasters are challenged. The stories told in sixteenth century maps, however, are slightly different and less about accuracy and state power.

An example of sixteenth century maps can be seen in Figure 1.2. These maps were not intended to be "the view from nowhere". The ideas, dreams and fears of the authors were ubiquitously present in the maps, for instance in the shapes of monsters and unicorns. We find this metaphor to be very fitting to the circular economy, in which the dreams of economic growth and fears of environmental catastrophes of its promoters, rather than a precise map, provide the rationale for the support of this concept.

Both the hopes and the knowledge gaps are evident in EU regulation. For instance, in the amendment of the waste directive, focus is put on municipal solid waste, even though this source of waste accounts for at most 10% of total waste. Policies focus on municipal solid waste, because this type of waste is accounted for in statistics and is easier to monitor than industrial waste, which may be traded between countries. The lack of reliable information on the remaining 90% of waste is not seen as a problem. Rather than considering the different challenges associated with different sources of waste, potential success in the management of municipal solid waste is seen as a proxy for success elsewhere.

> Municipal waste constitutes approximately between 7 and 10% of the total waste generated in the Union; however, this waste stream is amongst the most complex ones to manage, and the way it is managed generally gives a good indication of the quality of the overall waste management system in a country.
> (European Commission, 2015a)

The consequence of navigating by a sixteenth century map is that the good intentions behind the circular economy may result in contradictory policies.

Figure 1.2 The sixteenth century map

Source: https://commons.wikimedia.org/wiki/File:Carta_Marina.jpeg

For instance, non-recyclable waste may be used in incinerators to produce electricity, a loop called waste-to-energy. Incineration, however, requires a minimum input of waste to function determined by its technical specifications, which make the technology incompatible with varying quantities and qualities of waste, and economically unviable for sporadic use which depends on waste that cannot be used otherwise. Incineration, in other words, provides an incentive to avoid recycling (Finnveden & Ekvall, 1998; Morris, 1996). This tension is recognised in European policy, which refers to incineration as an option for non-recyclable waste (European Commission, 2017).

The difficulties associated with the definition of the circular economy and with contradictory policies will bring us to a discussion of the challenges of complexity and uncertainty for governance. In the final part of the book, we will consider whether it is possible to have a complete map that guides policy making, or whether a twenty-first century map is better understood as guidelines through the difficult debates, controversies, the disagreements in values and the high stakes involved in ambitious projects that aim to restructure the economy.

Part I: The circular economy as a policy concept

As it often happens with policy proposals in the European Union, the concepts used are not precisely defined, different member states have different stakes in the circular economy and different visions of what the circular economy should be. We will return to this question in all the chapters (1–4) of Part I, to understand how different the ideas of what the circular economy is, or should be, are presented and influence each other.

As part of the empirical material for this book, we conducted research interviews with policy officers in the Directorate General for the Environment, the Directorate General for Growth, and the European Environment Agency, and we organised: i) a focus group (June 2017) with representatives of the Directorate General for the Environment, the Directorate General for Growth, the Directorate General for Agriculture and the Directorate General for Energy, and two workshops; ii) one hosted by the Joint Research Centre at Ispra, Italy (February 2018); and iii) one by the European Environment Agency in Copenhagen, Denmark, (May 2018). The two workshops had representatives from the Directorate General for the Environment, the Directorate General for Agriculture, and from the environmental agencies of member states of the European Union.

We combine the insights gained from the conversations we had with policy officers during interviews and workshops, with text analysis of documents related to the policy development of the circular economy, including official communications of the European Commission, staff working documents and implementation reports made publicly available by the Commission, and reports written in support of circular economy policies, such as the Ellen MacArthur Foundation publications.

In Chapter 2, we review the academic debates from which the circular economy emerged and present this concept as a new iteration of the tension between planetary boundaries and economic growth. We will show that the theoretical bases of the circular economy are in tension: according to some ecological economists, the economy is an entropic process that is linear by definition. The circular economy is a theoretical impossibility, from this point of view. From the point of view of industrial ecology and business models, the circular economy is a guiding principle for designing new products, production processes and services.

In Chapter 3, we trace the development of the circular economy policy in the European Union. The Ellen MacArthur Foundation played an important role in mainstreaming the concept in European policy. The policy has later evolved in accordance to the political priorities of the European Commission, and is characterised by caution, moderation, it is presented as a realistic goal, while at the same time ambitious in economic terms, and requiring a systemic change. The multiplicity of, sometimes contradictory, adjectives used to define the circular economy speaks to the multiple actors and stakes that influence this policy. The analysis of the policy development is more telling of the political landscape of the European Union than of what the circular economy is supposed to achieve as a policy.

From both the academic and the policy perspectives, we find that it is easier to say what the circular economy is not, than to say what it is. For this reason, in Chapter 4 we set aside the concept of circular economy and refer to *dflkjdrl haqwnmz*, a fictive term we use as a rhetorical device to move the discussion away from the definitions and contradictions of the circular economy. Our interest in this book is the circular economy as a policy concept. We do not aim at giving any ultimate definition. Rather, we are interested in understanding why such an ambiguous and contested concept has become so successful in European policy and politics. What does the idea of a circular economy offer to policy-makers? Why is it gaining ground in the European context? Which types of negotiations does it enable and which interests does it conceal?

Part II: Critical perspectives

In the second part of the book (Chapters 5–8), we turn to the criticisms of the circular economy.

In Chapter 5, we return to the academic debate and the disagreement about the (im)possibility of the economy being circular. We revisit this debate from an epistemological perspective, enquiring about the arguments and knowledge base mobilised by each side of the debate. What can be learned by taking the argument of the economy as an entropic process seriously? What can be learned by taking the techno-optimist argument seriously? Both sides may be interpreted as agreeing on the fact that the current economic model in unsustainable and existing technology cannot solve the sustainability question. Can current impossibilities be overcome in the future?

In order to answer this question, in Chapter 6 we analyse the imaginative resources that are being mobilised to build the circular economy policy. We use the analytical concept of sociotechnical imaginaries (Jasanoff & Kim, 2009; 2015) to assess how ideas about the future are articulated, which role technology is supposed to play in these imagined futures, and to critically assess what type of work the circular economy imaginary is doing in the present.

In Chapter 7, we ask how the circular economy is being implemented in practice. An important strategy for the implementation of the circular economy policy through to 2019 has been the development of indicators to measure material throughput and circularity. We analyse the role of indicators in enacting a particular model of governing based on accounting, reporting and monitoring. We show how indicators and technocratic/bureaucratic modes of governance are co-produced.

In the final chapter of this section, we turn to the question of who is making the circular economy. We present the circular economy policy as a nexus policy, which reflects the wish for cooperation and mutually beneficial policy solutions that characterises the European Commission and European Union in a time of crisis of the European project. We argue that the circular economy helps understand what is at stake in European policy, rather than offer a solution to practical problems. Because the stakes are high, the circular economy is framed as a win-win policy, and invites an apparent consensus which makes criticism difficult to voice, and all the more necessary.

Part III: The future of change

In the third and final part of the book (Chapters 9–11), we take a more philosophical turn and reflect on the implications of the criticisms raised, of the uncertainties surrounding the circular economy and of complexity for governing for change. This book does not aim to speak truth to power, and we do not claim to know the truth about the circular economy. We do have serious concerns, though, about the scientific legitimacy of the circular economy, and we will try to channel those into recommendations going forward, reflecting more on the *way* than on concrete suggestions of what should be done.

Chapter 9 relates the criticisms articulated in the book to the wider debate between "stop" and "go" narratives. We will call this grand narratives Geos and Bios, one focusing on limits and the need to stay within those boundaries, and the other focusing on progress and growth. The criticism of the circular economy easily falls within a "stop" narrative, which does not say what should be done, and just says that what is being attempted is wrong. We raise the point that blaming policy makers for doing something that does not work (according to the critics) is an unfair criticism. We are also worried, however, about the action imperative, or solution-ism, that characterises a lot of policy making. We thus wonder, is the European Union a system in crisis that tries to solve problems because it does not want to recognise that it is coming to an end? Or is the European project not coming to an end, and will we (citizens of Europe) have to suffer the consequences of morbid solutions like the circular economy?

In Chapter 10, we return to the idea of complexity and argue that the science-policy interface should aim at governance *in* complexity, rather than governance *of* complexity. Governance of complexity is the attempt to describe and model all the complexities of the circular economy, in which science has the role of informing policy about how to manage the system. Governance in complexity is a recognition of the irreducible uncertainties in the knowledge base, which invites a different relationship between science and policy that moves away from apparent consensus and is open to criticism of ideas such as the circular economy. The problem of complexity is that more knowledge does not mean action, it means more ambiguity. We argue that there cannot be a perfect map, the alternative to the sixteenth century map is a messy knowledge base that is more aware of uncertainty and of the limits of governing in a changing world.

In the final chapter of the book, we reflect on the way forward, taking inspiration from the literature on the logic and ethics of care and from Eastern philosophy. We understand that policy makers try to find a solution not because they are naïve about the limits of the circular economy proposal or sold to the neoliberal cause, but because there is a narrow range of things that can be done and they chose from the options that are known. We posit that our responsibility as scientists is not just to communicate the uncertainties and the complexities, pass on the bad news, and then let others deal with the difficult choices, but it is also to care for the policy processes and policy makers that may be affected by our criticism. We understand the good intentions behind the circular economy, and sympathise with them. This is not a book about let's burn the planet now, but it is cautious (maybe even sceptical) about how far good intentions can go. For this reason, we resist the urge to provide recommendations for policy, and offer instead a view from Eastern philosophers about the way (the Dao) of governance, rather than the specific situation of the circular economy.

How to read this book

The making of this book was a highly enjoyable exercise. The three authors were all working on the circular economy as a case study inside a much larger research project on governance of the water-energy-food nexus. This project was funded by Horizon 2020, the 8th framework programme of the European Union. It was called MAGIC; its many results and activities can be found at www.magic-nexus.eu. Coordinated by ecological economist and complexity theorist Mario Giampietro, MAGIC developed a uniquely original approach to interdisciplinary research on environmental governance, combining STS and neighbouring social science approaches with comprehensive socio-biophysical data collection and analysis by so-called MuSIASEM, Multi-Scale Integrated Analysis of Societal and Ecosystem Metabolism, a method developed by Giampietro and his co-workers. What MAGIC produced, was a hybrid of quantitative environmental science and qualitative social science called "quantitative story-telling" (which we will describe in Chapter 10). The purpose of quantitative story-telling is to be able to deal discursively with policy narratives while at the same time providing rigorous checking of their biophysical feasibility and economic viability. This book has the borrowed the style and purpose of quantitative story-telling, while there was no need for a lot of number crunching to craft our argument. We do recommend, however, the interested reader to visit the MAGIC website and consult the formal report on the circular economy that we delivered to the European Commission (Giampietro, Kovacic, Strand, & Voelker, 2019) as well as the analytical paper that our project coordinator, Mario Giampietro, prepared (Giampietro, 2019).

In addition to these more formal project outputs, we felt that our case study had given us an incredibly rich material that allowed itself for a lively story to be told. When the opportunity came to produce a book out of this material, our primary goal was to offer an interesting reading, one with rich descriptions, a broad range of theoretical perspectives and unusual couplings between them. This is not a dry treatise with a crisp clear and consistent theoretical framework. Neither is it a handbook in how to achieve circularity in the economy or how to succeed in policy. In that respect it differs from most other books written about the circular economy.

This is our most important advice, then, to readers of this book: Read as you wish, but we recommend you to enjoy unusual perspectives and to leave aside the expectation that the book will provide the final answer on what to do. We do not intend to speak truth to power or indeed to anyone else.

The second and final advice is that we expect some of the theoretical perspectives to be quite demanding reading. We invoke everything from ecological economics à la Georgescu-Roegen to science and technology studies à la Sheila Jasanoff and Bruno Latour. Indeed, quite a lot of the argument breaks with common sense opinions in neoclassical economics and in mainstream science. These are all necessary aspects of the big picture that we try to convey; however, they are not additive as parts of a puzzle. The big picture is a complex one, in which the aspects are entangled into each other. This called for an iterative approach to the structuring of the book. Above, we presented the three parts as if they have a rather distinct and tidy division of labour: Part I, describe; Part II, analyse and criticise; Part III, make constructive proposals. Although there is a grain of truth in the division of labour, it is also possible to see the three parts as three iterations in the dissemination of the complex picture. Already by Chapter 4, the reader will have a general feeling of the argument, which then will be filled in with more empirical detail and more theoretical refinement in Chapters 5–8. The final three chapters, although constructive, also adds acuity and gravity to the critique. And finally, each of the final Chapters 9, 10 and 11 develop the analysis of the challenges of governance in a progressively broader context. Taking the nexus context of Chapter 8 as our point of departure, we move to the political context and the meta-narratives of Bios and Geos in Chapter 9, to the broader issue of how to know and act in a complex world in Chapter 10, and finally moving beyond modern concepts of knowledge and action in Chapter 11.

Finally, we hope that the readers will share the book. Some will enjoy a printed copy, while others will read it on a digital platform. It has been a great inspiration to know that this book will remain available to everyone on the internet, thanks to the open access agreement with Routledge. Whether such an arrangement could be said to be part of the circular economy, we do not know. We do hope, though, that the book will circulate both in physical and digital forms, and that some responses, thoughts and criticisms will also circulate back in a feedback loop to the authors. We are readily found on the internet and hope that some of you will reach out to us.

References

Ellen MacArthur Foundation. (2013). *Towards the Circular Economy*. Retrieved from www.ellenmacarthurfoundation.org/assets/downloads/publications/Ellen-MacArthur-Foundation-Towards-the-Circular-Economy-vol.1.pdf

European Commission. (2015a). *Proposal of Directive of the European Parliament and of the Council amending Directive 2008/98/EC on waste*. Brussels: European Commission. doi:10.1708/1175.13030

European Commission. (2015b, December 2). *Closing the loop: Commission adopts ambitious new Circular Economy Package to boost competitiveness, create jobs and generate sustainable growth*. Press Release. Brussels: European Commission. Retrieved from http://europa.eu/rapid/press-release_IP-15-6203_en.htm

European Commission. (2017). *Communication from the Commission to the European Parliament, the Council, the European Economic and Social Committee and the Committee of the Regions. The role of waste-to-energy in the circular economy* (No. COM (2017) 34). Brussels: European Commission. Retrieved from http://ec.europa.eu/environment/waste/waste-to-energy.pdf

European Commission. (2019, March). *Closing the loop: Commission delivers on Circular Economy Action Plan*. Press Release, pp. 2019–2021. Brussels: European Commission.

Finnveden, G., & Ekvall, T. (1998). Life-cycle assessment as a decision-support too: The case of recycling versus incineration of paper. *Resources, Conservation and Recycling*, 24(3–4), 235–256. doi:10.1016/S0921–3449(98)00039–00031

Giampietro, M. (2019). On the circular bioeconomy and decoupling: Implications for sustainable growth. *Ecological Economics*, 162 (April), 143–156. doi:10.1016/j.ecolecon.2019.05.001

Giampietro, M., Kovacic, Z., Strand, R., & Voelker, T. (2019). *Report on Narratives Behind the Circular Economy Concept*. Barcelona/Bergen/Ispra. Retrieved from https://magic-nexus.eu/sites/default/files/files_documents_repository/magic_deliverable-5.7_revision_24.06.2019.pdf

Jasanoff, S., & Kim, S.-H. (2009). Containing the atom: Sociotechnical imaginaries and nuclear power in the U.S. and South Korea. *Minerva*, 47(2), 119–146.

Jasanoff, S., & Kim, S.-H. (2015). *Dreamscapes of Modernity: Sociotechnical Imaginaries and the Fabrication of Power*. Chicago, IL: University of Chicago Press.

Morris, J. (1996). Recycling versus incineration: An energy conservation analysis. *Journal of Hazardous Materials*, 47(1–3), 277–293. doi:10.1016/0304–3894(95)00116–00116

2 Limits to growth

Historical antecedents of the circular economy

In this chapter, we analyse the academic debates that gave context to ideas about circularity and we trace the historical development of the concept of circular economy. The historical antecedents of the circular economy are linked to debates sparked by the work of the likes of Thomas Malthus (1766–1834) and Henry George (1837–97), who brought to light questions of scarcity and of the role of innovation in economic growth and depression cycles. The debate came to fruition during the Cold War as a confrontation between the Cornucopians and the Prophets of Doom, in which economic growth and the environment were framed as being at odds with each other. According to the Prophets of Doom, resource scarcity and biophysical limits would put an end to economic growth, as exemplified by the publication of *The Limits to Growth* report by the Club of Rome in 1972. On the other hand, the Cornucopians argued that environmental constraints could be overcome through technological progress and human ingenuity. Against this backdrop, ideas about circularity started to emerge through Kenneth Boulding's essay "The Economics of the Coming Spaceship Earth" (1966), Stahel and Reday-Mulvey's proposal for a closed-loop economy in 1976, the development of ideas about industrial symbiosis from industrial ecology, and the cradle-to-cradle narrative from life-cycle assessment. Through this historical overview, we identify the disciplines, narratives and intellectual debates that have informed and shaped thinking about the circular economy. We conclude the chapter by discussing the tensions that exist between the different schools of thought that inform the circular economy, and the emerging criticisms from the social sciences.

Introduction

The term "circular economy" started being used in the 1990s, drawing from two seminal works: Kenneth Boulding's (1966) economics of spaceship earth, and Stahel and Reday-Mulvey's (1976) closed-loop economy. The circular economy appeared in the policy realm in Germany and Sweden in the late 1990s and was part of the 2002 five-year plan in China. As Murray et al. note, "one interesting difference between circular economy and most of the other schools of sustainable thought is that it has largely emerged from legislation" (Murray et al., 2017). Notwithstanding the relatively recent origin of the term itself, the circular economy draws from, and rehearses, long held debates on sustainability and the question of (in)compatibility between the economy and the environment. In this chapter, we are interested in the schools of thought that inform research on the circular economy and on the ideas and debates that have led to the emergence of the concept.

The context: the tension between the economy and the environment

The circular economy is a concept that emerges from the debate about sustainability and the finite nature of natural resources. This debate has its roots in concerns raised by Thomas Malthus in 1798. Malthus observed that while food production increased arithmetically, population grew exponentially. This situation would eventually lead to overpopulation and famine. Malthus' predictions were not realised, because technological improvements made it possible to increase food production and because Western societies underwent a demographic transition, which revealed that exponential growth was a temporary phase. The argument was discredited also by the fact that Malthus was concerned with population growth among lower classes, whose growth was attributed to lack of virtuous behaviour. Malthus thus argued for population control through education of the lower classes.

In 1898 Henry George published *Progress and Poverty* (George, 1898), which became one of the most read books of its time. George observed that technological advances lead to a concentration on wealth, especially in cities, and that the problem of poverty was not one of scarcity but one of inequality. George's work was of great influence in contemporary thinking. George was one of the first economists to theorise that fluctuations in economic growth were due to business cycles. George remarked the role of technology and innovation in both leading to economic growth and concentration of wealth. Scarcity was thus linked to inequality, not to lack of resources. His study of inequality contributed to the focus of economic sciences on issues of distribution through trade and taxation. The debate was shifted from availability of resources to allocation, free trade and, later on, the market mechanism.

The debate about environmental limits developed into two schools of thought. Even though the growth rate of the population declined, in absolute terms, European countries were much more populous in the nineteenth and twentieth centuries than at the time of Malthus, and required more resources. Demand grew not just for food, but also for energy, water, raw materials and land. At the same time, technological innovation in all fields, from agriculture, to industry, transport, healthcare, information and communication technologies, made for great changes both in production techniques and in consumption habits. As a result, changes became hard to predict, and a growing faith in innovation and its capacity to overcome barriers emerged. Giampietro, Mayumi, and Sorman (2012) describe this ongoing debate as a confrontation between the "Cornucopians" and the "Prophets of Doom". According to the Prophets of Doom, resource scarcity and biophysical limits will eventually put an end to economic growth. On the other hand, the Cornucopians argued that environmental constraints could be overcome through technological progress and human ingenuity. The label refers to the cornucopia, the horn of plenty in Greek mythology, which provides endless nourishment.

The confrontation between these two opposite views became particularly acute during the Cold War. During that time, the Cornucopian view was an important part of the imaginary of the West, associated with the American dream of prosperity for all and unlimited growth potential. Boulding defined this vision as the "cowboy economy", alluding to the seemingly infinite plains – the prairie and beyond – of the United States. At the same time, concerns also mounted about the unsustainability of economic growth on a global level, exemplified par excellence by the publication of *The Limits to Growth* report by the Club of Rome in 1972 (Meadows, Meadows, Randers, & Behrens, 1972). The novelty introduced by this publication was the planetary perspective, which revealed that economic growth cannot continue indefinitely in a finite planet. The report used system dynamics to simulate long-term trends of population growth, food production, industrialisation, pollution, and non-renewable natural resources. While population, food and resource consumption were predicted to grow exponentially, technological innovation was assumed to grow linearly. The report therefore rehearsed Malthus' argument by incorporating innovation, and predicted a collapse of population, food supply, and natural resources. The report set also the example for global level simulations, which are nowadays widely deployed in climate change assessments. With the collapse of the USSR, however, it seems fair to say that the Cold War was resolved to the advantage of the cowboy economy imaginary.

The circular economy: building blocks of the concept

There are two emerging trends in the intellectual landscape that set the ground for the circular economy to appear: systems thinking and social metabolism. Systems thinking draws on mid-twentieth century intellectual developments such as those in cybernetics, ecology and sociology and perhaps above all the work of von Bertalanffy starting in the 1930s. Von Bertalanffy was a theoretical biologist and is often considered the father of general systems theory, which influenced biology, ecology, the complexity sciences and the branch of economics associated with ecological economics, among others. Von Bertalanffy develops a systems perspective in opposition to the Cartesian approach of breaking down a problem in many separate and independent elements. The idea of system invokes interconnectedness and focuses on organisation, which cannot be deduced from the study of the parts. From the perspective of systems theory, the question of organisation is central to understand life and to develop biology from a study of instances and natural history to a scientific discipline that aims to formulate laws of living nature. Von Bertalanffy (1972) notes that *organisation* is constitutive of *organism*, and is thus a fruitful concept for theoretical biology. Systems thinking has been taken up by a variety of disciplines and in economics, it has influenced the understanding of the economy as a *system*, embedded in a higher-level ecosystem, and composed of parts that interact with each other. Another important contribution to systems thinking came from the work of Howard T. Odum, who introduced the concepts of feedback and loops in ecology (Odum, 1996: 370). One of the ideas of the circular economy is to promote industrial symbiosis, exploiting the interactions between the parts of the system, rather than just optimising individual behaviour.

The second influence comes from social metabolism and industrial ecology. The idea of metabolism is used to describe the economy "not as a set of independent inputs and outputs, but as a unified larger 'organism'" (Murray et al. 2017: 372), which depends on an embedding ecosystem for its inputs and which discharges waste into this ecosystem. Applied to a society, the idea of metabolism studies the material and energy throughput that is needed for a society to reproduce itself. The metabolism metaphor has been broadly applied to social metabolism, in ecological economics, to urban metabolism and industrial metabolism, in industrial ecology. The focus on inputs and outputs mobilises both the idea of resource extraction (and the limits posed by absolute scarcity) and of carrying capacity (how much output can be absorbed by the ecosystem). The relationship between the economic systems and the ecosystem is schematically represented in Figure 2.1. This framework makes the circular economy a relevant concept also for scholars concerned with waste management, both from an environmental engineering point of view, and from industrial ecology. In fact, as we discuss in the following chapter, the concept of circular economy has originated from waste management in European regulation.

The circular economy blends in the concepts of system and throughput. The idea of the circular economy is to make the economic *system* more circular, by reducing *throughput* and transforming waste into an input. In the words of Boulding, the circular economy is about transforming the cowboy economy into a spaceship economy. The images of the earth seen from satellites as a finite planet

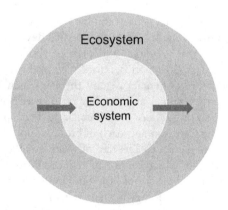

Figure 2.1 Metabolism of an economic system embedded in an ecosystem

have greatly influenced sustainability thinking in the 1960s and contributed to the creation of new metaphors, such as the spaceship. The finiteness of the earth becomes part of economic modelling and theorising. Economic growth means that the economic system transitioned from existing in an empty world to a full world (Daly, 2005). Herman Daly, one of the founders of ecological economics, argued for the need to reach a steady-state economy, which should maintain its size and not exceed the carrying capacity of the earth. Daly introduced the idea that the size of the economic system is limited by the size of the ecosystem, as represented in Figure 2.2. As the economic system grows in size, its pace of consumption of natural resources overtakes the regenerative capacity of the ecosystem. As a result, in a full world, the restorative processes through which natural resources are recycled needs to be internalised by the economic system.

Building on the full world metaphor, Boulding set the conceptual basis for the circular economy. In a full world,

> the earth has become a single spaceship, without unlimited reservoirs of anything, either for extraction or for pollution, and in which, therefore, man must find his place in a cyclical ecological system which is capable of continuous reproduction of material form even though it cannot escape having inputs of energy.
>
> (Boulding, 1966: 8)

The circular economy thus tries to close the loop between inputs and outputs, to reduce the need for inputs by decoupling economic growth from resource consumption, and to re-insert outputs into the economic cycle as inputs. Outputs can be recycled and used for the same purpose, used for different purposes if the quality decreases with reprocessing (as is the case with textiles for instance), or used as waste-to-energy if no other use is possible. Stahel and

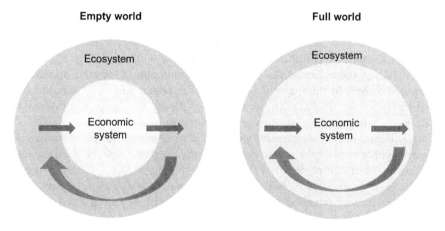

Figure 2.2 From an empty world to a full world
Source: Adapted from Daly, 2005

Reday-Mulvey (1976) argue that the substitution of energy for labour was sustainable in a context in which energy resources were thought to be abundant, but in a context of limited resources labour should substitute energy and recycling of energy intensive products should be encouraged.

According to Murray et al. (2017), an important feature of the circular economy is that it is supposed to be restorative. That is, the circular economy aims not only at reducing waste and pollution, but also at repairing previous damage through better product design. Innovation through eco-design is central to the circular economy. Eco-design is supposed to produce goods that last longer, that require less material and energy inputs, to improve substitutability of scarce inputs by more readily available ones, and to restore the ecological status of the embedding environment.

The circular economy is also linked to visions of a more just and equitable society, echoing the debate raised by George about the unequal distribution of gains from innovation and the business management perspective of the circular economy as a means to improve social corporate responsibility. Yet other alliances are built between the circular economy and the sharing economy, and with ideas of repair and maintenance cultures. Both the sharing economy and the idea of a repair and maintenance place the accent on consumer behaviour and behavioural change, suggesting that consumers do not need to buy new things all the time, and that old things can be repaired, used for longer and shared. These concepts articulate a criticism of the assumption that more is better, and are associated with an ethos of voluntary simplicity. The idea of the sharing economy invokes collaborative consumption and a democratisation of the market.

Stahel and Reday-Mulvey (1976) also see the circular economy as a means of reversing the "social problem" of maladjusted workers, that is, the fact that even though more unskilled labour was hired in industrial production in the 1960s and 70s in France, people did not want these jobs, industries increasingly hired immigrants, and unemployment went up. The closed-loop economy proposal sees repair and maintenance as means of "substituting labour for energy", by investing in less energy intensive and more labour-intensive activities. Repair and maintenance, thus create more jobs by reversing the loss of jobs and the increase in unskilled labour due to automation of industries such as the car industry and construction (Stahel & Reday-Mulvey, 1976). Moreover, in the case of the construction industry, modernisation of existing houses was supposed to benefit the unprivileged part of the population, who lived in substandard housing (ibid.). Also, in this case, closing the loop is supposed to improve questions of equity between skilled and unskilled labour.

It is important to distinguish between these relatively simple notions and their putative real-world counterparts, which invariably will be meshed into various types of complexity. For instance, to the extent that Uber and Airbnb can be seen as attempts to implement the notion of a sharing economy, they have been heavily criticised for their disruptive and paradoxical effects. In the case of Uber, the availability of cheap taxi services may provide an incentive to use more taxis and less public transport, thereby increasing the number of cars in cities (Malhotra & Van Alstyne, 2014). Airbnb has been associated with real estate speculation and increased rentals, as private homes can be converted into businesses and increase the demand for housing. In both cases, the new business models are hard to monitor and tax, converting the sharing economy into an informal economy in which workers are not protected by labour laws. Indeed, to the extent that Uber and Airbnb indeed are examples of "disruptive innovation", a claim that by no means is uncontroversial, the whole idea of disruptive innovations is that they are supposed to disrupt the market of a high-grade product or service by introducing something simpler and cheaper that will drastically increase the demand and ultimately, the consumption. For this reason, it is difficult to imagine how disruptive innovation may be reconciled with goals of sustainability.

Also, in the case of repair and maintenance, the circular economy carries some ambiguity. Repair and maintenance can spur initiatives such as the Repair Café and Fairphone (Hobson, 2016), in which people can learn how to repair and operate things, but can also be interpreted as types of services to be provided by businesses. The idea of repair and maintenance is well received by some businesses, because it allows to provide new, or more, services to consumers and therefore increase the market. As Valenzuela and Böhm (2017) argue, Apple uses a circular logo to indicate that its products are recycled, and therefore provide a moral justification for the purchase of newer models of its products. The circularity of Apple's products is used as a means to support its market expansion. Similarly, repair and maintenance are not incompatible with continued consumption.

The vision of the circular economy takes the issue of limits to heart, and solves it with technology and ingenuity, turning the stand-off between Cornucopians and Prophets of Doom into an alliance. The circular economy can be seen as the latest iteration of recurrent attempts at reconciling environmental concerns and economic growth. Earlier examples of attempts to reconcile the environment and the economy are captured by concepts such as sustainable development, the green economy, and the more recent bioeconomy, which is sometimes associated to the circular economy. Sustainable development has been heavily criticised for leading to a green washing of economic practices and neoliberal development models (Reinert, 2007), and has also been mainstreamed in the policies and goals of international organisations such as the United Nations, and of the European Union itself. The circular economy may follow a similar path, due to its popularity in policy discourse and the interest the concept draws from business management. How solid is the alliance between environmental doomsters and economic Cornucopians from a scientific point of view?

A fragile alliance

In terms of disciplines, the circular economy draws from ecological economics and industrial ecology and is increasingly attracting attention from business and management studies, not least with important contributions coming from Chinese scholars (Geng, Sarkis, Ulgiati, & Zhang, 2013; Yuan, Bi, &

Moriguichi, 2006). This combination of disciplines is not without tensions. For instance, there is a fundamental disagreement about the possibility of circularity. We will expand on this discussion in Chapter 5, but in a nutshell, ecological economics is based on the understanding of the economy as an entropic process (Georgescu-Roegen, 1971; Martinez-Alier, 2015), that is, a process through which inputs are degraded. Entropy introduces irreversibility in the economic process: once the toothpaste is out of the tube it cannot be put back in (unless one spends an amount of energy equivalent of emptying an even bigger tube of toothpaste). This means that the throughput of energy and materials can only go in one direction. Energy cannot be recycled once fuels are burnt, food cannot be recycled once it is eaten, etc. According to this view, the economic process can only be linear. On the other hand, Murray et al. (2017) see the circular economy as a useful framework to address corporate social responsibility by using less resources, responding to global warming and tackling social justice. Hence views on the circular economy from the scientific community differ sharply.

At the heart of the controversy over the possibility of circularity is the question of recyclability of different inputs. While materials such as plastics, metals, paper and cardboard can be recycled, the idea of circularity does not apply to energy and food flows, which are degraded through use. Technology for the recycling of construction materials is also missing, because bricks and concrete "cannot be remelted nor decomposed into their basic elements" (Stahel & Reday-Mulvey, 1976). Recyclability also comes in different degrees, because materials such as paper and textiles loose quality when recycled and cannot be recycled over and over again. Only part of the material throughput can be recycled. Acknowledging that what can be recycled also loses quality over time, definitions of the circular economy refer to maintaining the value of materials in the economy for "as long as possible" (Merli, Preziosi, & Acampora, 2018). The term circular economy, therefore, does not indicate a change in overall economic activity, but rather seems to be a means of labelling the circular part of the economy, which studies have shown to be about 6% of the overall throughput at the world level (Haas, Krausmann, Wiedenhofer, & Heinz, 2015).

The role of energy and energy accounting in the circular economy is debated (Geng, Sarkis, Ulgiati, & Zhang, 2013). Because the use of energy is necessarily linear (emissions cannot be recycled into fuels or electricity), some proponents of the circular economy argue that energy should not be part of the circular economy accounting (workshop, May 2018). Others argue that circularity with regard to energy can be reached by using renewable energy sources (Ellen MacArthur Foundation, 2013). The juxtaposition of renewable and non-renewable resonates with the concepts of circular and linear, yet are not synonyms. Renewable energy sources such as wind, water gradients and solar radiation are not produced by recycling, they are resources extracted from the global cycles of the earth and from the sun. The reproduction of global cycles does not depend on whether the economic system is circular or linear, but rather may be influenced by anthropogenic changes induced by the size of the economic system and its emissions. An obvious example of how anthropogenic activity may disrupt global cycles is climate change. Finally, some proponents of the circular economy see the use of waste as an energy source, referred to as waste-to-energy, and as a way of increasing the circularity of the economy (Pan et al., 2014). In this case, circularity is increased by the fact that non-recoverable materials are used as input for energy production, rather than discarded into landfills, but the energy produced can only be used linearly, that is, once. This means that energy cannot be produced only once either and that new material inputs (including in the form of waste) need to be generated, which may go against the waster hierarchy of reducing waste in the first place.

The degree of circularity may be increased through technological innovation, but is also constrained by the limited substitutability between different inputs. Substitution is one of the arguments that distinguished strong sustainability and weak sustainability. Strong sustainability assumes that natural inputs cannot be replaced by labour and technology. Weak sustainability allows for a greater degree of substitution between different types of inputs, so that if natural resources become scarcer, other inputs can be increased. The two visions have different implications for the management of natural resources. If different inputs can be substituted, resources can be managed by the market. In neoclassical economic analysis, a firm can use more or less of different production factors, such as labour and capital, depending on the cost that each factor has. If labour becomes more expensive, firms will invest more in mechanisation and substitute human labour with machinery. If natural resources become scarcer, their price will increase, and firms will substitute them for cheaper inputs. If different inputs cannot be substituted, natural resources cannot be managed by the market mechanism and necessitate specific policies for their conservation and to regulate their use. As a consequence, different analytical concepts will support very different policies.

The substitutability debate introduces qualitative differences between different inputs. For instance, in agriculture one cannot substitute water with any other input. Technology can help reduce water consumption by limiting losses, but it cannot change evapotranspiration and the associated water requirement of crops. Genetically modified organisms (GMOs) may marginally alter crop water requirements, but even in countries with wide spread use of GMOs, the agricultural sector retains the lion share of water use. According to the United States Department of Agriculture, agriculture accounts for about 80% of the country's consumptive water use (United States Department of Agriculture, 2019). Water inputs cannot be factored out. Qualitative distinctions are lost in economic analysis through the use of generic categories such as "inputs" and because of the possibility of substituting one input for the other. The role of technology is therefore limited in the strong sustainability perspective. Returning to the debate on the limits to growth, innovation cannot overcome biophysical limits. This is why the Club of Rome argued that resource consumption increases exponentially, while technological innovation contributes linear improvements in resource use.

An alternative reading of the circular economy, based on business management, is that circularity can expand the function of firms from suppliers of goods to supplier of repair and maintenance services associated with the goods they commercialise. Services are associated with higher value added, which helps the business case for the circular economy, and requires less material inputs, which contributes to social corporate responsibility and the greening of businesses. The circular economy contributes to the service economy. Once again, it is not clear whether the circular economy represents a new business model or is just a different way of describing the tertiarisation of the economy. From the point of view of ecological economics, the tertiarisation of European economies has been associated with the outsourcing of secondary activities to Third World countries and emerging economies, particularly to China. The shift to a service economy in Europe has thus been criticised as a displacement of high material consumption and polluting activities elsewhere (Giampietro et al., 2012; Magalhães et al., 2019; Peters, Minx, Weber, & Edenhofer, 2011; Roberts & Grimes, 1997). If the circular economy is to be a solution to the environmental problems at the global level, tertiarisation and displacement of polluting activities does not contribute to sustainability.

Industrial ecology is also affected by the ambiguity of the circular economy. Industrial ecology focuses on the analysis of industrial processes and on waste management. The circular economy has acquired popularity in the discipline as a means to refer to waste management studies, and to highlight the positive contribution of waste management to the economy. Industrial ecology contributes to the understanding and enhancing of recycling possibilities, and on the restorative potential of the circular economy through research on eco-design and eco-efficiency. Ancillary concepts used to refer to the contribution of industrial processes to the circular economy are remanufacturing, refurbishing and repurposing. At the same time, social metabolism approaches are widely used in industrial ecology, which has developed a variety of analytical tools for the accounting of material inputs and shares some of the theoretical assumptions of ecological economics on the limited substitutability of material inputs. This discipline provides both supportive and critical arguments for the circular economy.

Industrial ecology has contributed to the imaginary of the circular economy thanks to analytical tools such as life-cycle assessment (LCA) and material flow analysis (MFA). LCA aims at analysing the environmental impacts associated with all phases of a product's lifetime. Part of the LCA assessment is to define the boundaries of the process to be analysed. An analysis of the whole lifespan of a product is described as cradle-to-grave. When the products analysed can be recycled, the boundaries can be extended to cradle-to-cradle. The formulas cradle-to-grave and cradle-to-cradle are primarily descriptions of the boundaries of the analysis. In the circular economy narrative, however, these descriptions are used prescriptively. The shortcoming of the prescriptive use of the cradle-to-cradle metaphor is that the types of processes analysed by LCA cannot always be scaled up from industrial processes to the whole economy and from materials to energy, water and food.

LCA also contributes to the knowledge base of the circular economy with its methodology. LCA takes a functional unit, which may be defined as one kilogram of a final product such as a bottle, paper, a clothing item, and makes an inventory of all the inputs and outputs associated with the processes included in the system's boundaries. The analysis of processes and the interactions between different processes has contributed to the identification of potential for industrial symbiosis, in which one industry's wastes are transformed into another industry's inputs, thus changing the notion of waste into a resource. However, the focus on a functional unit makes the analysis blind to scale issues. For instance, an example of industrial symbiosis is the use of waste heat from glass production in industrial greenhouses for food production (Andrews & Pearce, 2011). The fact that the excess heat of one process can be used as input for another process masks the issue that industrial greenhouses necessitate considerable amounts of energy inputs, and this synergy does not eliminate the need for other inputs of energy. Additional energy inputs require additional energy production processes, which are often not built ad hoc for a specific industry but are part of the energy infrastructure of a region, or a country. Moreover, energy power plants, such as nuclear power and coal powered power plants, cannot be switched on and switched off on demand, but may require up to three days to be turned on or off. The energy production industry operates at a much larger scale than individual production processes, making energy production unadaptable and unresponsive to process-level innovations. Therefore, the creation of symbiotic synergies for specific processes cannot be taken as a proxy for economy-wide symbiosis and does not reduce the losses and wastes of energy production as a whole.

The second approach which is broadly used both in ecological economics and in industrial ecology is material flow analysis, MFA. MFA provides an accounting of the inputs and outputs of an economy, measured in tons, by aggregating all types of material flows. This accounting technique provides a biophysical reading of the economy, by measuring economic activity in tons rather than in monetary terms. MFA assumes that matter is conserved and uses the mass balance principle to account for inputs, which are matched either by additions to stock or outputs. The accounting distinguished between domestic extraction and inputs, which add up to domestic material inputs. Domestic material inputs are used for exports and for domestic material consumption. Eurostat, the statistical office of the European Commission, produces annual data about material domestic consumption. MFA has been widely used to measure the circularity of European economies and the world economy, and has strongly influenced European policy making and the imaginary of the circular economy (see Chapter 6). Interestingly, MFA also shows how little circularity there is (estimated at 6% for the world economy) and how little room for improvement there is, given that half of the material flows represented are energy inputs, and another 40% are construction materials which are added to stocks (buildings) (European Commission, 2014; Haas et al., 2015).

Criticisms

The ambiguities and contradictions of the circular economy concept have been observed by scholars, and criticisms of the concept are voiced both within the disciplines that give the theoretical and methodological foundations to the circular economy, such as ecological economics and industrial ecology, and from other academic fields. We conclude this chapter by mentioning some of the critiques raised by other disciplines. Later in this book, we will articulate our own critiques of the circular economy, inspired from analytical concepts of entropy, imaginaries, indicator politics and governance.

The majority of the existing literature on the circular economy comes from organisation and planning studies and deals with proper ways to manage a transition from a linear towards a circular economy (Bakker, Wang, Huisman, & Den Hollander, 2014; Bocken, de Pauw, Bakker, & van der Grinten, 2016). Over recent years, also social science scholars have studied the development of circular economy policies (for an overview see Ghisellini, Cialani, & Ulgiati, 2016). The contributions of the social sciences have focused mainly on: i) the challenges of implementation of the vague circular economy policy; ii) the limits of policies directed at changing consumer behaviour, and the analysis of the complexity and variety of factors that influence people's practices; iii) the parallels between the circular economy and sustainable development, an argument that we will pick up in Chapter 8; and iv) the expectations and imaginations linked to the circular economy.

We opened the book with a discussion of the vagueness of the circular economy concept. A number of studies have focused on a micro level and on comparative studies of the circular economy initiatives in cities. These studies argue that because the concept is ambiguous or even ill-defined, it is in need of interpretation by the actors responsible for its implementation (Petit-Boix & Leipold, 2018; Prendeville, Cherim, & Bocken, 2018). The ambiguity of the circular economy concept is remedied in its practical application by reference to predecessor concepts such as sustainability. Marin and De Meulder (2018) identify different sustainability framings and political positions that guide the implementation of circular economy initiatives: objectivist framings relate to technocratic management and foreground a "technology and entrepreneurial 'applied' circular economy" (Marin & De Meulder, 2018: 13), while constructivist framings focus on the social organisation of consumption and direct attention to practices of sharing, re-use and collaboration.

Building on practice theory, others have argued that the framing of the circular economy is too narrow and tends of overlook social aspects of the envisioned transition and questions about its 'social desirability' (Murray et al., 2017; Sauvé, Bernard, & Sloan, 2016). In particular, the focus on consumption and on the rational choices by 'consumers' is criticised (Mylan, Holmes, & Paddock, 2016; Welch, Keller, & Mandich, 2017). Mylan, Holmes, and Paddock (2016) argue from a sociotechnical perspective that food consumption needs to be understood as a social practice consisting of combinations of routines and habits, shared cultural meanings and understandings, and available infrastructures. Simplistic initiatives that focus on changing consumer behaviour through information campaigns are necessarily bound to fail. In a similar manner, the role of plastics for contemporary societies and for socio-material ways of living has been problematised by showing how waste is not only a by-product, but a fundamental aspect of Western society's current ways of living (Gabrys, Hawkins, & Michael, 2013).

Different scholars, hailing from human geography and Marxist studies, have enquired about the type of governance and political regime that the circular economy implies. Hobson (2016) warns that policy interventions can create a governance lock-in, and that the circular economy may become another instance of neoliberal environmental governance that is practiced through the labelling of products, ecological modernisation, and the promotion of individualised action such as recycling. The critique is that the circular economy fails to challenge existing modes of governance and of consumer behaviour, which are deemed to be fundamentally unsustainable. Valenzuela and Böhm (2017) argue that the circular economy reproduces capitalist logics of othering, and does not challenge the current model of production and consumption. Circularity makes consumption acceptable and green, and does not challenge the identity of the consumer, nor of the capitalist system.

More conceptual engagements with circular economy policy have traced the lineage and relation of the concept to notions like sustainable development, sustainability, post growth, or zero waste (Corvellec & Hultman, 2012; Hultman & Corvellec, 2012; Valenzuela & Böhm, 2017). During the development from sustainable development to zero waste and circular economy, not only the policy objectives have changed, but also the shared meaning of the very concepts that underlie these policies. Waste has become an object of manageable sustainability and is no longer a signifier of unsustainable practices. Even more, it has become a resource in what has been labelled an "optimization business" (Hultman & Corvellec, 2012). Importantly, through this reconceptualisation of waste it has been possible to naturalise and de-politicise the idea of permanent growth in an "economic naturalism" (Valenzuela & Böhm, 2017). Circular economy policy shares some of the problems of predecessor notions such as sustainable development, i.e. that it is "appropriating critique and then selling it back to the ethically-driven, sustainability-wary subject" (Valenzuela & Böhm 2017: 50). Criticism like this resonates with arguments made by ecological economists, who, influenced by the work of Georgescu-Roegen (1971), have pointed out that notion of a circular economy is misleading since perfect circularity is a theoretical impossibility (Haas et al., 2015; Martinez-Alier, 2015). We also draw the parallel between the circular economy and sustainable development in Chapter 8, but we will argue that the circular economy is a new phenomenon because recasts the tension between sustainability and growth in terms of synergy.

Finally, a number of authors take the imaginative resources and the promissory logics involved in the development of circular economy policy as their starting point. These studies also stress the need to critically engage with the multiple meanings and futures of circularity that are currently being negotiated and start to manifest, e.g. in the distribution of R&D funding. Lazarevic and Valve (2017) describe how circular economy documents describe a hero's journey of transitioning to an economy that builds on ideas about a perfect circle of slow material flows, a shift from consumers to users, visions of decoupling economic growth from environmental protection and ideas of security and competitiveness. In a similar manner, Welch, Keller, and Mandich (2016) direct attention to the imagined everyday futures of circular economy policies and argue that these policies bring together conflicting orders of worth in a way that marginalises ecological matters. They diagnose a "crisis of political imagination" (Welch et al., 2017: 51) and call for critical engagement with these futures and especially the incompatible orders of worth that are potentially naturalised through them. Other authors stress that circular economy policies rest on a moral economy that brings together "discourses of ecological modernisation, environmental justice and resource (in)security" (Gregson, Crang, & Fuller, 2015). We will also use the idea of imaginaries in Chapter 6, and draw attention to how future visions are shaping present practice, institutional arrangements and negotiations about the meaning of circularity.

Overall, there is a general agreement that a fully circular economy is not possible. If that is the case, what does the concept of partial circular economy do? In the next chapter, we start looking for the answer by analysing the role of the circular economy imaginary in European policy.

References

Andrews, R., & Pearce, J. M. (2011). Environmental and economic assessment of a greenhouse waste heat exchange. *Journal of Cleaner Production*, 19(13), 1446–1454. doi:10.1016/j.jclepro.2011.04.016

Bakker, C., Wang, F., Huisman, J., & Den Hollander, M. (2014). Products that go round: Exploring product life extension through design. *Journal of Cleaner Production*, 69, 10–16. doi:10.1016/j.jclepro.2014.01.028

Bocken, N. M. P., de Pauw, I., Bakker, C., & van der Grinten, B. (2016). Product design and business model strategies for a circular economy. *Journal of Industrial and Production Engineering*, 33(5), 308–320. doi:10.1080/21681015.2016.1172124

Boulding, K. (1966). The economics of the coming Spaceship Earth. In H. Jarrett (Ed.), *Environmental Quality in a Growing Economy* (pp. 3–14). Baltimore: Johns Hopkins University Press.

Corvellec, H., & Hultman, J. (2012). From "less landfilling" to "wasting less". *Journal of Organizational Change Management* (pp. 297–314). doi:10.1108/09534811211213964

Daly, H. E. (2005). Economics in a full world. *Scientific American*, 293(3), 78–85.

Ellen MacArthur Foundation. (2013). *Towards the Circular Economy*. Retrieved from www.ellenmacarthurfoundation.org/assets/downloads/publications/Ellen-MacArthur-Foundation-Towards-the-Circular-Economy-vol.1.pdf

European Commission. (2014). *Communication from the Commission to the European Parliament, the Council, the European Economic and Social Committee and the Committee of the Regions. Towards a circular economy: A zero waste programme for Europe* (No. COM (2014) 398). Brussels: European Commission. Retrieved from http://eur-lex.europa.eu/resource.htm l?uri=cellar:50edd1fd-01ec-11e4-831f-01aa75ed71a1.0001.01/DOC_1&format=PDF

Gabrys, J., Hawkins, G., & Michael, M. (2013). *Accumulation: The Material Politics of Plastic.* London: Routledge.

Geng, Y., Sarkis, J., Ulgiati, S., & Zhang, P. (2013). Measuring China's circular economy. *Science*, 339(6127), 1526–1527.

George, H. (1898). *Progress and Poverty.* New York: Doubleday and McClure Company.

Georgescu-Roegen, N. (1971). *The Entropy Law and the Economic Process.* Boston: Harvard University Press.

Ghisellini, P., Cialani, C., & Ulgiati, S. (2016). A review on circular economy: The expected transition to a balanced interplay of environmental and economic systems. *Journal of Cleaner Production*, 114, 11–32. doi:10.1016/j.jclepro.2015.09.007

Giampietro, M., Mayumi, K., & Sorman, A. H. (2012). *The Metabolic Pattern of Societies: Where Economists Fall Short.* London and New York: Routledge.

Gregson, N., Crang, M., & Fuller, S. (2015). Interrogating the circular economy: the moral economy of resource recovery in the EU. *Economy and Society*, 44(2), 218–243. doi:10.1080/03085147.2015.1013353

Haas, W., Krausmann, F., Wiedenhofer, D., & Heinz, M. (2015). How circular is the global economy? An assessment of material flows, wste production and recycling in the European Union and the world in 2005. *Journal of Industrial Ecology*, 19(5), 765–777.

Hobson, K. (2016). Closing the loop or squaring the circle? Locating generative spaces for the circular economy. *Progress in Human Geography*, 40(1), 88–104. doi:10.1177/0309132514566342

Hultman, J., & Corvellec, H. (2012). The European waste hierarchy: from the socio-materiality of waste to a politics of consumption, *Environment and Planning A*, 44, 2413–2427. doi:10.1068/a44668

Lazarevic, D., & Valve, H. (2017). Narrating expectations for the circular economy: Towards a common and contested European transition. *Energy Research and Social Science*, 31(February), 60–69. doi:10.1016/j.erss.2017.05.006

Magalhães, N., Fressoz, J. B., Jarrige, F., Le Roux, T., Levillain, G., Lyautey, M., … Bonneuil, C. (2019). The physical economy of France (1830–2015). The history of a parasite? *Ecological Economics*, 157(March), 291–300. doi:10.1016/j.ecolecon.2018.12.001

Malhotra, A., & Van Alstyne, M. (2014). The dark side of the sharing economy … and how to lighten it. *Communications of the ACM*, 57(11), 24–27.

Marin, J., & De Meulder, B. (2018). Interpreting circularity. Circular city representations concealing transition drivers. *Sustainability (Switzerland)*, 10(5). doi:10.3390/su10051310

Martinez-Alier, J. (2015). La economía no es circular sino entrópica. *La Jornada.* Retrieved from www.jornada.com.mx/2015/06/14/opinion/026a1eco

Meadows, D. H., Meadows, D. L., Randers, J., & Behrens, W. W. (1972). *The Limits to Growth: A Report for the Club of Rome's Projects on the Predicament of Mankind.* Washington, DC: Potomac Associates Book.

Merli, R., Preziosi, M., & Acampora, A. (2018). How do scholars approach the circular economy? A systematic literature review. *Journal of Cleaner Production*, 178, 703–722. doi:10.1016/j.jclepro.2017.12.112

Murray, A., Skene, K., Haynes, K., Murray, A., Skene, K., & Haynes, K. (2017). The circular economy: An interdisciplinary exploration of the concept and application in a global context. *Journal of Business Ethics*, 140(3), 369–380. doi:10.1007/s10551–10015–2693–2692

Mylan, J., Holmes, H., & Paddock, J. (2016). Re-introducing consumption to the "circular economy": A sociotechnical analysis of domestic food provisioning. *Sustainability*, 8(8). doi:10.3390/su8080794

Odum, H. T. (1996). *Environmental Accounting: Energy and Environmental Decision Making*. New York: Wiley.

Pan, S. Y., Du, M. A., Huang, I.T., Liu, I. H., Chang, E. E., & Chiang, P. C. (2014). Strategies on implementation of waste-to-energy (WTE) supply chain for circular economy system: A review. *Journal of Cleaner Production*, 108, 409–421. doi:10.1016/j.jclepro.2015.06.124

Peters, G. P., Minx, J. C., Weber, C. L., & Edenhofer, O. (2011). Growth in emission transfers via international trade from 1990 to 2008. *Proceedings of the National Academy of Sciences*, 108(21), 8903–8908. doi:10.1073/pnas.1006388108

Petit-Boix, A., & Leipold, S. (2018). Circular economy in cities: Reviewing how environmental research aligns with local practices. *Journal of Cleaner Production*, 195, 1270–1281. doi:10.1016/j.jclepro.2018.05.281

Prendeville, S., Cherim, E., & Bocken, N. (2018). Circular cities: Mapping six cities in transition. *Environmental Innovation and Societal Transitions*, 26, 171–194. doi:10.1016/j.eist.2017.03.002

Reinert, E. S. (2007). *How Rich Countries Got Rich … And Why Poor Countries Stay Poor*. New York: Public Affairs Press.

Roberts, J. T., & Grimes, P. E. (1997). Carbon intensity and economic development 1962–1991: A brief exploration of the environmental Kuznets curve. *World Development*, 25(2), 191–198. doi:10.1016/S0305–0750X(96)00104–0

Sauvé, S., Bernard, S., & Sloan, P. (2016). Environmental sciences, sustainable development and circular economy: Alternative concepts for trans-disciplinary research. *Environmental Development*, 17, 48–56. doi:10.1016/j.envdev.2015.09.002

Stahel, W. R., & Reday-Mulvey, G. (1976). *Jobs for Tomorrow: The Potential for Substituting Manpower for Energy*. Brussels: European Commission.

United States Department of Agriculture. (2019) *Irrigation & Water Use*. Retrieved from www.ers.usda.gov/topics/farm-practices-management/irrigation-water-use/

Valenzuela, F., & Böhm, S. (2017). Against wasted politics: A critique of the circular economy. *Ephemera Journal*, 17(7), 23–60.

von Bertalanffy, L. (1972). The history and status of general systems theory. *The Academy of Management Journal*, 15(4), 407–426.

Welch, D., Keller, M., & Mandich, G. (2017). Imagined futures of everyday life in the circular economy. *Interactions*, (March–April), 46–51.

Yuan, Z., Bi, J., & Moriguichi, Y. (2006). The circular economy: A new development strategy in China. *Journal of Industrial Ecology*, 10(1-2), 4–8.

3 Enter Ellen

The circular economy hits the European scene

Following from the previous chapter, we analyse how the concept of circular economy was mainstreamed both in academic research and in European policy in the 2010s. The concept of circular economy gained prominence in Europe in 2013 with the first report of the Ellen MacArthur Foundation. Defined both as a blessing and as a curse, the work of the Foundation has impacted policy-making and supported the advancement of a number of communications on the circular economy by the European Commission. The circular economy first appears in a communication in 2014 as a cautious transition pathway towards sustainability, characterised by moderation. The new presidency of the European Commission recasts the circular economy as an ambitious project in 2015, which is supposed to deliver economic growth. We show how the recent development of the circular economy concept drives towards a reconciliation of economic and environmental objectives, shifting the discourse from a problem of trade-offs and difficult choices to a language of "win-win" and opportunities for synergy. We argue that, despite the ambition of the European Commission, the circular economy policy has mainly consisted of the development of a sociotechnical imaginary, and has fallen short of moving beyond waste management in terms of policy implementation.

Introduction

Following from the previous chapter, we analyse how the concept of a circular economy was mainstreamed both in academic research and in European policy starting in the 2010s. The term itself – circular economy – had been in use at least since 1991, and notably so in Chinese policy since 1998. However, its prominence in Europe came in 2013 with the first report of the Ellen MacArthur Foundation. This foundation, whose aim is to promote and support the circular economy, has been a major player in mainstreaming the concept from restricted academic circles to the wider public. The early 2010s were also difficult times for the European Union, which was still recovering from the economic crisis ensued from the 2008–2009 financial crisis. The post-crisis context has played a significant role in the framing of the circular economy and in the negotiation of its stated aims. In this chapter, we consider the circular economy a policy "in the making" and retrace the emergence of this concept in European policy, paying attention to the initial policy priorities that set the path for the circular economy.

Circular economy policies combine a vast array of policy areas, policy objectives, scientific disciplines and communities with various promises and also dystopian visions. While as a policy proposal in the European Union, the circular economy concept grew out of waste management, current ambitions go significantly beyond waste and draw on a broad variety of culturally situated meanings. Right now, there are many different meanings, definitions and visions of circularity. The on-going policy-making processes, including the choice of indicators, will determine not only how to define circularity but also how it will be measured and ultimately how it will be implemented. The circular economy draws on various imaginative resources and thus is closely tied to a particular "sociotechnical imaginary" (Jasanoff & Kim, 2009). Socio-technical imaginaries are understood as collectively shared visions of desirable societal and technological futures. The emphasis is on the futuristic orientation of policy narratives, especially those in which future, hitherto undeveloped, technology is expected to play a major role. Since the solutions do not exist yet, the combined political and scientific challenge is to invent them, and this is inherently a creative task that calls for imagination. This is what is intended by the concept sociotechnical imaginaries, namely to understand contingencies in science and technology (and related policy) in their joint effort to envision as yet non-existing solutions, and then try to realise these solutions by using the imaginaries as the source for plans of action. Famously, Jasanoff and Kim comparatively analysed the development of nuclear energy both in the United States and South Korea and found that the vastly different development paths of nuclear energy could be partially explained by diverging ideas of how nuclear energy is related to collective identities and imagined futures. Whereas South Korea saw nuclear energy as a possibility for economic and democratic development of the country, the United States framed the technology in terms of risk and thus followed an imaginary of containment in contrast to the South Korean imaginary of development. In this line of thought it will be important in later chapters to ask which collective ideas of the future of Europe and "Europeanness" are co-produced with circular economy policies together with certain risks and benefits. This chapter will lay the groundwork by tracing the institutional development of this policy, that is the main actors involved and the broad shifts in focus that have occurred so far.

The circular economy has its policy antecedents in waste management. One of the first legislative proposals related to the circular economy was an amendment to the waste directive in 2015 (European Commission, 2015c). Efforts have been directed at creating a *"new narrative"* (interview, 11 Jan 2017) for the circular economy, making it clear that the circular economy is much more than the economy of waste, and offers opportunities for economic growth. However, as we will argue throughout the chapter, the initial association with waste management created a path dependency, and the move beyond waste happens more in rhetoric than in practice. The chronology of different activities that contributed to the development of the circular economy policy is described in Figure 3.1.

In the development of the concept, the circular economy has become a site for the establishment of collaborations between different agencies and directorates of the European Commission, bridging the gap between environmental policies and economic policies, historically in tension with each other. Environmental policies are often aimed at correcting economic growth, keeping it within the limits of planetary boundaries, blocking the way when industry becomes too polluting, and when substances are too toxic. The circular economy, instead, is a nexus policy: it promises to change the terms of dialogue between these two different policy realms, making it possible to work together, and overcome policy silos. In the circular economy narrative, environmental "problems" become "opportunities", waste is turned into a resource of recycled primary materials, of rare earth metals, and of fuel for energy production. As the scope of the circular economy is expanded beyond waste management, more interests come into play.

In this chapter, we trace the emergence of the circular economy in European policy and we analyse how political negotiations have shaped the definitions of the circular economy, the regulations issued, and the type of language used. The chapter will go through the development of the policy year by year as described in Table 3.1, starting with the 2013 report of the Ellen MacArthur Foundation, which precedes and opens the ground for the Communications of the European Commission.

2013 – Ellen MacArthur Foundation

The Ellen MacArthur Foundation was created in 2010, by Ellen MacArthur, who was given the title of Dame after breaking the non-stop round the world solo sailing record. Sailing made Ellen MacArthur experience in very concrete sense what it means to live with finite resources, and later she translated her experience to the vision of a circular economy as a means to cope with finite resources on earth. The Foundation states that its mission is to "accelerate the transition to the circular economy" (www.ellenmacarthurfoundation.org/). To that purpose, the Foundation actively engages with academics and public governments.

In 2013, the Ellen MacArthur Foundation published a report entitled *Towards the Circular Economy*. The report includes a foreword by the European Commissioner for the Environment, which signals interest in the circular economy from the European policy scene. In this report, the circular economy is defined as:

> an industrial system that is restorative or regenerative by intention and design. It replaces the 'end-of-life' concept with restoration, shifts towards

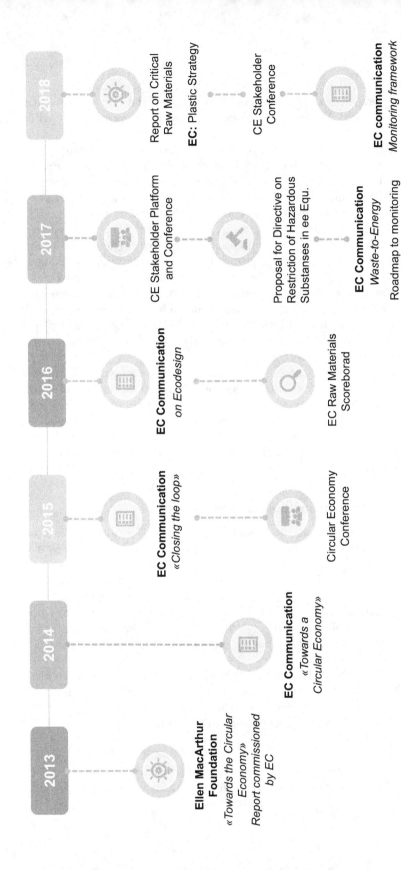

Figure 3.1 Timeline of the circular economy

Table 3.1 Summary of the regulations and communications linked to the circular economy

Year	Regulations and communications
2014	Communication from the Commission to the European Parliament, the Council, the European Economic and Social Committee and the Committee of the Regions. Towards a circular economy: A zero waste programme for Europe (No. COM (2014) 398)
2015	Communication from the Commission to the European Parliament, the Council, the European Economic and Social Committee and the Committee of the Regions. Closing the loop – An EU action plan for the Circular Economy EN (No. COM (2015) 614) amending Directives 2000/53/EC on end-of-life vehicles, 2006/66/EC on batteries and accumulators and waste batteries and accumulators, and 2012/19/EU on waste electrical and electronic equipment on electrical and electronic waste, landfill waste, packaging and waste amending Directive 1999/31/EC on the landfill of waste amending Directive 94/62/EC on packaging and packaging waste amending Directive 2008/98/EC on waste legislative proposal to extend legal guarantees on goods sold online to 2 years
2016	Proposal for a Regulation of the European Parliament and of the Council laying down rules on the making available on the market of CE marked **fertilising products** and amending Regulations (EC) No 1069/2009 and (EC) No 1107/2009 Launch of the "**Innovation deals** for a circular economy", which was open between 26 May and 15 September 2016, to identify perceived regulatory barriers to innovation Adoption on 30 November 2016 of the **Ecodesign Working Plan** 2016–2019 as part of the Clean Energy for All Europeans package Launch of the stakeholder's platform on **food waste** prevention, development of an EU methodology to measure food waste, and preparation of EU guidelines to facilitate food donations and use of former foodstuff as feed
2017	Proposal for a Directive of the European Parliament and of the Council amending Directive 2011/65/EU on the restriction of the use of certain **hazardous substances in electrical and electronic equipment** Communication on **waste-to-energy** processes and their role in the circular economy, (European Commission, 2017b) Launch of the platform to support the **financing of circular economy**
2018	Monitoring Framework

the use of renewable energy, eliminates the use of toxic chemicals, which impair reuse, and aims for the elimination of waste through the superior design of materials, products, systems, and, within this, business models.

(Ellen MacArthur Foundation, 2013)

The representation of the circular economy used by the Ellen MacArthur Foundation explains circularity as mimicking the ecosystem. Just like water and nutrients are recycled by the ecosystem to reproduce living processes, the argument goes that the economy should also recycle its "technical nutrients". The analogy with the ecosystem is rendered through a "butterfly diagram" of the circular economy (Figure 3.2).

The Ellen MacArthur Foundation concept of the circular economy is focused on industrial processes, rather than on the economy as a whole. As can be observed in Figure 3.2, the system boundaries are defined by specific production processes, such as mining or manufacturing, or by a sequence of production processes, in which technical inputs are used for further manufacturing, assembling, service providers and final use. The specific focus on industrial processes can also be observed in the reference to a "restorative industrial system". This representation draws on life cycle assessment (LCA), a technique to assess environmental impacts associated with all the stages of a product's life cycle, from raw material extraction through materials processing, manufacture, distribution, use, repair and maintenance, and disposal or recycling.

The Ellen MacArthur Foundation merges the LCA approach with the use of business models and explores the potential business interest in offering recycling, reuse and repair services for manufacturing companies. The report does not study circular business models for the primary sectors (food and energy production). It is limited in scope to industrial processes that use recyclable components. Innovation plays an important role, both by imagining new business models and the transition towards a high-value added service economy, and by promoting the development of more advanced recycling systems.

The case presented by the Ellen MacArthur Foundation has been important in putting the circular economy on the policy agenda as a business opportunity. The focus on manufacturing and business opportunities supports the idea of making the circular economy more than just waste, and powerfully takes the proposal out of the environmental protection realm and turns it into an instrument of economic growth.

2014 – A cautious transition to the circular economy

The circular economy officially appears in European Union policy in 2014, with the publication of the Communication *Towards a circular economy: A zero waste programme for Europe* (European Commission, 2014c). In this communication, the circular economy is defined as:

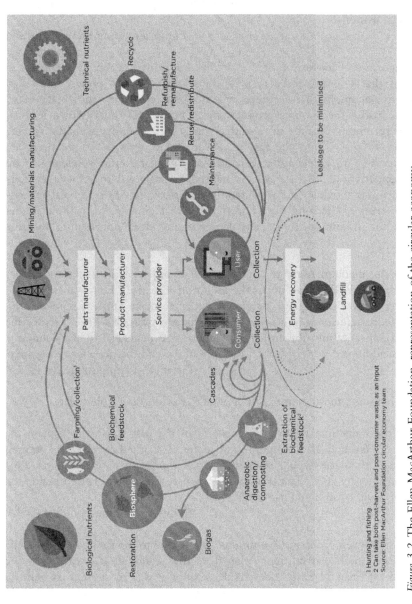

Figure 3.2 The Ellen MacArthur Foundation, representation of the circular economy
Source: Ellen MacArthur Foundation, 2013

Circular economy represents a development strategy that entails economic growth without increasing consumption of resources, deeply transform production chains and consumption habits and redesign industrial systems at the system level. It relies on innovation being it technological, social and organisational.

(European Commission, 2014b: 2)

An important characteristic of the circular economy concept as it appears in 2014 is that it is presented as a cautious and moderate project. The staff working document that accompanied the 2014 communication, elaborated three scenarios for resource productivity: i) business as usual (which leads to moderate improvements in resource use); ii) transition scenario (which requires going back to the resource productivity growth of the pre-2008 crisis period); iii) acceleration scenario (improving resource efficiency above levels experienced in the past). Scenario 2 is projected to achieve the circular economy, while the acceleration scenario is not as beneficial in economic terms in the long run. The message that emerges from these studies is that the transition to the circular economy does not require extreme efforts.

In the medium term, this [rapid acceleration] scenario delivers a smaller increase in GDP than under the transition scenario. The reason why rapid acceleration is less good for growth is that to make further improvements, resource efficiency policies need to be put in place that have costs for the economy. Whilst the first improvements are beneficial to the economy, the additional steps come at a cost and in the end the net effect is negative.

(European Commission, 2014b: 15)

Furthermore, the transition is presented as realistic and achievable:

If the same annual rate of increase as in the past was to be kept in the future (around 2% per annum) as occurred over the last economic business cycle, then this would result in a 30% improvement in Resource Productivity by 2030. The [European Resource Efficiency Platform] endorsed this level of ambition as realistic.

(European Commission, 2014b: 15)

The cautiousness of the first Communication is due to the fact that in 2014, the European Union was still recovering from the economic crisis caused by the 2008–2009 financial crisis. The circular economy was an attempt to reinstate environmental concerns in the political agenda. European public policy was faced with high unemployment, the Greek debt crisis, and threats of exit from the European Union and from the Euro zone. In this context, the European Commission created the strategy of "smart, sustainable and inclusive growth" (European Commission, 2010). Due to the unfavourable economic climate, environmental concerns were brought up by making a business case for the circular economy, with the support of the Ellen MacArthur Foundation, and by stating very clearly that the circular economy would not halt economic growth and did not require an acceleration. The circular economy was a realistic goal, a moderate goal.

Early work on the circular economy was supported by the European Environment Agency and the Directorate General for the Environment. The origins of the proposal can be associated with a school of thought informed by ecology and environmental studies, and that is in opposition to the economic management of the environment, associated with environmental economics. In environmental economics, instruments such as taxes (called Pigouvian taxes), polluter-pays principle and cap-and-trade are used to correct market failures. The European Environment Agency, by contrast, considers that the environment is better managed through targeted policies (www.eea.europa.eu/about-us), not economic policies. Examples of targeted policies may include improving material and energy efficiency, supporting environmental legislation and conservation efforts. The tension between economic instruments and environmental initiatives can be observed in the mild criticism of the self-regulating capacity of the market, in the 2014 Communication. The communication reports:

> Despite the argument that increasing commodity prices will deliver resource savings, both theoretical and empirical evidence suggests that there are *significant market failures* due to externalities, information deficits, adaptation and coordination deficits:
>
> - Positive externalities associated with eco-innovation that pose barriers to entrepreneurs and product innovation,
> - Wide-spread information deficits as regards to potentials for saving material purchasing costs within companies and across industries,
> - Information deficits concerning uncertainties about future demand for new eco-innovations, including in critical areas such as construction,
> - Adaptation and coordination deficits with regard to existing market power, path dependencies and difficulties to finance mass market development of radical innovations.
>
> (European Commission, 2014b: 11 – our emphasis)

The criticism of the economic management of the environment disappears from later versions of circular economy policy proposals. In November 2014, Jean-Claude Juncker was elected president of the European Commission, and pressures increased on the European Commission to set in place measures that would help the Union recover from the economic slowdown. In December 2014, the European Commission withdrew its policy proposal on waste, promising to deliver a new proposal.

2015 – A more ambitious vision of the circular economy

In late 2014, the European Commission changed presidency to Jean-Claude Juncker, and the change in presidency was accompanied by a revision of existing policies. The Juncker Commission considered that the first proposal for the circular economy, *Towards a circular economy: A zero waste programme for Europe*, was not ambitious enough. A new communication was published in 2015, entitled *Closing the loop – An EU action plan for the circular economy*. In contrast to the first Communication, which spoke of moderation and continuity, the second Communication is a public display of the change in presidency and speaks of renewal and break with the past.

An important priority of the Juncker Commission was to ensure that the circular economy could be delivered by the end of the mandate (2019). According to a policy officer,

> We got a number of sort of instructions which basically said, you know, you will look at things that we are confident we can deliver until the end of this Commission. You will look at things that have added value at the EU level. You will not look at giving instructions in some way to Member States, what they should do at a national, local or regional level. And you will obviously look very much at what you can do with the existing tools and policies.
>
> (Interview, 11 Jan 2017)

The new policy proposal moves away from target setting (giving instructions to Member States) towards producing a new vision for Europe, while at the same time maintains continuity with the past by relying on existing tools and policies.

The main novelty of the second Communication is a clear focus on economic growth. This change reflects also in part the change in sponsors, as the circular economy narrative found allies in the Directorate General for Growth, within the European Commission. The European Union is depicted as supporting an existing process: "Economic actors, such as business and consumers, are key in driving this process. Local, regional and national authorities are enabling the transition, but the European Union also has a fundamental role to play in supporting it" (European Commission, 2015a: 2). The protagonists of the circular economy are economic actors, businesses and consumers. The environment is left in the background.

There is a subtle switch of narrative in the second Communication, which presents the circular economy as a transition that is under way. The definition of the circular economy thus focuses on transition, on enhancing the already existing circularity of the economy:

> The transition to *a more circular* economy, where the value of products, materials and resources is maintained in the economy for as long as possible, and the generation of waste minimised, is an essential contribution to

the European Union's efforts to develop a sustainable, low carbon, resource efficient and competitive economy.

(European Commission, 2015a: 2 – our emphasis)

This definition is mainstreamed in later policy documents, and the 2015 communication is often cited as the point of departure for the circular economy action plan. We emphasise here the idea that the economy needs to become *more* circular, which implies that the economy is already circular and that this policy package does not represent a disruption of the current system. *"So it's not a revolutionary concept. So it's not questioning the fundamentals of our system and it never was"* (interview, 11 Jan 2017). The more ambitious plan is still framed as an economic opportunity, to maintain the alliance between environmental and economic policy.

The very mild criticism to market failures is substituted by parlance of opportunities, as in "Such transition is the opportunity to transform our economy and generate new and sustainable competitive advantages for Europe" (European Commission, 2015a: 2). The idiom of opportunities is also a characteristic of successive policy documents. We argue that the focus on opportunities and "win-win" solutions are fundamental aspects of how the circular economy is being framed in order to gather support. The circular economy, first and foremost, is described as offering opportunities for economic growth and increased competitiveness of Europe internationally. The main rationale for the pursuit of circularity is the business case. This way, the Directorate General for the Environment seeks an alliance with the Directorate General for Growth, overcoming the political dead end of environmental limits to growth. According to those involved in the process, the circular economy does not create additional policy priorities, but is seen as a means to achieve existing priorities:

So I think that was, it was a very interesting development, that something that was outside of the political priorities as established by President Juncker made its way, not by creating an additional priority, but saying it's actually part of a number of the big priorities we have.

(Interview, 11 Jan 2017)

The greater level of ambition appears in the presentation of the circular economy as a systemic change, in contradiction with the 2014 idea that the circular economy is a moderate project, and with the claim that the circular economy attends to existing policy priorities. According to the 2015 communication, "The transition to a circular economy is a systemic change" (European Commission, 2015a: 18), that needs a vigorous push.

The Commission will assist Member States, regions and local authorities in strengthening their circular economy approach in this context through targeted outreach. Private finance needs to be directed towards new opportunities created by the circular economy. For the financial sector, such projects can *differ significantly from "business as usual"*.

(European Commission, 2015a: 19 – our emphasis)

Differing from business as usual means that the mainstream economy should be made circular, not that the economic aims of the European Commission are questioned or reviewed in any way.

The broad vision of the circular economy is manifested in the projections of what the circular economy should achieve by 2030:

- A reduction of 17–24% in material inputs by 2030
- An increase of 3.9% in GDP thanks to material cost-saving opportunities
- A reduction of 2–4% in total annual greenhouse gas emissions
- A potential annual savings of €600 million for European industry

In practical terms, the circular economy starts to inform also legislative proposals. The communication *Closing the loop – An EU action plan for the circular economy* was accompanied by the proposal to review several existing directives, on batteries and accumulators, on waste landfill, on packaging and packaging waste, and on waste. There was also a new proposal to extend legal guarantees on goods sold online to two years, which takes up the idea of increasing product durability. The implementation of the circular economy is at odds with the narrative of proposing a new package. In financial terms, the circular economy is supported through €650 million under Horizon 2020 and €5.5 billion under the Structural Funds.

The goal was to establish the idea of a circular economy as not being exclusively about waste. Existing policy instruments, however, are about waste management and the circular economy struggles to move away from this practice. As a result, there is somewhat of a mismatch between the rhetoric and the practice. The 2015 Communication is meant to move away from the idea of a *"zero-waste society"*, which was described by a policy officer as *"unachievable in an economically viable way"* (interview, 11 Jan 2017). The focus switched to *"maximise the reuse, recycling and remanufacturing possibilities"* (ibid.). As public policy scholars Robert Geyer and Paul Cairney (Geyer & Cairney, 2015) argue, initial decisions and events contribute to the formation of institutions that influence practice in the long term. As people build institutions around initial decisions, it becomes increasingly costly to change path and the bulk of policy making tends to be repetitive.

2016 – Implementing the circular economy

Following the 2015 communication, policy efforts focus on the implementation of the circular economy and in the formulation of a Circular Economy Action Plan. In this phase, the circular economy concept is deployed outside of waste policy, and is used to build connections with more policy realms. Many Directorates General were asked to contribute to the initiative, including the Directorates

General for Agriculture, for Health and Food Safety, for Research and Innovation, for Mobility and Transport, and for Regional and Urban policy.

The implementation reveals two important features that contribute to the making of the circular economy. First, the circular economy becomes linked to the security narrative. Security refers to the ability of a nation to secure access to resources, either through production or by having access to suppliers, which depends on purchasing power and geopolitical relations (Buzan, Waever, Waever, & De Wilde, 1998). A notable example of the use of the term is energy security, a concept used to relate the availability of energy sources (both in physical and geopolitical terms) to the affordability of energy for a country and its citizens (Chester, 2010). The concept of security is thus closely related to a multiplicity of risks and uncertainties (Kovacic & Di Felice, 2019). The rising demand for raw materials at the global level increases the competition for scarce resources and has consequences for the European Union's security of supply. Specific attention is paid to the recycling of rare earth metals, and of increasingly scarce resources, such as fertilising products. The implementation of the circular economy package includes a proposal for a regulation of fertilising products. The security narrative mobilises geopolitical concerns and makes the circular economy palatable to broader political concerns.

Second, innovation emerges as a central feature. Innovation refers both to the creation of new regulations and institutional arrangements, and to technological innovation and the pursuit of new solutions that would make the economy (more) circular. The initiative "Innovation deals for a circular economy" was launched between 26 May and 15 September 2016, to identify perceived regulatory barriers to innovation, and directed at "innovators" and Member States. Businesses are invited to the frontline of implementation of the circular economy. In November 2016, the Ecodesign Working Plan for 2016–2019 was adopted as part of the Clean Energy for All Europeans package. Ideas of ecodesign have been part of the circular economy imaginary from the start. Ecodesign is supposed to increase product durability, reduce the use of toxic materials so that more products can be recycled safely, and improve production processes towards less energy and primary materials use, and less pollution. In this case, the role of innovation is that of providing solutions, or promises of solutions, for the technical bottlenecks that may impede the circularisation of products. The promises of innovation play a fundamental role in policy negotiations and in the mainstreaming of the circular economy concept, by making the proposal less vulnerable to criticism about what can and cannot be done. Innovation promises to transpose the boundary of what can be done.

Notwithstanding the role of innovation to gloss over some of the unclear paths for the implementation of the circular economy, knowledge gaps are also acknowledged. An important linear element in the economy is food, which is degraded through digestion and cannot be recycled. At best, some manure can be used as fertiliser, but, in any case, the production of new food requires natural resources including, water, soil, and secondary agricultural inputs including, energy, fertilisers and pesticides. Efforts are thus directed at limiting food waste, so that the processes that cannot become circular are at least minimised. However, there are no statistics on food waste for the European Union. To correct this knowledge and policy gap, a number of initiatives were launched: i) a stakeholder's platform on food waste prevention; ii) the development of a European Union methodology to measure food waste; and iii) the preparation of European Union guidelines to facilitate food donations and the use of former foodstuff as feed. The focus on food waste is one of the only acknowledgements of the sixteenth century map in the development of the circular economy imaginary.

Notably, indicators start to emerge as an important site of policy making. In 2016, the European Commission published a scoreboard of 24 indicators that would help monitor, among other things, the development of the circular economy. The report constructs a new economic sector, namely the raw materials sector, which comprises not only the extractive industries (e.g. mining, forestry) but also those industries that use raw materials in their production processes (e.g. manufacturing and construction).

2017 – Public performance of the circular economy

According to the European Commission, 2017 was a crucial year to develop a policy dialogue with stakeholders. To this purpose, the Commission launched a circular economy stakeholders' platform, with the purpose to "gather stakeholders' input and views" (European Commission, 2017c: 2), raising awareness and sharing best practices. The effort to involve stakeholders contributes to another feature of sociotechnical imaginaries, namely the public performance of the vision. To this purpose, the first Circular Economy Stakeholders Conference was organised in 2015, followed by a second conference in 2018. The Stakeholder Platform is an initiative that builds on the Stakeholder Conferences. Both conferences and platform are organised by the European Commission, signalling that these are not means through which ideas are discussed, but public performances.

Public performance revolves around the presentation of the circular economy as a matter of fact, something that is already happening and whose benefits are clear and beyond doubt. The assumption that the circular economy has obvious benefits goes back to 2015, as can be observed in the statement by Karmenu Vella, the European Commissioner for Environment, Maritime Affairs and Fisheries:

> I was very impressed by the enormous societal and economic benefits which the report found could stem from the transition to a circular economy. So the question is not whether we want to set Europe on a circular path of growth. It is rather about how to help our economies to get there, and how quickly.... Once people are convinced of the impact on their pocket, on the services they receive, they will be much more receptive to listen to the wider benefits like CO2 reductions.
>
> (European Commission, 2015b)

This vision is then used to "convince" people of the benefits of the circular economy.

The novelty of the 2017 phase is the launch of a platform to support the financing of circular economy. The public performance of the circular economy imaginary has also the aim of raising financial support. This initiative rehearses the commitment of the European Commission to the economic benefits of the circular economy, which are presented as a given. Efforts are not directed at making the business case but at spreading the word: "While the business case for the circular economy is clear, this message still has to reach a good part of businesses in the EU and of the financial and banking sector" (European Commission, 2017b: 7).

With regard to implementation, efforts continue to be directed at the production of regulation in support of the Circular Economy Action Plan. New regulations include an amendment to the directive on the use of hazardous substances in electrical and electronic equipment, and a communication on waste-to-energy processes and their role in the circular economy. The main objective of the latter is that of ensuring that "the recovery of energy from waste in the EU supports the objectives of the circular economy action plan and is firmly guided by the EU waste hierarchy" (European Commission, 2017d: 2). In both cases, the heritage of waste management is very clear, as well as the path dependency created by the early focus on waste.

A report by the Directorate General for Research and Innovation (European Commission, 2017a), summarises the "reality" of the circular economy policy. Circular economy targets are all linked to waste management and include:

- Increase recycling of municipal waste to a minimum of 65% by 2030
- Increase the recycling rate for packaging waste to 75% by 2030
- Reduce landfill to 10% by 2030 (binding target)

These targets are accompanied by measures that include action beyond waste, such as increasing standards for secondary raw materials, measures that promote repair, durability and recycling of products, a plastics strategy, and mentions of wastewater and food waste reduction.

2018 – Measuring the circular economy

The most notable advancement in 2018 has been the publication of the Circular Economy Monitoring Framework in January (European Commission, 2018), which adopts a series of indicators through which to monitor progress towards the circular economy. The monitoring framework includes elements of waste management as well as innovation and economic growth, and is representative of the attempt to mainstream waste management into economic narratives. The indicators were the result of a collaboration between the Directorate General for the Environment and the Directorate General for Growth. By 2018, the circular economy had evolved from the aspiration of connecting different policy realms to an active collaboration, becoming a nexus policy.

Indicators have two functions in the development of the circular economy policy. One the one hand, they provide the evidence base to support and justify support for the policy. Since the policy came before the indicators, this can be seen as a case of policy-based evidence (Saltelli & Giampietro, 2017). The indicators have an instrumental role. Quantitative measures are used to indicate the way forward, not to set precise targets for the circularity of the economy. Their role is strictly of support in the creation of the circular economy imaginary.

> *The Commission decided that we would not have the quantitative objectives and goals that we want to meet by a certain time but that we would have a qualitative description of where we want to go and that we would have a set of indicators in the long-term framework that would allow us to say over time, have the measures that are put in place had an effect in changing certain parameters of the European economy.*
>
> (Interview, Jan 11 2017).

On the other hand, indicators are used for monitoring progress, and they become part of the bureaucratic machinery of the European Union and of the reporting obligations of Eurostat, the statistics agency of the European Commission. This way, indicators institutionalise the circular economy, and create those paths that lock policy making in a specific discourse. As progress towards the circular economy must be monitored, more and more policies, measures, and initiatives mention the circular economy, or are mentioned by the implementation reports. In this context, it becomes increasingly difficult to see whether policies are created to make the economy circular, or whether the reporting obligations create a tendency to pay lip service to the circular economy while continuing with business as usual. Because of the central role of indicators and of the important efforts devoted to the creation of indicators for the circular economy by the European Commission and its statistical agency, Eurostat, we will return to the discussion of indicators in Chapter 7.

Careful of what you wish for?

The circular economy has become an all-purpose label. The term is widely used both in academic research and in European policy. The two trends are related. As funding is devoted to research on the circular economy, it provides an incentive for academics to enter this research field. We conclude this chapter by reflecting on whether the popularity of the circular economy is a blessing or a curse. The editor of a scientific journal told one of the authors that the circular economy has made the once unknown discipline of industrial ecology very popular but has also cannibalised the field. He concluded, "you should be careful of what you wish for".

The Ellen MacArthur Foundation has played an important role in popularising the term "circular economy" and in mainstreaming the concept in European policy. As a result, even though the circular economy has gathered support both from academia and from the European Commission, the policy has been constrained by the concept that made it popular. We found similar sentiments in our interviews: *"So I'm not sure circular economy was the right term to be coined but here we are, it is what it is. I think it's in, there is still some work to do to convince everybody that it's actually not waste but it's actually the circular economy that we're talking about"* (interview, Jan 11 2017).

In European policy, the 2015 definition is repeated in most policy documents. The circular economy is an economy "where the value of products, materials and resources is maintained in the economy for as long as possible, and the generation of waste minimised" (European Commission, 2015a: 2). This is, however, a vague definition that makes it possible to enlist broad support and be used in a variety of contexts (Cairns & Krzywoszynska, 2016). The policy of the circular economy takes the form of a sociotechnical imaginary, which is future oriented, highly reliant on innovation, and publicly performed. So far, most efforts have been directed at convincing consumers and businesses of the benefits of the circular economy, at creating a new narrative, and at making alliances with different agencies and directorates within the European Commission, and interest groups and lobbies from outside the European Commission.

Even though the circular economy promised to be about more than waste, implementation is based on setting targets for waste management, and projections of economic benefits. The recurrence of waste management in policy implementation is a case of path dependence in policy implementation and creates a discrepancy between the rhetoric of systemic change and the practice of policy making. As the Juncker presidency comes to its end at the time of writing (2019), the sociotechnical imaginary of the circular economy has been greatly developed and mainstreamed in European policy, but practical implementation lags behind. Practical results could certainly be delayed and may be observable in the future, but for the time being, we observe a policy developed on the basis of promises that resonate very well with the idea of a sixteenth century map.

References

Buzan, B., Waever, O., Waever, O., & De Wilde, J. (1998). *Security: A New Framework for Analysis*. New York: Lynne Rienner Publishers.

Cairns, R., & Krzywoszynska, A. (2016). Anatomy of a buzzword: The emergence of 'the water-energy-food nexus' in UK natural resource debates. *Environmental Science and Policy*, 64, 164–170. doi:10.1016/j.envsci.2016.07.007

Chester, L. (2010). Conceptualising energy security and making explicit its polysemic nature. *Energy Policy*, 38(2), 887–895. doi:10.1016/j.enpol.2009.10.039

Ellen MacArthur Foundation. (2013). *Towards the Circular Economy*. Retrieved from www.ellenmacarthurfoundation.org/assets/downloads/publications/Ellen-MacArthur-Foundation-Towards-the-Circular-Economy-vol.1.pdf

European Commission. (2010). *Europe 2020: A strategy for smart, sustainable and inclusive growth* (COM (2010) No. 2020 final). Brussels: European Commission.

European Commission. (2014a). *Annex to the Communication from the Commission to the European Parliament, the Council, the European Economic and Social Committee and the Committee of the Regions. Towards a circular economy: A zero waste programme for Europe* (No. COM (2014) 398).

European Commission. (2014b). *Commission Staff Working Document. Analysis of an EU Target for Resource Productivity Accompanying the Document. Communication from the Commission to the European Parliament, the Council, the European Economic and Social Committee and the Committee of the Regions* (No. SWD (2014) 211).

European Commission. (2014c). *Communication from the Commission to the European Parliament, the Council, the European Economic and Social Committee and the Committee of the Regions. Towards a circular economy: A zero waste programme for Europe* (No. COM (2014) 398). Brussels: European Commission. Retrieved from http://eur-lex.europa. eu/resource.html?uri=cellar:50edd1fd-01ec-11e4-831f-01aa75ed71a1.0001.01/ DOC_1&format=PDF

European Commission. (2015a). *Communication from the Commission to the European Parliament, the Council, the European Economic and Social Committee and the Committee of the Regions. Closing the loop – An EU action plan for the Circular Economy EN* (No. COM (2015) 614). Brussels: European Commission.

European Commission. (2015b). Introductory remarks by Karmenu Vella, 25 June. Retrieved from https://ec.europa.eu/commission/commissioners/2014-2019/vella/a nnouncements/closing-loop-conference-circular-economy-introductory-remarks-ka rmenu-vella-25-june-2015_en

European Commission. (2015c) *Proposal for a Directive of the European Parliament and of the Council amending Directive 2008/98/EC on waste.* (COM/2015/0595 final). Brussels: European Commission.

European Commission. (2017a). *Circular Economy Research and Innovation: Connecting Economic & Environmental Gains.* Brussels: European Commission. doi:10.2777/416618

European Commission. (2017b). *Communication from the Commission to the European Parliament, the Council, the European Economic and Social Committee and the Committee of the Regions. The role of waste-to-energy in the circular economy* (No. COM (2017) 34). Brussels: European Commission. Retrieved from http://ec.europa.eu/environment/ waste/waste-to-energy.pdf

European Commission. (2017c). *European Circular Economy Stakeholder Platform.* Retrieved from https://circulareconomy.europa.eu/platform/en/dialogue/cg-nam es-contacts?page=2

European Commission. (2017d). *Report from the Commission to the European Parliament, the Council, the European Economic and Social Committee and the Committee of the Regions on the implementation of the Circular Economy Action Plan* (No. COM (2017) 33). Brussels: European Commission.

European Commission. (2018). *Commission Staff Working Document. Measuring progress towards circular economy in the European Union – Key indicators for a monitoring framework. Accompanying the document Communication from the Commission to the European Parliament, the Council, the European Economic and Social Committee and the Committee of the Regions* (No. SWD (2018) 17).

Geyer, R., & Cairney, P. (2015). *Handbook on Complexity and Public Policy.* Cheltenham: Edward Elgar.

Jasanoff, S., & Kim, S. H. (2009). Containing the atom: Sociotechnical imaginaries and nuclear power in the United States and South Korea. *Minerva,* 47, 119–146. 10.1007/ s11024–11009–9124–9124

Kovacic, Z., & Di Felice, L. J. (2019). Complexity, uncertainty and ambiguity: implications for European Union energy governance. *Energy Research & Social Science,* 53, 159–169.

Saltelli, A., & Giampietro, M. (2017). What is wrong with evidence based policy, and how can it be improved? *Futures,* 91, 62–71.

4 The circular economy

A concept in the making

This chapter is an intermezzo that weaves together the different strands and argues that it is useful to think of the circular economy not merely as something that either can be achieved or not, but as policy concept that is currently being assembled or "in the making". That means, we analyse not only attempts of achieving circularity but also how, as a part of these negotiations, different visions and versions of a circular economy are also negotiated. For doing so we use Clarke's concept of "situation" and map the institutions, actors and ideologies involved and interested in this concept and the discursive framings attached to it. In order to shift the focus away from the definitions and (im) possibility of the circular economy, we use the concept of *dflkjdrl haqwnmz* – a rhetorical device that allows us to discuss the situation. We argue that *dflkjdrl haqwnmz* policy sticks because of vagueness, which can be interpreted to the advantage of multiple actors, can be adapted to changes in policy officers and policy agendas, and is broad enough to represent a generic goal for the economy, escaping the accountability of more concrete promises.

Introduction

We started this book by noting that the circular economy is a vague and undefined concept, which resembles a sixteenth century map in as far as it describes the wishes and fears of the cartographer more than the territory. In Chapter 2 we have traced the emergence of the circular economy concept in academia and argued that there are important discrepancies between the academic fields that inform the circular economy. In Chapter 3 we have discussed how the concept is being shaped in European policy.

The next part of the book, with Chapters 5–8, will zoom into particular aspects of the circular economy and perform critical analyses of its policies and imaginaries. The current Chapter 4 aims to be a short intermezzo to consolidate the point of departure for the analyses to follow. Chapter 4 has one goal: We wish to create an effect of alienation to increase the distance from involved debates on what the circular economy is or might be, and whether it is desirable or at all possible. We will take a step back from definitions, and argue that the "circular economy", whatever that may be, is of interest in policy processes not because of the present content of this contested concept, but precisely because the concept is vague. Its vagueness and ambiguity create space for negotiation and the creation of imaginaries about the future.

To achieve that effect of alienation we shall use a rhetorical device. We mentioned in the introductory chapter that this book emerged out of a larger research project called MAGIC – Moving towards adaptive governance in complexity. European Union's circular economy policies was one of the case studies of MAGIC. In the initial phase of the case study, discussions between the ecological economists and the social scientists in the project frequently stranded. The social scientists (including the authors of this book) argued that one had to approach the subject of the circular economy with an open mind, to try to find out what the policy-makers wanted to achieve. The ecological economists argued that the whole idea of the circular economy was ill-conceived and simply wrong.

After months of not understanding each other well, one of us (Roger Strand) sent an e-mail to the group where he jokingly introduced the rhetorical device that we shall apply throughout this chapter: He gave the circular economy policy a nonsensical name:

> From the bioeconomics perspective [alluding to the tradition in ecological economics originating from Georgescu-Roegen] the policies on circular economy make no sense, that is clear. From the social scientist perspective they are interesting policies in-the-making. I endorse both perspectives.
>
> The social science point can be easier to grasp if you just pretend that they are not called "circular economy policies" but "*dflkjdrl haqwnmz* policies". For people such as me it is interesting to find out what policy-makers and other actors think of and define by "*dlfkjdrl haqwnmz*", what they want to achieve (which is surely NOT *dlfkjdrl haqwnmz* but something else), and how we meaningfully can interact with them.
>
> So this is not a situation of "we bioeconomists know that ★**this**★ is bullshit but we leave it to you social scientists to tell them in a nice way". It is a situation of us trying to discover what ★**this**★ (the policies on *dlfkjdrl haqwnmz*) is on its way to becoming and how we can help shape that becoming in a good way (or help divert or abort it).
>
> (E-mail by Roger Strand, 13 September 2017, lightly edited)

This trick resolved the problem of communication. Even if one has studied ecological economics and knows that the economy cannot be circular, one can still be curious about what the European Union is up to in their new policies on "*dflkjdrl haqwnmz*". In this intermezzo, we will insist on this rhetorical device, hoping that the readers will enjoy a bit of text that is somewhat more tongue-in-cheek inside an otherwise quite serious academic treatise.

Dflkjdrl haqwnmz

In what follows, then, we argue that the *dflkjdrl haqwnmz* has acquired relevance in European policy because it is a concept "in the making". With this observation, we shift our attention from what the *dflkjdrl haqwnmz* might mean to the wider context in which discourses and imaginaries are shaped through the interaction of different stakeholders. We are interested in what policy-makers and other actors think of and define by "*dlfkjdrl haqwnmz*" and what they want to achieve. The shift in attention from the circular economy to the *dlfkjdrl haqwnmz* is a shift from subject matter to the situation (Clarke, 2005), rooted in the traditions of pragmatist philosophy and symbolic interactionism. These traditions assume that the meaning of a phenomenon, *dlfkjdrl haqwnmz* in our case, is not to be found in an essentialist way. There is no "true" circularity that can be achieved or not. Rather, its meaning is constructed interactionally and dependent/co-constitutive with the situation in which it emerges. This doesn't mean, of course, that the meanings *dlfkjdrl haqwnmz* will assume are completely arbitrary. Much to the contrary, there is a very narrow range of meanings particular phenomena can take on (this narrowing down of potential meanings of *dlfkjdrl haqwnmz* will be a central line of critique throughout this book), which also significantly narrows down possible material effects. Because, and this is another important feature of this line of thought, meaning and meaning making (or sense-making) are necessarily material activities in a material world. The meanings *dlfkjdrl haqwnmz* will take on will have consequences in the "real" world. This can happen for example in terms of allocated funding resources, or international companies claiming to change their modes of production. This theoretical perspective is labelled "relational materiality" and is relentlessly post-essentialist (Law, 1994, 2004).

Highlighting the situation then means looking not at the degree to which circularity is being achieved or not. It focuses on the meanings as they are ascribed to a particular configuration or assemblage of institutions, groups of actors and their beliefs. As Adele Clarke puts it, there are

> multiple collective actors (social worlds) in all kinds of negotiations and conflicts in a broad substantive arena focused on matters about which all the involved social worlds and actors care enough to be committed to act and to produce discourse about arena concerns.
>
> (Clarke 2005: 37)

This means asking questions about the (institutional) actors involved, their stakes and concerns, and about lines of conflict and controversy. Importantly, all of this is not "the context" of *dlfkjdrl haqwnmz*, all of this is *dlfkjdrl haqwnmz*.

Therefore, throughout the remaining chapters of this book we draw inspiration from this line of thought and will describe the different meanings of circularity in terms of institutional settings, or collectively shared ideas about legitimate objectives, goals and futures. Importantly, this perspective also implies representing the phenomena under scrutiny through their own perspectives. To do so we will draw on our interactions with actors engaged in developing circular economy policy and its epistemic basis.

This perspective with its focus on the situation of inquiry is also closely tied to the situatedness of knowledge which seeks to position scientific knowledge in its cultural, political, economic, geographic and historical context (Haraway, 2006). This perspective postulates that there simply is no view from nowhere. A recurrent observation of studies of situated knowledge is that things could have been otherwise. This observation challenges the modernist idea of science as the view from nowhere, which provides clear and unique "solutions" to the "problems" it studies. What is defined as a "problem" depends on the political and economic context (Bacchi, 2009), on the identity, gender and sexuality of the scientist (Harding, 1993), on the institutional culture and historical antecedents (Jasanoff, 2004) that influence which questions can be asked and which questions are perceived as important. Similarly, the "solution" carries with it prescriptions about how the world should be, hopes for change and/or political interests for the stabilisation of the status quo. As philosopher Ian Hacking famously pointed out, representation is intervention (Hacking, 1983). As knowledge is always interwoven with the situation of its production, it also intervenes with this exact situation.

In the case of the *dflkjdrl haqwnmz*, the otherwise that could have been is being shaped together with *dflkjdrl haqwnmz*. By using an ambiguous and yet undefined concept, which we express as *dflkjdrl haqwnmz*, it becomes clear that the distinction between what *dflkjdrl haqwnmz* is and what the otherwise could be, is blurred itself. The *dflkjdrl haqwnmz* concept is emerging from a process in which different political interests are negotiated, irreducible uncertainties are present, and the legitimacy of the bureaucratic machinery of the European Union is being questioned.

Rather than diagnosing the situation after it has occurred, we analyse the situation in which the circular economy is being made, while it is in the making. The circular economy is not a finished project in European policy, and the interviews, policy documents and focus groups we refer to throughout the book are early formulations of the circular economy concept, which are being developed and are changing even as we write. By referring to *dlfkjdrl haqwnmz*, we take a step back from the elusive and changing concept of circular economy and take a closer look at the discourses, imaginaries, power relations and political debates among which *dlfkjdrl haqwnmz* is being shaped. Because the *dflkjdrl haqwnmz* is in the making, we will apply a critical lens to the analysis of the scientific claims mobilised (Chapter 5), the imaginaries used (Chapter 6), the indicators created (Chapter 7) and we will pay attention to the policy actors that are included (Chapter 8) in the governance of the *dflkjdrl haqwnmz*.

The legitimacy crisis of the European Union

As we mentioned in Chapter 3, the *dflkjdrl haqwnmz* was reformulated in 2015 with the specific aim of supporting the economic recovery after the 2009 financial crisis and the economic crisis that ensued, especially in Southern

Europe. As the *dflkjdrl haqwnmz* policy was being developed, the European project itself entered a severe legitimacy crisis, which has manifested in the rise of extremist parties, anti-immigrant and separatist discourses. The crisis of the European Union was epitomised by Brexit, the (democratic) decision of the United Kingdom to exit the European Union in 2016. At the time of writing, the conditions for the exit of the United Kingdom are being negotiated, and the crisis of European institutions is still unfolding.

In this context, it is useful to remind ourselves that *the dflkjdrl haqwnmz* is a European policy. The need for the *dflkjdrl haqwnmz* to deliver economic growth can thus be seen as an attempt to restore the legitimacy of the European project by making clear its economic advantages. The *dflkjdrl haqwnmz* establishes a dialogue between environmental concerns and economic needs, and transforms a tension between opposing goals into the joining of forces towards a common goal – a point we will return to in Chapter 8. We suggest that part of the common goal is to demonstrate the unity and strength of the European project, and to de-emphasise tensions. This is why what the policy is called is irrelevant, and we can speak of *dflkjdrl haqwnmz*. What matters is the ability of the European institutions to show that they can work together, and that they are unaffected by the threat of disintegration of the European Union. The success of the *dflkjdrl haqwnmz* policy represents not just a golden medal for the Juncker administration, it is also a much-needed proof that the European project can work.

For this reason, the *dflkjdrl haqwnmz* is a message of hope, in which the content is of secondary importance. One may speak of circular, as well as elliptical, square, flat, full economy. Things could have been otherwise by acknowledging the legitimacy crisis of European institutions, the fading trust in the European project and the return of nationalisms and xenophobic discourses. Acknowledging these trends would not be pleasant, but silencing them through messages of hope may be reckless.

The fact that the legitimacy crisis of the European institutions is not openly acknowledged does not mean that it is unnoticed. We do not aim at "revealing" that the emperor has no clothes (we do not claim to know the "truth" about the circular economy), but rather at providing an alternative reading of the Andersen's story. In the story, the adults remain silent not because of ignorance, but because they willingly take part in the emperor's illusion. By speaking up, the kid breaks the illusion, as well as the community that is held together by a common ideal. We suggest that the emergence of extremist parties in the political spectrum in many European countries is similar to the shout that the emperor has no clothes. The political turmoil reveals that the illusion is in crisis. However, there is no clear alternative. Proposals such as *dflkjdrl haqwnmz* may be seen not as a denial of the crisis, but as a desperate attempt to keep the illusion alive. As Antonio Gramsci wrote in his Prison Notebooks: "The crisis consists precisely in the fact that the old is dying and the new cannot be born; in the interregnum a great variety of morbid symptoms appear".

The institutional context of the European Commission

When the first interviews were conducted (end of 2016 and beginning of 2017), we learned that the Directorate General for Growth and the Directorate General for the Environment were developing indicators for the circular economy, and later in 2017 attention shifted to issues of implementation and the involvement of private industry. The development of *dflkjdrl haqwnmz* policy has been very dynamic so far and the reflections we develop in this book refer only to the first steps of this process.

In addition, the policy officers that we interviewed have, in some cases, changed position and in other cases, changed tasks. There was only one instance in which we were able to continue the conversation with a policy officer, who was interviewed and attended the first focus group. The high turnover of officers both in the European Commission and in its agencies is part of the context in which policies are formulated and negotiated. In a conversation with a policy officer at the workshop conducted in February 2018, we learned that officers are moved every two years, in order to avoid corruption. As a result, policy officers do not manage to build strong expertise in their field of work, and have to rely on expert advice and lobbyists. In the words of an interviewee, Commission officers are made "intentionally weak" with regard to expertise.

Zahariadis (2008) argues that the multiplicity and the high turnover of actors, and the highly bureaucratic system of the European Union, cause a fragmentation of the policy process. In this context, ambiguity plays an important role in policy making. According to Zahariadis, ambiguity is due to three factors: i) policy officers have unclear goals, often due to the urgency of the policy process and the unresolved uncertainties in the evidence base; ii) participation is fluid, because of the high turnover, the same policy officers do not follow the same issue through the different policy stages; and iii) the organisational technology is opaque, as policy officers are familiar with their own responsibilities but have less knowledge of policy processes in the European Union and of its bureaucracy. In this context, new ideas may be taken up not because of their viability or feasibility, but because they appear during policy windows in which a "problem" needs to be solved and because policy actors champion that "problem". According to the policy window narrative, solutions chase problems. The ambiguous *dflkjdrl haqwnmz* solution is acquiring popularity precisely because of, and not despite of, its ambiguity, which makes it capable of chasing multiple problems.

The idea of policy windows is at odds with the linear model of the policy process. In the latter, policies are created in response to a problem. The situation in which solutions chase problems is referred to as the garbage can model (Cohen, March, & Olsen, 1972), which is defined as a chaotic policy process in which organisational preferences and institutional processes are unclear, and decision makers change frequently. In this case, problems, solutions and decision-makers are seen as three independent variables, which are thrown together like garbage in a can. Rather than an orderly process going from problem to solution, the garbage can describes a messy process, in which causality can go in many directions. According to the garbage can model, the decision-making process provides decision makers an understanding of what they are doing and what they have done (Cohen et al., 1972). The decision- or policy- making process is a way of generating meaning. What matters is not the meaning of *dflkjdrl haqwnmz*, but the processes that *dflkjdrl haqwnmz* enables and through which meaning is generated.

Climate change and the context of environmental concerns

In 2016, the United Nations Framework Convention on Climate Change signed the Paris Agreement, which was presented as an unprecedented success in climate change negotiations and has become a policy priority for the European Commission. In academic research, climate change has come to dominate environmental studies. Climate change makes environmental concerns a global issue, that require a system perspective and action at the higher levels of governing. Environmental agendas have similarly undergone an upscaling of problem framing, becoming economy-wide strategies. These economy-wide strategies include the circular economy, the bioeconomy, the blue economy, the green economy, and possibly more. What matters is the "economy" scope of environmental policies.

The change of scale from local issues of pollution control, water quality in the rivers of Northern Europe and water scarcity in Southern Europe, biodiversity loss in specific habitats, and so on, to economy wide issues, suits well the scale of governance of European institutions. Economy-wide environmental governance can be regulated at the European Union level through the creation of reporting schemes for member states, and allows for the formulation of goals for Europe, rather than of localised and marginal improvements. On the other hand, the broader focus makes local needs invisible. There is the risk that local environmental issues may be considered of secondary importance with respect to global and European issues, not as a result of a democratic or deliberative process, but due to a more convenient problem framing for policy.

The broader framing of environmental issues changes the mechanisms of accountability. A vague policy aim such as *dflkjdrl haqwnmz* may be achieved independently of whether local problems are attended to. Because of its wide scope, it is less clear who will benefit from *dflkjdrl haqwnmz* and who should be held responsible for its implementation. The promises of *dflkjdrl haqwnmz* are not concrete, they resonate with a vague ideology of sustainability. As we will discuss in Chapter 8, the European Commission has initiated over 50 actions (European Commission, 2019), which consist mostly of the development of indicators, quality standards, revisions of existing regulations and allocation of funding. These actions, however, are not yet linked to any change in the level of circularity of the economy. What has been implemented is the concept of *dflkjdrl haqwnmz*.

As environmental concerns become a global matter and national and European priorities focus on the economic crisis, efforts have been devoted to mainstreaming the environment and keeping the environmental dimension present in European policy. As a result, the adjective that accompanies the "economy" is of secondary importance, as long as it signals the will to maintain environmental concerns on the agenda. For this reason, the concept of *dflkjdrl haqwnmz* continues to be a useful description, in this case of environmental governance. What matters is not the specific problem that circularity tries to solve, as opposed to "bio" or "green" solutions, but the fact that environmental concerns are mainstreamed together with economic concerns. In fact, some publications speak of the circular bioeconomy (Carus & Dammer, 2018; European Environment Agency, 2018), focusing the attention on the multiple ways in which environmental needs can be mainstreamed in the economy, and away from the specificities of each concept.

What comes next (in the book)

In a situation of fluidity, multiple interests and high turnover as described above, what is noteworthy is that a policy idea "sticks". New concepts and ideas are brought up all the time, and fade away all the time, as their proponents move and as interests change. The circular economy, on the other hand, has caught on. Using the rhetorical device of *dflkjdrl haqwnmz*, we have hypothesised that the stickiness of the circular economy is not due to its specific content, but to its contribution to sociotechnical imaginaries that support the European project, its ambiguity that makes it a repository for different (and maybe otherwise incompatible) policy objectives, and its ambitious scope, which resonates with grand challenges, rather than localised and less visible policy needs. In this book, we try to discover what the policies on the circular economy are on their way to becoming and hope that our critical reflections may help shape that becoming in a reflexive and responsible way (or help divert or abort it). We will do so by referring to analytical concepts and lenses drawn from science and technology studies and from post-normal science.

References

Bacchi, C. (2009). *Analysing Policy: What's the Problem Represented To Be?* Frenchs Forest: Pearson Australia.

Carus, M., & Dammer, L. (2018). *The Circular Bioeconomy – Concepts, Opportunities, and Limitations* (2018–2001 No. 9). Nova Papers (Vol. 14). Huerth: Nova Institute. doi:10.1089/ind.2018.29121.mca

Clarke, A. (2005). *Grounded Theory after the Postmodern Turn: Situational Maps and ANALYSES*. Thousand Oaks, CA: Sage.

Cohen, M., March, J., & Olsen, J. (1972). A garbage can model of organizational choice. *Administrative Science Quarterly*, 17(1), 1–25. doi:10.2307/2392088

European Commission. (2019, March). *Closing the loop: Commission delivers on Circular Economy Action Plan*. Press Release, pp. 2019–2021. Brussels: European Commission.

European Environment Agency. (2018). *The Circular Economy and the Bioeconomy: Partners in Sustainability*. Copenhagen: EEA.

Hacking, I. (1983). *Representing and Intervening: Introductory Topics in the Philosophy of Natural Science*. Cambridge, UK: Cambridge University Press.

Haraway, D. (2006). Situated knowledges: The science question in feminism and the privilege of partial perspective. *Feminist Studies*, 14(3), 575. doi:10.2307/3178066

Harding, S. (1993). Rethinking standpoint epistemology: What is "Strong Objectivity"? In L. Alcoff & E. Potter (Eds.), *Feminist Epistemologies*. London and New York: Routledge.

Jasanoff, S. (Ed.) (2004). *States of Knowledge: The Co-Production of Science and the Social Order*. New York: Routledge.

Law, J. (1994). *Organizing Modernity*. Cambridge, UK: Cambridge University Press.

Law, J. (2004). *After Method: Mess in Social Science Research*. London and New York: Routledge.

Zahariadis, N. (2008). Ambiguity and choice in European public policy. *Journal of European Public Policy*, 15(4), 514–530.

Part II
Critical perspectives

5   Postulating circularity

Biophysical flows and the problem
of entropy

From a biophysical point of view, a "closed loop" is an impossibility. In this chapter, we begin by discussing what it at all may mean that the economy goes in circles, or indeed that anything goes in circles. The foundational issue at the bottom of the discussion is the relationship between model and reality, and in the case of a "circular" model, which properties of the geometric object known as the circle are included in that model. If "circular" merely means that there is something somewhere that travels in a loop, the economy may well be circular. If that loop is supposed to be a closed loop of biophysical flows, the problems begin.

For bioeconomists, who focus on biophysical flows, it is difficult to make sense of the vision of the circular economy. Here is why: Most basic materials for human consumption, such as food and freshwater, have to be taken from the environment and once used cannot be recycled by processes under human control. The reason is that materials and products for consumption have to be pure or ordered enough to be safe and useful. Economic activities are entropic (disordering) processes that only can run at the expense of gradients provided by nature (resources and environmental services). Indeed, since the industrial revolution, socio-economic systems have been optimised towards increasingly linear models of production and consumption because this has allowed to accelerate the rate of economic activities. This change was possible because of fossil energy. Linear economies grow faster and are more competitive. In fact, within the EU, agriculture, mining and industry are increasingly outsourced to other countries, and the fossil energy used in EU is almost totally imported. Increase in productivity in Europe depends on linear economies outside Europe and on the capacity and opportunity of Europeans to import them.

In conclusion, the ideal of a circular economy is known to be incompatible with a developed, affluent economy in growth. Overall circularisation implies de-growth, or a slowdown of economic growth. As a consequence, the current level of recycling is very low.

Introduction

In the previous chapters we have traced the historical antecedents of the notion of the circular economy and described how and by whose efforts the notion came into political prominence in the European Union in the decade of the 2010s. We have pointed out debates and disagreements about circularity as well as the economy, and shown how certain conceptions of the circular economy came to dominate over others as policies were developed inside EU governmental institutions but also outside, notably with the Ellen MacArthur Foundation as a catalyst.

It would have been entirely possible to produce a historical and sociological account of the circular economy that did not penetrate more deeply into the matter, that is, that limited itself at displaying the variety of opinions and then the political work and interests that closed the discussions. Next, one could follow the implementation process and try to characterise the outcomes and impacts of the policies, and perhaps also "evaluate" and possibly suggest adjustments and improvements. There is in general no scarcity of this type of superficial policy analysis.

Throughout this book, however, we aim to show that a deeper analysis is called for in order to understand the circular economy as a policy concept in the making but also in order to govern its process of making in a promising direction. One way of explaining why there is such a need is to show that the disagreements about the circular economy are not just "simple" differences in conceptual and/or political preferences. Rather, they correspond to a more fundamental question: Is it at all possible to have a circular economy? Is it at all a meaningful concept? Already in Chapter 2 we presented academic traditions that will answer the question in the negative: *The economy cannot be circular!* Indeed, in the previous chapter we employed a rhetorical device that we developed in order to be able to talk about the policy concept within these academic traditions, since most attempts at debate stranded with vehement objections that the circular economy is an impossibility and an absurdity.

If this is to be the conclusion, then a superficial, common sense understanding of "the circular economy" as, indeed, an economy that is or tries to be circular, will fail to grasp the subject matter. If the circular economy is not an economy that is circular, what is it? What is the content of the concept? This radical insight opens up for an STS-inspired analysis that looks for the processes by which a *prima facie* empty, meaningless or otherwise undetermined concept acquires meaning and content through social, technical and political work of imagination, calculation and institutionalisation. This analysis we will present in the subsequent chapters, 6–8. The task of this chapter, however, is to consolidate the radical insight that was already indicated in Chapter 2 and presupposed in Chapter 4. We shall revisit the intellectual debates prior to and surrounding the recent concept of the circular economy, this time not by a historical account. Instead, we shall take the immanent perspective and introduce the key scientific content to discuss the sense in which the economy cannot be circular. Readers who are proficient in ecological economics will have to bear with us as the exposition will need to begin from elementary concepts (or alternatively, consider to jump directly to Chapter 6).

Can the economy go in circles? What would that mean?

Can the economy go in circles? The superficial answer is: Of course, it can. Numerous textbooks of economics will include diagrams similar to the one below, representing what is sometimes called "the circular flow of economic activity".

To be clear, this figure has nothing to do with the policy concept of the circular economy. We will use this example, however, to make what philosophers would call an epistemological point, that is, a theoretical point about the properties of (scientific) knowledge. The point is an instance of a very general and elementary insight in the philosophy of science, which nevertheless is not at all well appreciated in modern culture or even science itself, namely that science is not about what the world really is (whatever that means) but rather about what descriptions it is possible to make of the world, and what they are good for.

The figure above shows two circles. The outer circle depicts how money flows from consumers to firms and back again to consumers (in their capacity as workers). So, we might say that money flows in a circular motion between firms and consumers. The inner circle depicts another type of flow. The flow starts with goods and services flowing from firms through the market to consumers, and continues with "productive resources" flowing from consumers back to firms. This second flow goes via a market that is sometimes called a labour market but which involves also other so-called production factor, namely capital and land. Workers are of course not the source of land or natural capital in the form of as raw materials. If one puts emphasis on labour as a key production factor, as we did, this inner circle makes more sense, perhaps.

Let us reflect for a moment in which sense these circles represent something that is "really circular" in the world. First, "circular" here does not mean anything more than "continuously back and forth between consumers/households on one hand, and firms on the other". Any closed loop – elliptic, square, hexagonal or simply represented by two arrows, one in each direction – would state the same point. In geometry, a circle is defined as the infinite set of points in a plane that all share the property of having a certain Euclidian distance from one given point, namely the circle of that centre. Any other type of set would not in any way be a circle from a geometrical point of view. The "circles" that we just described, are not at all geometrical circles. The concepts of "circle" and "circular" is used in economics in a *metaphorical* sense. In our current example, they just mean that something goes back and forth without stop and without ending up somewhere else.

Our second observation is that the circles in Figure 5.1 are not really meant to depict loops that are entirely closed. The money loop is not closed between firms and consumers, because in almost all modern societies both firms and consumers will pay taxes and may also receive various kinds of governmental support; furthermore, the value of money may also be dynamic due to financial policy and the financial market. As for the inner circle of Figure 5.1, it is not even a loop of the same things going back and forth. Above all, material products are made by physical materials that hardly ever come from the consumers. A tiny part of food materials consumed may be reintroduced into the production factor market as integral parts of the workers' bodies; the

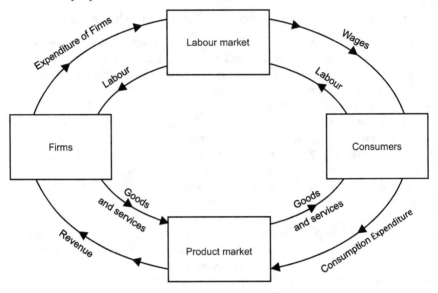

Figure 5.1 The circular flow of economic activities

rest is disposed as waste in one way or the other. In economics education, it may also be more common to emphasise the outer circle of the figure. The inner circle is only sustained because of continuous supply from the natural world outside of the firm-consumer system, as well as constant disposal of waste into this natural world. And still we have not even begun to address the issue of energy. Firms do not make food and other products out of their workers' bodies.

Everybody knows what was explained in the previous paragraph, including all students and practitioners of economics. What the latter may argue, is that representations such as Figure 5.1 are useful because of their heuristic value. The representations direct our thoughts towards the high degree of connectedness and interdependence between firms and citizens, the latter in their dual role as consumers/workers. For instance, these representations may help understand how an increase in wages may lead to an increase in demand of goods and services as well as increased prices, assuming that other factors are kept constant – the famous *ceteris paribus* clause. The fact that there is nothing in this real world of firms and consumers that "is" a circle or even a closed loop, is in that sense beside the point. The circle is a theoretical construct, an idealised model. The statistician George E. P. Box (1987) is remembered for his statement that all models are wrong but some are useful.

Economics is no different from other sciences in this respect. Textbooks and research articles of biology, sociology, chemistry, and other disciplines also contain circular diagrams and many other forms of idealised models that emphasise certain features of a system while ignoring others. This is how science works. In order to use the model correctly, one needs to know its intended meaning and use, and in particular which types of inferences that legitimately can be drawn from it. This type of knowledge is difficult to get by mere reading; rather it is imparted to students by the informal processes of training by which the students become socialised into the discipline. The philosopher Thomas Kuhn used the concept "paradigm" to describe such informal knowledge. For example, in biology one can find figures of circles and loops to describe "metagenesis" or alternation of generations. In humans, we alternate between our diploid generation (in which we grow to full human organisms) and our haploid generation (eggs and sperm cells). In biology textbooks, this is often depicted as a "circle". We have produced our own version of this type of illustration in Figure 5.2.

Everybody can understand, though, that the circle depicted in Figure 5.2 is more of a spiral. During conception, an egg from a woman and a sperm cell from a man fuse and become a zygote, a diploid unicellular organism that can divide and grow into a new human being. However, this new human being – the offspring – is neither the original woman nor the man. He or she is somebody else, similar but also different from the parents and composed of molecules that largely originate elsewhere than their bodies. To the extent that there is a "circle" from humans to eggs and sperms and back again, it runs back and forth between two other theoretical constructs, namely the sets (or equivalence classes) of the haploid and diploid organisms,

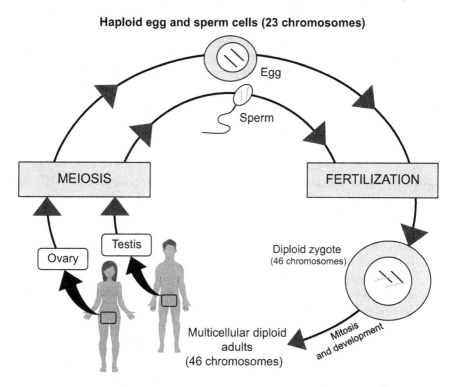

Figure 5.2 Alternation of generations in the human species

respectively. In contrast, circles in astronomy are more like in geometry. When past astronomers discovered that planets do not move in circular orbits, they were attending to more of the geometrical properties of the circle. It was not sufficient to observe that planets go back and forth in the sense of ending up in the same place in the solar system; the shape of the trajectory was important and so Kepler concluded that Copernicus was wrong and that planetary orbits were elliptical and not circular.

This philosophical detour is highly relevant to the issue of the circular economy. If we are content with observing that some money flows from consumers to firms and that most of it then flows back again to some (other) consumers, we may indeed conclude that the economy is circular in that particular sense. Of course, in reality it is also the case money and goods flow in other directions. We learned in Chapter 2 that the economy is not circular "really". That is, however, besides the point that we are stressing in this paragraph. The point is a formal one and not concerned with Reality as such: it is always possible to model a system with almost any model, provided that this model is sufficiently idealised and empty, and that we are willing to be content with focussing only on those aspects of reality that are grasped by that idealised model.

The same holds if we are merely interested in the back-and-forth exchange between workers' labour and the results of this labour, in services and the added value of goods being sold to consumers (who are also, by and large, workers). What is at stake in the discussions about the circular economy, is something else and more, namely the exchange of matter and energy between the economic system and the natural world outside the economic system. Furthermore, the issue of sustainability is at stake. These issues were introduced in Chapter 2 but we will pursue them at some more length in what follows in order to clarify the main controversies. For that purpose, we will need sharper concepts of the economic system and the natural world as well as sustainability.

Can the economy be a closed system?

There are many definitions of "economy" and "economic system". For the purpose of this chapter we may just as well apply a Wikipedia entry:

> An economy (from Greek οἶκος – "household" and νέμομαι – "manage") is an area of the production, distribution, or trade, and consumption of goods and services by different agents. […] Economic agents can be individuals, businesses, organizations, or governments. […] Economic activity is spurred by production which uses natural resources, labor, and capital.
> (Retrieved from https://en.wikipedia.org/wiki/Economy on 3 July 2019)

At quite low precision, one may say that the argument about the circular economy revolves around the issue of whether or not the economy can be a closed system with respect to natural resources. The argument at the low precision level runs as this:

A: Production requires natural resources to be collected ("internalised") from the natural world. Consumption produces waste, that is, materials that are worthless and unwanted in the economy and consequently are released ("externalised") into the natural world. Accordingly, the economy is and has to be a materially open system. And insofar as the economic activity and growth depend on the use of natural resources of limited supply, the natural world sets limits to growth. The transformation of natural resources into waste is an entropic process that is irreversible: materials lose their value through use.

B: The circular economy can overcome the limits to growth because it will no longer deplete the supplies of natural resources. In the circular economy, consumption will not render products and materials worthless and unwanted. The products and materials will be reused and recycled and so their value will be kept within the economy.

At the level of low precision and ordinary common sense, interlocutor B is simply wrong and loses this debate. As a matter of fact, from everyday life experience, consumption does indeed degrade products by mechanical wear and tear, ingestion and digestion, corrosion, evaporation and many other physical and chemical processes.

B could argue, though, that they are not referring to the economy as it is today, but as it may become when the appropriate technology has been developed. Furthermore, they could invoke the "spaceship" metaphor that was introduced by Kenneth Boulding (see Chapter 2) and use it to criticise an underlying premise in the argument of interlocutor A above. A seems to presuppose a worldview in which the world can be divided into two parts: the economy and the natural world. In reality, however, these two concepts – economy and nature – are not logical counterparts. If we consider the Earth as a huge set of elements, it is not so that the economy and nature are the set-theoretical complements of each other. Rather, the economy as we tried to define it above (with the aid of Wikipedia) is a social phenomenon but one that of course also is composed by material entities that can be described by the natural sciences. Just as many social scientists would refrain from a clean divide between Nature and Culture, one could argue that there is no clean divide between Nature and the economy. In that sense, disregarding the arrival of meteorites and the departure of space rockets, one can indeed consider Planet Earth as one economic system that actually is materially closed (although of course not with respect to energy). The economy would then be a materially closed system by definition. It is interesting and perhaps even amusing to see that Boulding's spaceship metaphor, which was introduced in the context of a strong critique of Western capitalist growth models (during the Cold War, as was noted in Chapter 2), can be adopted in this way by proponents of Western capitalists who now argue for endless economic growth by transition to a circular economy.

Indeed, interlocutor B above can make Boulding's words to their own – "man must find his place in a cyclical ecological system which is capable of continuous reproduction of material form even though it cannot escape having inputs of energy" (Boulding, 1966: 8) – and argue that this is what the circular economy aims to deliver, by hitherto unknown technological and social innovations, given our current realisation that Earth indeed is a spaceship.

At this level of precision and generality, the debate does not get much further. Interlocutor A can insist on our current reliance on limited supplies of natural resources and interlocutor B can continue to insist that it is not impossible to overcome these limitations by developing new technologies and new social and political institutions and practices. The former sees themselves as realist and their opponent as one engaging in fantasies and wishful thinking. The latter sees their opponent as one who fails to recognise humanity's track record for creativity and for again and again developing science and technology that our predecessors would swear to be impossible, as judged from their level of understanding and knowledge. The ideological dimension of this debate is very similar to the one described in Chapter 2, between neo-Malthusians and Cornucopians.

From the perspective of the philosopher of science, it is no surprise that this particular version of the debate does not get further. The problem is not only a low level of precision but again that there is a slippage from descriptions ("the economy as a closed system") to statements of what the world "is" ("the economy IS a closed system"). It shows us that the issue at stake is not what the world "really is" but how we would like to live as humans on this planet – what we would like to change and what we would like to sustain. For that issue, more specific knowledge is needed. Those who argue that the economy cannot be circular, have a particular economic system in mind, and invoke a particular body of knowledge that originates in thermodynamics and that got its formulation with the field of ecological economics. They would typically agree that a stone-age economy with a small human population might be circular.

Humans and their economic activities are dissipative systems

Classical (including "neo-classical") economics is a social science. Its concepts are developed to refer to phenomena in the social domain – actors, consumers, firms, goods, money and so on. All of these phenomena are social and can be characterised in terms of their social meaning. Utility is a key type of meaning in economics. However, all of these phenomena, as encountered in the real world, also have material properties. Money, for instance, may be composed of metal, paper or plastic, or exist as electromagnetic inscriptions on hard drives or perhaps even currents in electromagnetic circuits. Classical economics is a science that tries to find law-like behaviour and other regularities of these phenomena by measuring their social meaning (above all utility) and abstracting away their material properties. This is the whole point of (this type of) economics: That the same equations can be applied to different types of goods and services.

For this reason, economics is particularly prone to suffer the consequences of what complexity theorist Dominique Chu and colleagues called contextuality:

We will call a system contextual if it:

- includes one or more elements that also occur in a different system(s) or if it is itself a shared element between more than one system
- In this other system(s) the shared elements take part in causal processes different from those included in the original system.

(Chu, Strand, & Fjelland, 2003: 25).

Everything in classical economics is contextual by Chu et al.'s definition. Every element also takes part in chemical and physical processes, and through their interaction with humans and other living beings, also biophysical processes. For instance, paper money that circulates in the outer circle of Figure 5.1, is subject to wear and tear and has to be substituted quite frequently by some other process. In modern societies there is usually a national bank that takes care of the process of substitution, which requires its own sources of materials, energy and labour. Contextuality is difficult to model and is a constant source of mismatch between economic models and the real world. For example, real human beings are not merely rational actors who try to maximise their utility but also animals that have a range of other abilities, sensibilities and desires. One way to deal with contextuality is to be attentive to knowledge from other domains and consider how that knowledge may pose constraints on the validity and usefulness of the knowledge from one's own discipline.

One way to describe ecological economics is that it was born as the study of the constraints posed on classical economics by knowledge from the natural sciences, in particular with regard to biophysical (material) flows. The most basic piece of knowledge has been invoked several times already, through the informal concepts of "wear and tear" and degradation. Such concepts invoke the Second Law of thermodynamics, the so-called Entropy Law.

There are many formulations of the Second Law of thermodynamics. Max Planck's (1914) formulation is among the more accessible ones: Whenever a change occurs in nature, "the entropy of all systems taking part in the change, must increase" (p. 60). Entropy can be seen as a measure of disorder, so what this means is that all spontaneous change in the Universe as such, or any isolated part of it, move towards a higher degree of disorder. Simple illustrations of this principle are that whenever energy is used to produce mechanical work, there will be some friction that converts part of the energy into heat. No energy is really lost since the heat will contain the same amount of kJ as the chemical, mechanical or electrical energy that it was converted from. But the heat cannot be converted back to work without an additional energy cost, because heat is a degenerate, disorderly form of energy compared to other energy forms.

Ecosystems, human societies, human beings and living organisms in general are all highly ordered structures that themselves create order. The same is true of economic systems. Production in the economy creates highly ordered objects. Pure silver is one example; digital computers another. The creation of order can only take place by coupling it to a process that creates even more disorder. This is a direct implication of the Second Law of thermodynamics. Green plants create chemical and anatomical order through photosynthesis and growth. For this, they need supply of available ("free") energy in the form of sunlight, which is created by solar fusion, which again creates massive disorder on the Sun. So, the creation of order – which is reduction of entropy – is coupled to an even higher entropy creation. A similar situation holds for herbivore animals, which need a constant supply of order in the form of the free energy stored in the chemical bonds of plant materials. Carnivores, in the next instance, feed on the high-order free chemical energy stored in the bodies of other animals. In all these processes, there is dissipation: Chemical and mechanical energy is converted to heat. Atoms are rearranged so that high-energy chemical bonds (as in sugar, fat and oxygen) are converted to low-energy bonds (as in water and carbon dioxide). The dissipation will always exceed the creation of order. The study of the interesting properties of such dissipative systems that concentrate order far from equilibrium, was the basis for the Nobel Prize awarded to Ilya Prigogine.

Economic activity feeds on various sources of low entropy. The raw materials for production will either have to be orderly, as pure natural stocks, or a high-order form of energy, such as electricity or the chemical energy of oil, will have to be used to purify and order the materials in the desired way. The faster the economy, the higher the demand for low entropy/free energy, and the vaster creation of disorder through dissipation. So far in human history, there appears to be a clear correlation between how technologically and institutionally advanced a society is and how much energy it consumes. The current hi-tech civilisation did not develop until humans learnt how to utilise fossil fuels, which is an energy source with extremely high energy density.

To summarise, systems that create order – plants, animals, societies and economic systems – can only work by coupling the creation of order to processes that destroy order. Creation of order uses free energy made available by destruction of order.

Still, this does not in itself prove that the economy cannot be circular with respect to materials. If we view Planet Earth as materially closed but with a constant influx of free energy from the Sun, it is entirely imaginable that solar energy could fuel not only our production but also energy-consuming processes of recycling, ecosystem remediation and restoration, recovery of lost materials, et cetera. A proponent of the circular economy could launch the idea of gigantic solar panels in space that send enormous amounts of energy for our use in a perfectly circular economy, and nothing we have said so far could contradict that idea.

Stocks, flows and funds

There is, however, a lot more to be said from the perspective of ecological economics, regarding the particularity of human beings and the planet that we live on.

First, there is the well-known distinction between renewable and non-renewable resources. To the extent that humanity will depend on non-renewable resources such as minerals and carbon-based fossil fuels, these dependencies obviously constitute limits to growth and even to status quo. In the 1970s, there was a prestigious debate within ecological economics between one of its primary spokesmen, Herman Daly, and his teacher Nicholas Georgescu-Roegen. Daly advocated what he called a steady-state economy, in which humanity develops political institutions and wisdom sufficient to keep the human population and its consumption limited. Georgescu-Roegen argued that even a zero growth regime with a constant population would ultimately deplete the stocks of non-renewable resources. Even worse, even well before the stocks are empty, the resources will become harder to get at and there will be diminishing returns in mining and extraction. Daly had to concede to this criticism: "A steady-state economy cannot last forever, but neither can a growing economy, nor a declining economy" (Daly & Townsend, 1993: 378). Classical economists may postulate that technological innovation can solve particular dependencies on non-renewables but the problem remains in principle if the substitution depends on a different non-renewable. At the moment, electric cars are introduced as an alternative to fossil fuel-dependent cars, provided electricity is produced from renewable energy sources. It is unclear what this will mean in terms of dependencies and scarcities of metals such as lithium and cobalt. Lithium can in principle be recycled but the process is highly energy-demanding. Again, the proponent of the circular economy can postulate a future technology that can provide large amounts of "clean" solar energy. The ecological economist would then ask: How will the clean energy be provided? By which energy carriers? Which materials will be needed to produce those carriers? In the world of non-renewable resources there is no free lunch. The creation of new order, that is, new advanced technology, can only take place by coupling it to equivalent processes of dissipation. Ultimately, stocks will be depleted, with implications for the economy. And that even without invoking the problem of climate change. With respect to non-renewable resources, there is no perfect "sustainability", only prolongation and decline.

Renewable resources are accordingly a much more attractive topic for those who wish to be optimistic about the future of the economy. Perhaps the single most useful concept from ecological economics is that of *fund* (Georgescu-Roegen, 1971). The relationship between stocks and flows is simple: In a non-renewable system, the sum of stocks and flows are constant. When a flow goes out of a stock, the stock is diminished with the same amount as the flow carried. Funds, however, can produce or consume flows without necessarily changing themselves. A forest can provide a certain flow of berries and mushrooms every year without being damaged or depleted; a river can clean a certain amount of polluted water; a cow can produce so and so many litres of milk while maintaining its health; and a human individual can work a certain number of hours per day and consume a certain amount of food without compromising his or her health and integrity. Ecological economists study and try to quantify the properties of stock, fund and flow elements in the

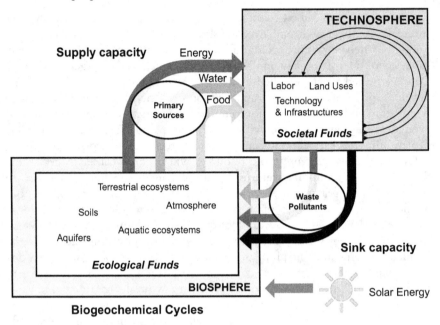

Figure 5.3 The biophysical narrative of the circular economy
Source: Adapted from Giampietro, 2019

interaction between economy and nature, reconceptualised in material terms as the technosphere and biosphere, respectively, as displayed in Figure 5.3.

Here, the technosphere is a dissipative structure that, in order to maintain and grow, has to destroy order and increase entropy. This creates waste and consumes water, energy and food ingredients. Water, energy and food ingredients have to be provided by the biosphere, which create order by exploiting the free energy from the sun. However, in order to be able to sustain that order, the ecological funds have to remain intact and provide what sometimes is called ecosystem services. The plants have to live and thrive, the bees have to survive and pollinate. The water cycle has to be able to supply clean water, et cetera. When the funds collapse and no longer maintain their integrity and identity, the resource becomes non-renewable. Sustainability from the perspective of ecological economics is accordingly a matter of ensuring that fund elements are protected from excessive use and other forms of destruction, and that the natural cycles that regenerate funds are protected and maintained. The current situation is, however, precarious. Fund elements are destroyed or compromised on a large scale. The same European Union that proudly presents its policy on the circular economy, has become reliant on importing food and energy supplied from the biosphere of other continents, and exporting waste from our technosphere into others' biospheres (Giampietro, 2019).

Squaring the circle: economic growth, sustainability and the circular economy

Barring the problem of non-renewables, we can now state a necessary condition for a "circular" economy in the sense of an economy that does not disrupt and compromise a sustainable interplay between the technosphere and the biosphere: The demand on ecological funds cannot exceed their carrying capacity, that is, what they can deliver without being damaged. Moreover, human activity has to be limited so as not to otherwise destroy or compromise the fund elements. Revisiting the "butterfly diagram" of the Ellen MacArthur Foundation (Ellen MacArthur Foundation, 2013) that we reproduced in Chapter 3, the perspective of ecological economics tells us that Ellen MacArthur Foundation sets the wrong target. The butterfly is the vision of making the technosphere analogous to the biosphere by becoming more "restorative". Likewise, the European Commission defined the circular economy as an economy "where the value of products, materials and resources is maintained in the economy for as long as possible, and the generation of waste minimised" (European Commission, 2015: 2). While this may give rise to new types of jobs and lifestyles, it is not necessarily relevant for the goal of sustainability. The economic activities of the circular economy will also by necessity be dissipative. Even if more materials are recycled, these activities do not help us towards sustainability unless they decrease the pressure on ecological funds.

The challenge of sustainability is accordingly to restructure the technosphere so that the fund elements in the biosphere are restored and maintained. Unfortunately, the limitation on human activity required appear to compromise the goal of economic growth. Rather, the evidence points towards the need for decreased production and consumption, also of goods that depend on renewable materials. Indeed, ecological economists have argued that the development of economic systems since the industrial revolution has gone in the opposite direction. Fast-growing, competitive economies are those that accelerate the rate of economic activities and increase the flows of energy and materials. The claim that the circular economy would be beneficial to economic growth is contrary to experience. Instead, a high degree of circularity in the biophysical sense, would slow down the economic process, for a variety of reasons.

First, ecological cycles of material recovery are very slow processes. As (Murray et al., 2017) point out

> it takes 9 days for water to cycle through the atmosphere, while it takes 37,000 years for the oceans to complete a cycle. Phosphorus takes 2000 years to cycle through the soil as does nitrogen. Carbon dioxide takes 4 years to cycle through the atmosphere while atmospheric oxygen takes 3.7 million years.
> (Murray et al., 2017: 371; inline references omitted)

Internalising these processes in the economic process would slow down economic activity.

One could even argue that economic growth has historically been linked to the extent to which economies have become linear. An economy based on agriculture, for example, is much more tied to the natural cycles of regeneration of soil, to the water cycle and to the (slow) seasonality of crops. Agricultural production has been accelerated in the short run through the use of fossil fuel-based fertilisers, although in the long run fertilisers, monocultures and the industrialisation of agriculture lead to loss in soil fertility. An even greater acceleration has come from the shift from agriculture to industry, which is not tied to seasonality, and from the use of resources that must be regenerated (soil, seeds, animal power et cetera) to the use of ready-made resources such as fossil fuels. The acceleration that comes from linearisation of production is evident also in Taylorism, which reorganised industrial production processes in assembly chains.

Second, linearity makes it possible for the pace of economic activity to be determined by the production of goods and services, while a circular economy would depend on the pace of production of the primary inputs required for the production of goods and services. This means that the rhythm of economic activity would not be determined by the production capacity of the industrial sector, but by the capacity to generate primary inputs.

In the linear economy, the limiting factor of production is the production capacity of an industry. Thanks to the introduction of work shifts, industrial factories can run 24 hours a day. An increase in production depends on the increase in machinery and workers, primary resources are assumed to be available. In the circular economy, the utilisation of production factors would depend on the availability of primary inputs. An increase in production would not be determined by technology, but by recycling capacity.

Third, part of the production resources used in the productive sectors would need to be moved to the recycling sectors, diminishing productive capacity of the economy. Recycling represents an opportunity cost, which reduces the productivity of economic funds and leads to a slower pace of economic activity. The economy cannot just produce new goods and services, but part of its resources has to be used for its own reproduction. Recycling implies that part of the resources devoted to "production" have to be diverted to "reproduction of funds". Because some production factors have a limited budget, such as labour, a circular economy would require that the labour force be redistributed, decreasing the labour available for productive activities in favour of recycling activities.

As will be seen in the following chapters, it is also the case that only a very small fraction of materials is actually being recycled in spite of decades of policy initiatives for recycling. The only economic activities that are even faster than massive material throughput fuelled by petroleum, seem to be financial services and other sectors that externalise the dependencies on material flows to other parts of the world (Kovacic, Spanò, Piano, & Sorman, 2018). It is easy to dematerialise the economy if one can convince other countries to supply one's food and energy.

The conclusion, then, of this chapter is that there is no clear relationship between the goal of sustainability and the policies for the circular economy. The circular economy is not going to deliver sustainable development in the biophysical sense. It may still be imagined to do so; the resulting beliefs, discourses and practices may have their own effects with their own vices and virtues. This is also why the circular economy is a fascinating topic: Once freed from the issue of sustainability in biophysical terms, it can be anything. The work of developing the policies and practices of the circular economy is a creative exercise, in which the notions sustainability and circularity will find new articulations, imaginations and framings. This is what we will investigate in the following chapters.

References

Boulding, K. (1966). The economics of the coming Spaceship Earth. In H. Jarrett (Ed.), *Environmental Quality in a Growing Economy* (pp. 3–14). Baltimore: Johns Hopkins University.

Box, G. E. P. (1987). *Empirical Model-Building and Response Surfaces*. New York: Wiley.

Chu, D., Strand, R., & Fjelland, R. (2003). Theories of complexity: Common denominators of complex systems. *Complexity*, 8(3), 19–30. doi:10.1002/cplx.10059

Daly, H. E., & Townsend, K. N. (1993). *Valuing the Earth: Economics, Ecology, Ethics*. Cambridge, MA: MIT Press.

Ellen MacArthur Foundation. (2013). *Towards the Circular Economy*. Retrieved from www.ellenmacarthurfoundation.org/assets/downloads/publications/Ellen-MacArthur-Foundation-Towards-the-Circular-Economy-vol.1.pdf

European Commission. (2015). *Communication from the Commission to the European Parliament, the Council, the European Economic and Social Committee and the Committee of the Regions. Closing the loop – An EU action plan for the Circular Economy EN* (No. COM (2015) 614). Brussels: European Commission.

Georgescu-Roegen, N. (1971). *The Entropy Law and the Economic Process*. Boston: Harvard University Press.

Giampietro, M. (2019). On the circular bioeconomy and decoupling: Implications for sustainable growth. *Ecological Economics*, 162(April), 143–156. doi10.1016/j.ecolecon.2019.05.001

Kovacic, Z., Spanò, M., Piano, S. L., & Sorman, A. H. (2018). Finance, energy and the decoupling: an empirical study. *Journal of Evolutionary Economics*, 28(3), 565–590. doi:10.1007/s00191–00017–0514–0518

Murray, A., Skene, K., Haynes, K., Murray, A., Skene, K., & Haynes, K. (2017). The circular economy: An interdisciplinary exploration of the concept and application in a global context. *Journal of Business Ethics*, 140(3), 369–380. doi:10.1007/s10551–10015–2693–2692

Planck, M. (1914). *The Theory of Heat Radiation*. Philadelphia: P. Blakiston's Son & Co.

6 Imagining circularity

The circular economy as a sociotechnical imaginary

This chapter builds on an understanding of the circular economy as a policy in-the-making, unravels the different elements that are associated with circular economy policies by different actors and provides an analysis of the multiple meanings of "circularity". In the previous chapter we noted that there can be no circular economy in the literal sense of closed loops of biophysical flows. To make sense of circularity and its current popularity, one accordingly has to ask for the cultural meanings that are attached to broadly shared ideas such as recycling, re-use, repair and quality of products. These culturally embedded meanings also entail ideas about desirable futures, ideas about which futures "we" want to make real and which ones to avoid. Such "sociotechnical imaginaries" guide policy-making, affect how people think about potential benefits risks, problems and solutions provided by novel technologies or scientific discoveries. Furthermore, they make visible the politics of innovation and the imagined roles (agency) of citizens in all of this. They are assembled and stabilised in material practices and become consequential in the "real world" as for example in the set-up of institutions and the development of particular networks and communities that stabilise these networks. By framing the cultural dimension of circular economy policy in terms of sociotechnical imaginaries this chapter provides insights into how these policies relate to broader cultural values and what potential challenges in a transition to a circular economy might be.

Introduction

Building on previous chapters, in which we showed that there can be no circular economy in the literal sense of closed loops of biophysical flows, we will direct our attention to the cultural meanings that are linked to circular economy policy. To make sense of circularity and its current popularity we argue that one has to ask for the meanings that are attached to broadly shared ideas such as recycling, re-use, repair and quality of products. These culturally embedded meanings also entail normative commitments in the form of ideas about desirable futures, ideas about which futures "we" want to make real and which ones to avoid. Such "sociotechnical imaginaries" (Jasanoff & Kim, 2009; 2015) guide policy-making, affect how people think about risks, problems and solutions, make visible the politics of innovation and the imagined roles (agency) of citizens in all of this. They are assembled and stabilised in material practices and become consequential in the "real world" as for example in the set-up of institutions and the development of particular networks and communities that stabilise these networks. By framing the cultural dimension of circular economy policy in terms of sociotechnical imaginaries this chapter provides insights into how these policies relate to broader cultural values and what potential challenges in a transition to a circular economy might be. Thus, this chapter explores current processes of assembling and stabilising an "imaginary of circularity" at the European Commission and asks for the multiple meanings of circularity that are currently being negotiated and the institutional configurations and materialities that are co-emergent with them. This will allow us to carve out the implicit (normative) ideas about the future within circular economy policy documents and statements of policy-makers for their imaginative capacity. This analysis reveals that while on a first level circular economy policy talks about sustainability and change towards a more ecologically conscious economy, the underlying ideas about European futures hardly challenge current patterns of consumption and production.

We will start the chapter by laying the groundwork with a detour to work about time and the future. Building on that, we will introduce different strands of literature on imagination in science, technology and politics. After discussing more recent work that has already started to tackle the issue of collective imagination in circular economy policy, we will empirically analyse how circularity is currently assembled and stabilised at the European Commission.

Imagination in technoscience and policy – imagining circularity

Usually when people talk about imagination and futures this is associated with science fiction or with fantasies. Imagining is understood as a practice that is something for leisure and not something that might be consequential or serious. Yet, imagining happens all the time and at different levels of society, it is a ubiquitous part of social life.

Times, futures, and collective imagination

In Chapter 5, we discussed the possibility that the circular economy may slow down economic activity, instead of promoting growth. Time, and the pace of time, is central to the circular economy imaginary and practice. Because of its importance, in this section we take a little detour to explore in more philosophical terms how the passing of time matters in scientific research.

Since imagination is usually concerned with the future, it is importation to be clear about what we understand by the term "future" before we introduce studies on the role of imagination in science and technology. Curiously enough the future, a temporal concept, is usually imagined in a spatial way through the metaphor of an arrow of time, where the past sort of lies behind us, the future ahead of us and we are occupying an area of this arrow labelled the present (moving on this arrow of time). Additionally, in this understanding, time as such is thought of as being external to or independent of human action.

And while it is true that there is constant change and becoming, scholars have pointed out that the concept of time and future itself is a social technology that became necessary at a particular point in societal evolution and fulfils certain functions. In their now classic paper "Social Time: A Methodological and Functional Analysis" Sorokin and Merton (1937) develop an innovative perspective on time by asking how "social time" is ordering social life. In contrast to a common understanding of time as independent of human actions they argue that:

> social time, in contrast to the time of astronomy, is qualitative and not purely quantitative; that these qualities derive from the beliefs and customs common to the group and that they serve further to reveal the rhythms, pulsations, and beats of the societies in which they are found.
>
> (ibid.: 623)

While they acknowledge the quantitative features of time, the also direct attention to time as something more "qualitative" and thus prepare the ground for an understanding of social time as something that is closely tied to particular societies and communities. They talk about "time systems" (ibid.: 627) to highlight this relation to what sociologists like to call socio-historical config- urations. But what exactly does it mean to say that time is not independent from certain communities? Such relations can be seen for example in different beginnings of the year in different societies or in the fact that systems of time reckoning are different in agricultural societies or societies based on hunting. Other scholars moved beyond this conception and argued that it is not enough to distinguish between different times and then define "social time" as the object of study for sociology (Elias, 1988). Norbert Elias criticised the idea of distinguishing between social and natural time and states that clocks (as well as other instruments for time reckoning) are not merely tools for measuring a somehow independent time (Elias, 1988: 94). It is time itself, which needs to be thought of as an instrument for orientation and regulation. One of the main issues in misconceptions of time is the fact, that it is usually a noun. To counter this convention, he focuses on practices of "Zeitbestimmen" and by doing so argues that what is usually called "time" are in fact practices of "synthesizing" different events. What does this mean? Synthesising as Elias describes it is the act of putting different events in relation to each other. Such events can be movements of the hands of a mechanical watch and the perceived movement of the sun. This understanding highlights the importance of a society's knowl- edge about recurring events: planetary movements and the development of technical devices for time measurement such as calendars or clocks are examples for knowledge necessary for time reckoning. What is important to understand here is that in Elias' conceptualisation time is neither a property of the human mind, nor is it something entirely independent of human action. He therefore moves beyond Sorokin and Merton as he emphasises the social nature of time reckoning understanding such practices as situated in particular socio-historic contexts. More importantly, he directs attention to the close relation of time reckoning and the knowledge available to the members of certain collectives. This shift of focus then asks which kinds of knowledge are used for time reckoning and which actors hold this knowledge. Is it for instance priests that hold the knowledge about the right time for harvest? Or is it a group of scientists who have the authority to determine the time to urgently move towards a more circular economy in order to save our environment? And how long do we as a society have until certain windows of opportunity are closing? These questions of course relate to intense controversies about the time-frames in which contemporary societies are embedded.

Time in this understanding is less a stable framework for human action, but a means of interpreting reality. It is in this sense that German sociologist Niklas Luhmann writes about time as a means of orientation and regards time as "the interpretation of reality with regard to the difference between past and future" (Luhmann, 1976: 135). If time is a way of interpreting reality then it follows that it is also contingent. Bruno Latour uses the term "temporality" to stress this act of interpretation. He differentiates time from this mode of interpretation and proposes to "call the interpretation of this passage [of time] temporality, in order to distinguish it carefully from time" (Latour, 1993: 68). Akin to such conceptions of time social science scholars from different disciplines build on the methodological implications of an understanding of time as a means of coordination and explore the temporal patterning of social life using time as an entry point for understanding social order (Nowotny, 1989; 1994; Wajcman, 2014; Zerubavel, 1985). In these accounts the essentialist question about the nature of time is turned on its head and becomes an invitation for empirical inquiry: time becomes timing and as such a mode of interactional and socio-material sense-making.

After this brief introduction into different understandings of time we now can get back to the future and direct our attention to practices of imagining. What, the reader might ask, does all this mean for our understanding of imagination and the future?

First and foremost, if time becomes a practice through which we as a society make sense of our being in the world, also the future needs to be understood as an object that is used for understanding and "managing" the present (Michael, 2000). Over the last decade the future has become a focus point of scholarly attention. Scholars talk about how a "breathless futurology" (Harrington, Rose, & Singh, 2006) and "anticipatory regimes" (Adams, Murphy, & Clarke, 2009) make it increasingly difficult not to take into account the "not yet" (Adam & Groves, 2007). Work in this line of research very often is centred around environmental issues and debates, arguing for a move beyond an understanding of the future as open and there for our (that is mostly Western industrialised societies) taking (Adam, 1998).

Similarly to the debates about time also "the future" is discussed as a temporal abstraction produced through social practices: the future is not a coherent temporal entity that we are moving towards (very often trying to get a grasp of temporal categories through spatial metaphors), but an object or a social artefact of sorts that we ourselves make up through various future-making practices. Think of making plans for the week, arranging appointments or buying insurance against potential future harms; or about targets for the reduction municipal waste by a certain date as it is done in the circular economy action plan.

If future-making is a collective social practice that different groups of actors are engaged in on different levels, it will be no surprise, that ideas about the future are constantly changing. And here we are talking not only about the content of visions about the future like the circular production processes that will be responsible for a steady supply of future SUVs in industrialised Western societies, or the political systems societies will be organised in. Also, the very ideas about what the future is and how we can and should position ourselves towards this temporal abstraction are subject to historical change. These differences, and this is the important sociological point, are by no means arbitrary. Much to the contrary, particular ideas about what the future is are tied to certain way of social ordering: "The relation of past and future will not have the same form in every society" (Luhmann, 1976: 136). If the future is not the same for every society, then necessarily there will be many different futures. It is for this reason that social scientists and philosophers usually talk about "futures" instead of speaking about "the future".

Current Western understanding of the future as open to human action and intervention is a relatively new "discovery" (Hölscher, 1999; Koselleck, 1979). Hölscher argues that the idea of the future as a single coherent entity emerged during the seventeenth and eighteenth centuries. This is not dissimilar to Elias' concept of time, especially when Hölscher argues that the ability to project oneself into a future is not an anthropological a priory but a historically and socially contingent mode of thinking (Hölscher, 1999: 10). We have argued before that conceptions of time and futures are closely related to varying societal orderings. This is also the way in which Hölscher explains the emergence of our modern future. This discovery is tied to the French Revolution, the rise of industrial capitalism and increasing secularisation. Additionally, this change in the conception of the future is tied to the emergence of a bourgeois society and related to notions of technological and social progress that are still prevalent today (Luhmann, 1976). The main difference is that former conceptions imagine the future as already existent – still visible in ideas about fate or destiny – the future as it is understood in modern Western societies is open and can be shaped to our will. This is important, because this very way of thinking about the future is the precondition for the idea of the future as a space of political contestation.

It is exactly this idea of the future, which is one of the defining features of modernity, that enabled what British sociologist Anthony Giddens famously calls a "colonisation of the future", understood as "the creation of territories of future possibilities, reclaimed by counterfactual interference" (Giddens, 1991: 242). The future is there for our taking, as the notion of "colonisation" suggests. It is not coincidental that Giddens talks about colonisation, the violent nature of colonial history echoes in Giddens' conception of the future as the emergence of the future as an object of political debate poses severe questions concerning the decisions we should or should not make and the ethical foundations for these decisions. It is in that sense that Giddens spots an "evaporation of morality" and states that "[m]orality is extrinsic so far as the colonisation of the future is concerned" (Giddens, 1991: 145). This ethical dimension of future-making is at the core of work that argues for a more "careful" approach towards the future (Adam & Groves, 2007; Felt et al., 2013). Additionally, Giddens' idea of "counterfactual interference" is worth pointing out here. It describes the necessity to make decisions under the condition of uncertainty. We will dive more deeply into what that means for governance in later chapters.

The ethical dimension of futures-thinking has been highlighted in the works of Barbara Adam and Chris Groves. Adam and Groves combine conceptualisations of the future with issues of knowledge and ethics. In doing so they relate different ways in which the future is known to particular conceptualisations of the future: "knowledge practices, and the implicit assumptions about the future that underlie them, linking diverse practices to one another" (Adam & Groves, 2007: 121). Whereas in ancient cultures pre-existing futures were "told" in oracles and prophecies, more recent approaches of dealing with the future include amongst other things the idea of insurances together with risk as a temporal concept, which means as a consequence of a geographically expanding market and the hazards of sea trade.

In their ethical thinking Adam and Groves develop a perspective of a "future present": the actual present that will be lived by actors in the future. There will be only one such future present. In contrast there are many "present futures", by which they mean current representations of what the future might be. The argument then is that is important to put more emphasis on the future present perspective in collective practices and decision-making processes. The question then becomes how to do this? In looking for possible answers to this question it is useful to look at a Science Policy Briefing published by the European Science Foundation a couple of years ago (Felt et al., 2013). The authors of this briefing refer to diagnosis of an "increasing attention given to anticipating, transforming and/or controlling societal futures through science and technology" (ibid.: 16) and call for "more collective forms of imagining" (ibid.: 17). Such novel forms of collective orientation towards the future, so their argument, will allow for a broadening of perspectives and thus enable societies to engage with futures in more responsible ways. In this way, this proposition relates to current discussions about Responsible Research and Innovation and care-oriented approaches (Mol, 2008; Mol, Moser, & Pols, 2015; Pereira & Saltelli, 2017; Puig de la Bellacasa,

2011) discussed in this book. Questions about whose futures are negotiated and who should take part in such discussions are put forward.

In these calls for consideration of ethical aspects in our occupation with the future an interesting and important shift becomes visible. While early work tends to focus on semantic issues, that is questions about how future is thought of in relation to socio-historical changes, we can see a different treatment of the future in more recent work. This work builds on a conception of the future that especially emphasises its material features and points out a process of constant emergence,

> the latent yet material dimension of that which already exists, and which is always at work, creating patterns for near and unimaginably distant futures. [...] When it is lived, once it becomes incorporated in bodies and in the social meanings by which humans project and organize their lives, it may emerge as beneficial or harmful.
>
> (Adam & Groves, 2007: 139)

In this quote the relation between latent and material is important. In socio-logical terms it means that the ontological difference between the present and the future is bridged through the materiality of our actions. Our actions in the present will become consequential in the future. Although the future might be latent now, it becomes a material reality once it is populated and lived by humans. Future here is a material and embodied reality, or as Adam and Grove put it: "latent flows of potential which, under specific conditions, congeal into organised physical structures with lived futures, such as organisms" (Adam & Groves, 2007: 132). This might sound quite abstract and academic, which is true but in this case not a bad thing. There is a very important implication for the work presented in this book and one of the main takeaways from this subchapter.

There are three important things to take away from the debates about time and the future: first, conceptualisations of the future are socially as well as his-torically contingent. The way we think about the "not yet" depends on where and when we live; hence, it is more accurate to talk about "futures" in the plural. However, while there might be an indefinite amount of present futures, there will be only one future present.

Second, these futures are closely entwined with the ways in which know it, be it through prophecies, quantitative risk assessments, metrics of waste streams, or participatory deliberation. These futures are constantly made and unmade in anticipatory practices and become consequential on a material level, which is especially important in thinking about environmental issues. When we talk about collective ideas about the future and visions of desirable futures, we argue from exactly this conceptual position; the position, that the ways in which we collectively imagine the future will become material reality for a future present. It is thus eminently important to take a careful approach to reflecting on the futures we envision and how we do so. This also touches on the "we" that does the imagining. Whereas the most dominant visions of the future are currently produced in Western industrialised societies, there is an argument to be made to make an effort to find more inclusive ways to imagine futures and broaden the "collective" in collectively imagined futures (Baptista, 2014).

Following from that and finally, thinking about or imagining futures is not to be confused with idly reflecting about a time to come. Much rather futures have become an object for negotiating societal orderings in the present; futures are a means of managing the present (Michael, 2000). Therefore, in a next step we turn to literature that has discussed the role of imagination in technoscientific developments.

Imagination as collective practice

Thinking about the role of imagining as a social practice and collectively held visions of the future as cultural resources has gained relevance in social science over the last decades. This is quite different from concepts such as fantasies in two important aspects: first, imagination is no longer situated within single individuals' minds and second, imagination can become consequential. What is more, collectively shared and accepted ideas about who "we" are and where "we" ought to go are regarded as constitutive in stabilising social order (Anderson, 1991; Appadurai, 1990; Jasanoff, 2001).

STS literature is in particular interested in the role of imagination in the conduct of science/scientific practice, meaning the production, use and distribution of knowledge. One of the central insights here is that scientists do not just engage in imagination occasionally in times of contemplation. Much to the contrary, we need to understand "both imagining and laboratory experimentation as practices in which scientists are regularly engaged" (Fujimura, 2003: 176). Joan Fujimura in her study about Japanese genome scientist writes about technoscientific imagining, which she considers "serious work done by serious people" (ibid.: 192); with potentially serious consequences. Fujimura focuses on "social practices of imagining" (ibid.: 176), which means that she explores collective imaginations on an actor level and asks how particular actors attempt to establish their ideas on a broader level. She shows how single genome scientists were in fact able to accumulate financial and cultural capital through establishing and stabilising particular imaginations about the future of their research field and thus gain support for their goals. These goals are mainly related to the establishment of a novel field of scientific activity. In this sense, her work might be compared to the interest in so-called "promise champions" in the sociology of expectations (Lente & Rip, 1998). In her work she raises important points about collective imagining. Scientists are producers of futures in (at least) two senses: first, they produce knowledge and innovation and second, they simultaneously always produce ideas about futures of particular fields like genome science or systems biology. Furthermore, she highlights that such imaginings might be related to other discourses prevalent in a given society at a specific time. Additionally, she directs attention to the historical situatedness of imaginings – "their present contexts" (Fujimura, 2003: 193). Thus, she understands collective imagining as a set of practices that is socially, culturally, and historically situated.

While Fujimura is interested in the practices of individual scientists other scholars focus more on the role that collectively shared imaginations play on an institutional or on a policy level. In her study about the development of nuclear energy (and particular reactor types) in France Gabrielle Hecht (2001) stresses that not only the personal, institutional and material elements need to be considered to understand the development of a technology. Additionally, the ideologies prevalent in a particular institutional setting provide an important aspect of what she calls "technopolitical regimes" (ibid.: 257). These regimes comprise: "the institutions, the people who run them, their guiding myths and ideologies, the artefacts they produce, and the technopolitics they pursue" (ibid.: 258).

Similar to Fujimura, Hecht also directs attention to implicit ideas about the futures that are embedded within such imaginations. However, she focuses more on questions of how practices of imagining the future are related to the stabilisation of certain collectives. She argues that ideas about the future of France are a crucial part of different technopolitical regimes and closely tied to the success of a certain vision for the nations' future. This means that technological development and political preferences about the future of France are co-dependent on each other. Imaginations about the future (and about the past) are thus closely tied to collective identities, or national identities in her case:

> Discussions of national identity typically refer back to the past. But ultimately, national-identity discourse is not about the past per se or even about the present. It is about the future. National-identity discourse constructs a bridge between a mythologised past and a coveted future. Nations and their suppo- sedly essential characteristics are imagined through a telos, in which the future appears as the inevitable fulfilment of a historically legitimated destiny.
>
> (ibid.: 255)

In contrast to Fujimura, Hecht accentuates her analysis of technopolitical regimes towards an institutional level (while of course being mindful of the fact that institutions are made up of people, artefacts and ideologies) and explores controversies between two different energy agencies and their visions of the technological future of France. Futures as collectively held imaginations become performative in this perspective by informing technological choices as well as influencing the relative significance of relevant institutional actors. In the case of nuclear energy in France discussion circled around whether to create a French technology or to make a foreign technology French:

> Both technopolitical regimes thus aimed at tightening the links between technological (nuclear) prowess and national identity. Both regimes

proposed visions of France's political and industrial future and, through this
future, France's identity. They did so not just with their language but also
by building reactors that where hybrids of technology and politics. G2 and
EDF1 were neither inevitable products of some inherent technological
logic nor infinitely malleable products of political negotiation. Rather,
each resulted from a seamless blend of political and technological goals and
practices.

(ibid.: 270)

Another influential strand of debate about practices of collective imagination
centres on the notion of "sociotechnical imaginaries". Introduced by Sheila
Jasanoff and Sang-Hyun Kim (2009; 2015) it brings together work on the role
of imagination in stabilising social orderings (Anderson, 1991; Appadurai, 1990;
Fujimura, 2003; Taylor, 2002) with work on technoscientific development
(Bijker, 1987; Winner, 1986). Sociotechnical imaginaries are defined as:

collectively held, institutionally stabilized, and publicly performed visions of
desirable futures, animated by shared understandings of forms of social life
and social order attainable through and supportive of, advances in science
and technology.

(Jasanoff & Kim, 2015: 4)

This quote addresses the main elements of imaginaries: they need to be collectively held and tend to be more stable when they are institutionalised in
some form. Imaginaries thus can become visible in the exercise of power such
as the allocation of resources, the development of research priorities or in particular institutional configurations. Then, imaginaries also need to be publicly
performed in order to be stable. This means that there is an emphasis on public
performance as central means in collective self-imagination (Anderson, 1991;
Pfotenhauer & Jasanoff, 2017). Finally, imaginaries focus on desirable futures
that are entwined with ideas about social order and scientific and technological
progress, but also the "monsters" (Dennis, 2015) that policy-making tries to
prevent from materialising.

Jasanoff and Kim distinguish imaginaries from policy agendas, master narratives, media packages or belief systems. Imaginaries, they argue, are "less issue-
specific, less goal-directed, less politically accountable and less instrumental"
than policy agendas (2009: 123). Imaginaries are also distinct from master narratives in their orientation towards the future. Furthermore, they are not as
focused on public spaces of communication as media packages. And unlike
belief systems, imaginaries need to be regarded as multiple and contending each
other. According to Jasanoff and Kim, imaginaries are situated "in the under-
studied regions between imagination and action, between discourse and decision, and between inchoate public opinion and instrumental state policy"
(ibid.). They can thus be thought of as underlying (normative) but rarely
explicated rationales and justifications of policy choices. As such this idea of

attainable or desirable futures is especially useful for looking at the normative ideas that underlie scientific, technological and political projects, "[f]or imaginaries not only help reconfigure actors' sense of possible spaces of action but also their sense of the rightness of action" (Jasanoff & Kim, 2015: 23). Sociotechnical imaginaries are thus explicitly designed to address the values and meanings that co-emerge with particular technological or scientific innovations and can be thought of as underlying (normative) but rarely explicated rationales and justifications of policy choices.

Jasanoff and Kim tend to share Hecht's interest in national identity. They are, however, interested more in comparing imaginaries on a national policy-level instead of historically tracing institutional boundary work and differences. In particular they show "how different imaginations of social life and order are co-produced along with the goals, priorities, benefits and risks of science and technology" (ibid.: 141).

Thus, imaginaries not only constitute visions of a desirable future, they necessarily do this against the background of a deficient past. Especially policies that are concerned with sociotechnical transitions and innovations are "routinely constructed as addressing a collectively felt and publicly diagnosed deficit. Such diagnoses are necessarily 'normative'" (Pfotenhauer & Jasanoff, 2017: 6). In addition to looking for the particular risks entailed in any given imaginary the concept also sensitises us to implicit narratives of deficiency and how they relate to ideas about potential endpoints of an envisioned transition (as well as models of change itself).

For the case of circular economy policy this means exploring its underlying rationales and justifications by asking how circular economy policy combines expectations and promises of (socially) desirable futures with particular models of sustainability and innovation, and with normative ideas about what constitutes the "public good". Put differently, how is circularity understood in European circular economy policy and what are the implicit goals, priorities, benefits and risks that shape or mediate different versions of circularity?

Imagining circularity in EU policy

In previous chapters we laid out the development of circular economy policy. We can now build on this groundwork and focus on the imaginative resources that are used in these policy documents, on the central notions and their framings, and on the shifts that occurred in the ongoing "making" of this policy. When talking about the policy development and the related shifts in the collective imagination of circularity, it is also necessary to consider the different definitions and visualisations of circular economy that are assembled in this imaginary. Thus, we will proceed by first describing the development of the imaginary of circularity in circular economy policies, then we will briefly address how different circularities become visible in some of the most prominent circular economy representations. In doing so we will carve out framings of future benefits and risks and show how these relate to ideas about sustainability, economy, innovation and governance.

Assembling imaginative resources

As we argued in previous chapters, circular economy policy at the moment is a policy "in-the-making" and as such a site in which both environmental and economic policy priorities are being negotiated. As we have shown in previous chapters, the notion of a circular economy entered the stage of European-policy making around 2013. The starting point for this is provided by a number of reports produced by the Ellen MacArthur Foundation (Ellen MacArthur Foundation, 2013). Two years later, in 2014, the European Commission published the communication *Towards a circular economy. A zero waste programme for Europe* (European Commission, 2014). Circularity at this stage is framed mainly in terms of resource efficiency and waste reduction with the goal to reduce material inputs into industry, which is supposed to provide an "overall savings potential of €630 billion per year" (European Commission, 2014: 2). A central issue and priority in this document, however, is to turn waste into a resource; a resource that is so far "leaking from our economy" (European Commission, 2014: 2). This prioritisation is also visible in a number of waste reduction targets.

This first circular economy package was cut when the Juncker Commission entered office. The rationale that is usually given for this by the actors from European Commission is that the Juncker Commission was very heavily influenced by the economic crisis and was thus determined to focus on economic issues. As a consequence, it became harder to get environmental concerns on the table. The only way to get environmental concerns on the agenda during the times of austerity, we were told, was by proposing an economically focused policy package. Thus, after criticism and protests from different sites within and from outside the Commission the circular economy package was brought back. There was a requirement though, it needed to be more economically focused. This means that instead of the initial package the new Commission asked for a "more ambitious package" that was less focused on waste management. The framing of "greater ambition" is most common within DG Environment when talking about the process of re-shaping the circular economy package. It was used for example by Jyrki Katainen in a speech delivered at the 2015 edition of the circular economy stakeholder conference. This process led to the publication of a second circular economy package called *Closing the loop – An EU action plan for the Circular Economy* in 2015 (European Commission, 2015). This document defines the circular economy as an economy "where the value of products, materials and resources is maintained in the economy for as long as possible, and the generation of waste minimised" (European Commission, 2015). Following the requirement for greater ambition, this definition builds on a close relation between economic narratives, resource efficiency and waste. Besides putting economic concerns centre stage, this

way of relating the economy to resource efficiency also points to a particular risk framing. Risk in circular economy policy documents is understood mainly in terms of volatile prices as a consequence of scarce
resources. This is one of the central risks that makes a transition towards a
circular economy necessary. Given this justification, it comes as no surprise
that *Closing the loop* primarily frames waste in economic terms as "lost
business opportunities" (European Commission, 2015: 4).

The Communication on Eco-design (European Commission, 2016a) and the
Raw Materials Scoreboard (Vidal-Legaz et al., 2016), which included first proposals for measuring the potential circularity in the use of materials, further extended
the understanding of circularity. Potential circularity is measured based on circular
economy indicator 15 called "Material flows in the circular economy", which
provides a measure of all the materials flows of the economy, aggregated by
weight. This representation draws from the ecological economics understanding of
the economy as an entropic process, in which total quantities of energy and
materials consumed are maintained (inputs must equal outputs) but degraded in
the process (energy inputs are balanced with emissions as outputs).

What is interesting to note in regard to sociotechnical imaginaries and the
elements that it assembles, it implicitly assumes that a transition towards more
circularity is a matter of improving product design and designing more sustainable modes of production and consumption (eco-design). Such a model
rehearses a techno-optimist understanding of innovation and problem solving
in which a seemingly inevitable technological progress provides solutions for
societal challenges (Strand, Saltelli, Giampietro, Rommetveit, & Funtowicz,
2016). This model builds on and at the same time rehearses a classical innovation narrative that depicts innovation as necessary for the EU to remain competitive in the international market. Innovation and technological progress
cannot be challenged. In the case of the circular economy, the narrative is used
to promote investment in research, R&D expenditure, patent applications, as
well as the number of programmes and graduates in mineral processing.

In partial response to criticism and worries about the limited circularity of
energy a range of different policy documents were published in 2017, including
a Communication on waste-to-energy (European Commission, 2017a), an
implementation report (European Commission, 2017c), and the first proposal
for a directive on the restriction of hazardous substances in electrical and electronic equipment (European Commission, 2017b). Additionally, a *roadmap to a
monitoring framework for the circular economy* was published (European Commission, 2017d), which then led to the Monitoring Framework (European Commission, 2018c), with the definition of ten indicators of circularity, and the
publication of the new European Plastics Strategy (European Commission,
2018b) that explicitly relates to attempts to transition towards a more circular
economic system. We will come back to this document in the next chapter.
For now, we just want to share the observation that the monitoring framework
mobilises a broader range of imaginative resources than the initial definitions
and includes a range of hopes and promises:

The transition to a circular economy is a tremendous opportunity to transform our economy and make it more sustainable, contribute to climate goals and the preservation of the world's resources, create local jobs and generate competitive advantages for Europe in a world that is undergoing profound changes. The importance of the circular economy to European industry was recently highlighted in the renewed EU industrial policy strategy. The transition to a circular economy will also help to meet the objectives of the 2030 Agenda for Sustainable Development.

(European Commission, 2018c)

In this quote a number of different imaginative resources is mobilised while the circular economy is more narrowly confined to the industrial sector (and hence primarily their issues of durability, recycling and repair). Economic visions are framed in terms of "tremendous opportunities" for "transformation".

The visions of change and transformation implied in this policy are striking as they also figured prominently in conversations with policy-makers involved in the development of circular economy policy. Transformation was explicitly mentioned as a contrast to more radical revolution of the economic system and thus needs to be understood as signifying gradual shifts in the European economic system and not fundamental critique. We argue that the mode of transformation, defined as gradual changes and in opposition to revolutions, is a crucial element in the assembly of the circular economy imaginary. Different, and sometimes opposing narratives, are brought together through moderation, setting the stage for "win-win" solutions, middle ground and compromises. What we also see in this quote is "boundary work" (Gieryn, 1983) that distinguishes Europe from the rest of the world, a world in which "profound changes" (sic) are taking place. These changes need to be mitigated through circular economy policy.

Attention has also been given to critical raw materials, invoking a security discourse and giving support to the circular economy as a means to keep critical materials in the economy for longer through targeted recycling. This indicates a risk framing of environmental policy in terms of resource scarcity that is prominent in a number of EU policy documents. The rising demand for raw materials at the global level has consequences for the EU's security of supply. Indicators measure concepts such as self-sufficiency (the EU's share in global production of raw materials, mining activity, monitoring the circularity of material flows and recycling rates), level of openness of the economy (the level of exports of mining equipment, export restrictions which may affect the EU's access to international markets), and vulnerability to geopolitical issues (the import dependency for critical raw materials which cannot be produced within the EU, and the quality of governance of exporting countries with which the EU has to trade). Such a "securitization" has been problematised in relation to EU environmental policy (Leese & Meisch, 2015).

Over the years we thus see a gradual shift and purposeful expansion of visions and imaginative resources that guide circular economy policy-making.

Starting from waste management and environmental concerns, the focus shifted towards economically-centred visions for future Europe and to security concerns. This implied a re-framing of sustainability issues in terms of economic viability, technological innovation and (European) resource security. The main strength of circular economy policy so far has been its ability to establish win-win scenarios for the future, visions of a transition that is at the same time profound, a mere evolution and a governance mode focused on moderation. However, while circular economy initially went from a waste management to an economy-centred policy, more recently environmental discourses seem to re-enter the policy as direct links to the Paris Agreement and the 2030 Agenda are made.

Visualising circularity

Sociotechnical imaginaries of course are not only visible in policy papers and public statements of policy-makers. They are also manifest in various kinds of visualisations. Thus, while so far we have only touched on two of the more common definitions to illustrate a broad range of imaginative resources that are mobilised in attempts at conceptualising circularity, the story gets even more interesting by including visualisations or "viscourses" (Knorr Cetina, 2001) of the circular economy in the analysis.

Already in early laboratory studies the importance of visualisation has been tackled. The notion of "inscription" as developed by Latour and a number of scholars from a line of thought usually labelled Actor Network Theory (Latour & Woolgar, 1986; Rheinberger, 1997) looks at visual representations of reality in terms of epistemological objectivation processes and consensus building. They argue that through inscription devices objects of study can be transformed into two-dimensional representations. This process, they argue, is fundamentally important as it allows for scientific discoveries to travel as "immutable mobiles" and to become reproducible.

Building on this work, Lynch and Woolgar (Lynch, 1998; Lynch & Woolgar, 1990) argue that representation is a core aspect of scientific practice. They add that visual representation cannot be understood independently from its use and its relation to particular discursive contexts. Knorr Cetina (2001) coined the term "Viskurse" to direct attention to the discourse embededdness of visual representations.

Additionally, STS scholars have directed attention to visual representations that blend the factual and fictional more directly. Nerlich argues in a study about images of so-called "nanobots" – fictional tiny machines that are able to perform particular tasks inside the human body – that these images are central to "the creation of meanings" (Nerlich, 2008: 290) that become part of emergent technologies like this.

The visualisation in Figure 6.1 is taken from the first legislative proposal on the circular economy called *Towards a Circular Economy*. According to the European Commission,

[t]he following conceptual diagram illustrates in a simplified way the main phases of a circular economy model, with each of them presenting opportunities in terms of reducing costs and dependence on natural resources, boosting growth and jobs, as well as limiting waste and harmful emissions to the environment. The phases are interlinked, as materials can be used in a cascading way, for instance; industry exchanges by-products, products are refurbished or remanufactured or consumers choose product-service systems. The aim is to minimise the resources escaping from the circle so that the system functions in an optimal way.

(European Commission, 2014)

This graph shows a neat circle with only a limited amount of "residual waste" and of primary inputs that come from outside the circle. The arrows in the graph are not represented to scale, thereby promising a great potential of circularity in consumption and production processes. The processes mentioned as examples are industrial processes, reflecting the influence of industrial ecology thinking in this representation, and reflecting the policy focus of the European Commission on industry. In this representation, one can observe the reference to waste management processes, which is the policy domain from

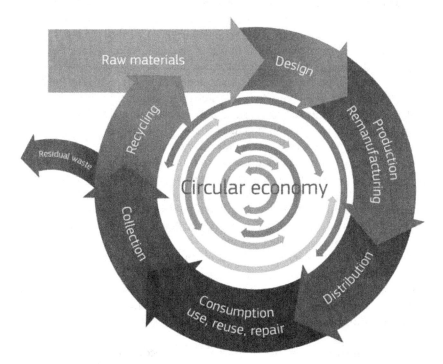

Figure 6.1 Representation of the circular economy in the Communication *Towards a Circular Economy*
Source: European Commission, 2014

which the first ideas about the circular economy have emerged, as well as the reference to design, signalling once more the important role of innovation and the imaginative function that the circular economy plays in policy-making.

In contrast, another frequently used representation of circularity tells a different story. One of the disciplines used to assess the potential circularity of the economy is ecological economics, which measures the economic process in biophysical terms, rather than in monetary terms as is done with GDP. A variety of biophysical units can be used, including materials, water and energy. In the case of the circular economy, Material Flow Analysis (MFA) has been widely used. Material Flow Analysis consists of accounting all the inputs and outputs of a system. All materials are aggregated by weight and the principle of mass balance is used to ensure consistency between input accounting and output accounting. The mass balance is represented using Sankey diagrams, which ensure that all inputs are consistently reported either as outputs or as additions to stocks (see Figure 6.2).

Aggregating material flows by weight means that construction materials account for about half of the material throughput of an economy. The quality of materials is not accounted for, so that this approach cannot provide information about hazardous materials or rare earth elements. MFA is most useful as a characterisation of the economic process as a whole, as a "bird's eye view", rather than as a means to obtain detailed information on, for instance, which economic sectors or processes have the greater potential for circularity.

This diagram depicts biophysical flows of materials, biomass and energy, and shows that the proportion of material flows that can be re-used or recycled is much less than often promised in policy documents. According to Haas et al. (2015), on a global scale about 45% of materials are destined to energetic use and are degraded, and about 42% of materials are construction materials that are added to stocks in the form of new buildings (hence the material inputs stay in the economy and are not circulated). Of the remainder, Haas et al. estimate that about 6% can be recycled, thus showing a very bleak picture of potential circularity.

This knowledge is part of the knowledge base through which the circular economy is being constructed: the Haas et al. paper was cited in the very first communication on the circular economy published by the Commission in 2013 and a new publication with a more detailed analysis of material flows by type of material stream is used to inform the 2018 Monitoring Framework. This vision of the circular economy stems from the understanding of the nexus as a material challenge.

Material flow analysis of the circular economy has been criticised for including energy flows, which cannot be made "circular" because energy is degraded through use. There is controversy also on the accounting of biomass, because the recycling is not performed by economic processes, but by the ecosystem, which blurs the notion of the circular economy.

In contrast to the previous representation, the Sankey diagram is scaled, meaning that the width of the arrows reflects the quantity of materials accounted for. In this case, the economy is not represented by economic

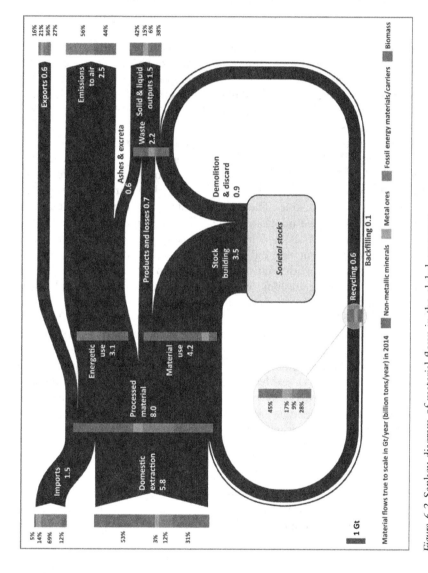

Figure 6.2 Sankey diagram of material flows in the global economy
Source: European Commission, 2018a

sectors, but is dominated by the materials consumed in greater quantities, namely energy and construction materials (dominant in the representations because of their weight).

Finally, the illustration in Figure 6.3 – taken from the first Ellen MacArthur Foundation report on the circular economy and found in most of their reports – further complicates the overall picture by speaking of a "restorative industrial system".

The representation of the circular economy used by the Ellen MacArthur Foundation, explains circularity as mimicking the ecosystem. Just like water and nutrients are recycled by the ecosystem to reproduce living processes, the argument goes that the economy should also recycle its "technical nutrients". The analogy with the ecosystem is rendered in the "butterfly diagram" of the circular economy.

This diagram recalls the industrial ecology perspective as well as one of the main messages of the Ellen MacArthur Foundation, namely to see sustainability practices as taking inspiration from nature and promote an economic model that mimics natural processes: nutrients are recycled in nature, therefore the economy should do the same. The parallel is drawn by using the concept of "technical nutrients". The mimicking is visually represented by mirroring natural and economic processes, which are visualised as a symmetrical butterfly in the picture. This representation differs from the previous two in that there are multiple processes, each with their own paces, which recycles nutrients – some are short term and some are long term. This representation makes explicit the fact that industrial recycling does not include natural resources such as water and biomass, for which the economy still depends on the ecosystem. Through the representation of faster and slower loops, this is the only representation that takes temporality into account.

The Ellen MacArthur Foundation concept of the circular economy is more focused on industrial processes than on the economy as a whole, as is the case in the MFA. As can be observed in Figure 6.2, the system boundaries are defined by specific production processes, such as mining or manufacturing, or by a sequence of production processes, in which technical inputs are used for further manufacturing, assembling, service providers and final use. The more specific focus on industrial processes can also be observed in the reference to a "restorative industrial system". This representation draws on life-cycle assessment (LCA), a technique to assess environmental impacts associated with all the stages of a product's life from raw material extraction through materials processing, manufacture, distribution, use, repair and maintenance to disposal or recycling.

The Ellen MacArthur Foundation merges the LCA approach with the use of business models and explores the potential business interest in recycling, reuse and repair services for manufacturing companies. The conceptualisation of the circular economy that emerges from the Ellen MacArthur Foundation report is, therefore, an embodiment of the aim of reconciling economic and environmental interests. The report does not study circular

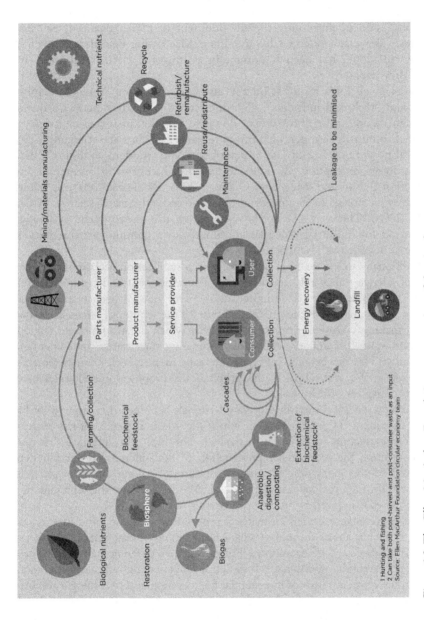

Technical nutrients

Mining/materials manufacturing

Recycle

Refurbish/
remanufacture

Reuse/redistribute

Maintenance

Parts manufacturer

Product manufacturer

Service provider

User

Collection

Consumer

Collection

Energy recovery

Landfill

Leakage to be minimised

Farming/collection¹

Biochemical
feedstock

Cascades

Biological nutrients

Biosphere

Restoration

Anaerobic
digestion/
composting

Biogas

Extraction of
biochemical
feedstock²

1 Hunting and fishing
2 Can take both post-harvest and post-consumer waste as an input
Source: Ellen MacArthur Foundation circular economy team

Figure 6.3 The Ellen MacArthur Foundation representation of the circular economy
Source: Ellen MacArthur Foundation, 2013

business models for the primary sectors (the food and energy of the nexus), but is limited in scope to industrial processes that use recyclable components. Innovation plays an important role, both in the sense of imagining new business models and the transition towards a high value-added service economy, and in promoting the development of more advanced recycling systems. The case presented by the Ellen MacArthur Foundation, even if limited in scope, has been important in putting the circular economy on the policy agenda.

Let us dwell for a moment on the distinction between "biological nutrients" and "technical nutrients". The distinction implicitly rehearses a divide between nature and culture and in doing so upholds an image of nature as external to human action, which brings in particular ideas about scientific and political power that Latour (1993) described as the "modern condition". This dichotomous conception provides the basis for discourses of restoration and protection (Hopwood, Mellor, & O'Brien, 2005; Robinson, 2004). It frames nature as an object of engineering, techno-fixes and natural science (Asdal, 2003; 2008). This way of visually representing the environment as a vague inspiration for industrial processes contributes to a framing that foregrounds nature as a source of raw materials.

Additionally this distinction contributes to a stabilisation a classical imagination of science-policy relations in terms of measurement and control (Porter, 1995; Turnhout, Neves, & de Lijster, 2014). This view of science and its relation to policy making is the implicit premise of the mantra of "evidence-based policy making". However, by neglecting that which it can't represent it tends to overemphasise certainty while underestimating uncertainty, ignorance and ambiguity. This can become highly problematic in areas such as environmental governance. We will return to this problem and propose some alternatives in the final chapters of this book.

The representation used in the Raw Materials Scoreboard is inspired by life cycle assessment (LCA) thinking, in which the whole life cycle of raw materials, from extraction to end uses, is tracked. The idea of a "life cycle" is rendered through the sequential representation of the different production steps involved in the extraction of primary resources, making and processing of products, through to final use and disposal. Also in this case, the representation of life cycles is inspired by industrial processes (see Figure 6.4).

This representation refers to material processes, but at the same time speaks more explicitly about the policy alliances and interests that intersect with the circular economy. The scoreboard brings together different narratives. These narratives reveal the interlinkages between imaginaries and indicators: it is about measuring waste in terms of its potential for recycling and becoming a resource for manufacturing processes. Nature returns as the site for extraction and pollution. It is also interesting to look at the boundaries in this representation. Waste leaves the system as a trading good or the form of economically irrelevant material (from the perspective of the system that is displayed). Global waste streams are out of the picture.

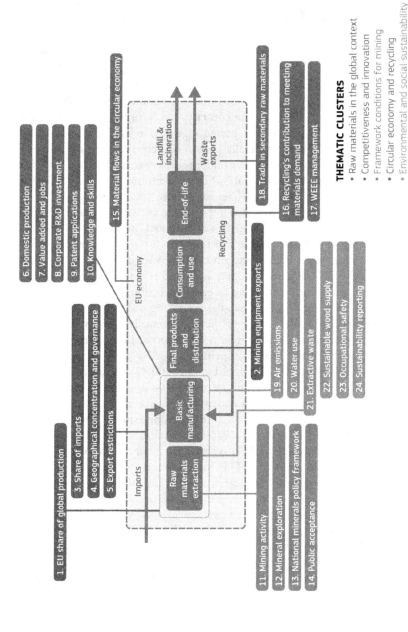

6. Domestic production
7. Value added and jobs
8. Corporate R&D investment
9. Patent applications
10. Knowledge and skills

15. Material flows in the circular economy

3. Share of imports
4. Geographical concentration and governance
5. Export restrictions

THEMATIC CLUSTERS

• Raw materials in the global context
• Competitiveness and innovation
• Framework conditions for mining
• Circular economy and recycling
• Environmental and social sustainability

1. EU share of global production

Landfill &
incineration

Waste
exports

18. Trade in secondary raw materials

16. Recycling's contribution to meeting
materials demand

17. WEEE management

EU economy

End-of-life

Consumption
and use

Recycling

Final products
and
distribution

Basic
manufacturing

Raw
materials
extraction

Imports

2. Mining equipment exports

19. Air emissions
20. Water use
21. Extractive waste

22. Sustainable wood supply
23. Occupational safety
24. Sustainability reporting

11. Mining activity
12. Mineral exploration
13. National minerals policy framework
14. Public acceptance

Figure 6.4 Representation of the circular economy in the Raw Materials Scoreboard
Source: European Commission, 2016b

Imagining circularity and rehearsing tropes

We started this chapter by taking a philosophically inclined detour into different conceptions of times and futures. This was necessary to carefully develop the reason for us analysing circular economy policy in terms of "imaginaries". The main lessons from this detour were that time is not the independent container in which our actions take place, but is intimately interwoven with how we organise ourselves as a society. We highlighted the importance of distinguishing between present futures and a future present: while there might be an indefinite amount of present futures, there will be only one future present. Following from that, imagining futures is not to be confused with idly reflecting about the "not yet". Much to the contrary, the future needs to be understood as an object, through which present (power) relations are constantly managed, which in turn has (potentially severe) consequences for a future present. Imagining futures therefore is best understood as a social practice that is an integral part of social interaction at various levels from our daily interactions to making business plans or creating policies for a more circular economy.

That, we argued, is precisely why it is important to better understand how and in which sites futures are being imagined and negotiated (in the next chapter, we will explore an additional site of collective imagination: indicator development). As such, imaginaries can be used to explain contingencies in policy making, help us understand why policies look like they look and reveal implicit assumptions that underpin certain policies. Looking at circular economy policy through the lens of imaginaries we argued that while the policy sets out to be "ambitious" in order to moderate "profound" changes there are actually a lot of imaginative resources and tropes that are neither new nor ambitious. In that sense there is a risk that the intended change remains superficial.

This becomes visible in the potential benefits and risks that are implied in these policies. Risk in circular economy policy documents is framed mainly in terms of volatile prices as a consequence of scarce resources. The rising demand for raw materials at a global level has consequences for the EU's security of supply. Thus, a security discourse is rehearsed that positions the circular economy as a means to keep certain materials in the economy for longer through targeted recycling. This indicates a risk framing of environmental policy in terms of resource scarcity that is prominent in a number of EU policy documents. The main potential benefits are pictured through win–win scenarios in which the preservation of the world's resources, the creation of local jobs and the generation of competitive advantages for Europe will be simultaneously possible. These win–win scenarios create visions for a transition to desirable futures that is at the same time profound and a mere evolution while stabilising a mode of governance focused on moderation. Also, the imaginative resources used to think about innovation and the sustainability rehearse classic policy tropes. Sustainability is described in a language of economic viability, technological innovation, and (European) resource security. This builds on a classical innovation narrative that depicts innovation as necessary for the EU to remain competitive in the international market. In this sense also waste has changed its meaning from a signifier of unsustainable practices to a resource in an "optimization business" (Hultman & Corvellec, 2012).

The problem is that stabilising a collective imagination of circular futures in this way might actually be counterproductive to the important objectives the policy aims to achieve. Such a framing for instance runs the risk of underestimating issues in regards to the social organisation of consumption and pay not enough attention to practices of sharing, re-use and collaboration (Marin & De Meulder, 2018). Also, such a narrow framing tends to overlook social aspects of the transition to a circular economy as well as concerns about its "social desirability" (Murray et al., 2017; Sauvé, Bernard, & Sloan, 2016). A focus on consumption builds on a rational choice model, in which individuals are understood mainly as "consumers". This is criticised for ignoring the fact that, for example, food consumption consists of complex combinations of routines and habits, shared cultural meanings and understandings, and available infrastructures (Mylan, Holmes, & Paddock, 2016; Welch, Keller, & Mandich, 2017).

This poses the question, why it seems to be so hard for the European Commission as a political institution to imagine a "circular society" instead of a narrow circular economy, as a discussant in a workshop remarked (workshop, May 2018). Without being able to offer a definitive answer to this question, literatures on collective imagination indicate that one might want to look at the actors doing the imagining and thus at contemporary ways of governing the future and how they can be improved. We will make some suggestions on how this could be done in the final chapters of this book.

References

Adam, B. (1998). *Timescapes of Modernity: The Environment and Invisible Hazards*. London and New York: Routledge.

Adam, B., & Groves, C. (2007). *Future Matters. Action, Knowledge, Ethics*. Leiden: Brill.

Adams, V., Murphy, M., & Clarke, A. E. (2009). Anticipation: Technoscience, life, affect, temporality. *Subjectivity*, 28, 246–265.

Anderson, B. (1991). *Imagined Communities: Reflections on the Origin and Spread of Nationalism*. London and New York: Verso.

Appadurai, A. (1990). Disjuncture and difference in the global cultural economy. *Theory, Culture & Society*. doi:10.1177/026327690007002017

Asdal, K. (2003). Kristin Asdal. *Nature*, 1(42), 60–74. doi:10.1046/j.1468–2303.2003.00257.x

Asdal, K. (2008). Enacting things through numbers: Taking nature into account/ing. *Geoforum*, 39(1), 123–132.

Baptista, J. A. (2014). The ideology of sustainability and the globalization of a future. *Time & Society*. doi:10.1177/0961463X11431651

Bijker, W. E. (1987). The Social Construction of Bakelites: Toward a Theory of Invention. In W. E. Bijker, T. Hughes, & T. Pinch (Eds.), *The Social Construction of Technological*

Systems. New Directions in the Sociology and History of Technology (pp. 159–187). Cambridge, MA: MIT Press.

Dennis, M. A. (2015). Our monsters, our selves: Reimagining the problem of knowledge in Cold War America. In S. Jasanoff & S. H. Kim (Eds.), *Dreamscapes of Modernity: Sociotechnical Imaginaries and the Fabrication of Power*. Chicago, IL: University of Chicago Press.

Elias, N. (1988). *Über die Zeit. Arbeiten zur Wissenssoziologie II*. Frankfurt am Main: Suhrkamp.

Ellen MacArthur Foundation. (2013). *Towards the Circular Economy*. Retrieved from www.ellenmacarthurfoundation.org/assets/downloads/publications/Ellen-MacArthur-Foundation-Towards-the-Circular-Economy-vol.1.pdf

European Commission. (2014). *Communication from the Commission to the European Parliament, the Council, the European Economic and Social Committee and the Committee of the Regions. Towards a circular economy: A zero waste programme for Europe* (No. COM (2014) 398). Brussels: European Commission. Retrieved from http://eur-lex.europa.eu/resource.html?uri=cellar:50edd1fd-01ec-11e4-831f-01aa75ed71a1.0001.01/DOC_1&format=PDF

European Commission. (2015). *Communication from the Commission to the European Parliament, the Council, the European Economic and Social Committee and the Committee of the Regions. Closing the loop – An EU action plan for the Circular Economy EN* (No. COM (2015) 614). Brussels: European Commission.

European Commission. (2016a). *Communication from the Commission. Ecodesign Working Plan 2016–2019* (No. COM (2016) 773).

European Commission. (2016b). *Raw Materials Scoreboard*. Luxembourg: European Commission.

European Commission. (2017a). *Communication from the Commission to the European Parliament, the Council, the European Economic and Social Committee and the Committee of the Regions. The role of waste-to-energy in the circular economy* (No. COM (2017) 34). Brussels: European Commission. Retrieved from http://ec.europa.eu/environment/waste/waste-to-energy.pdf

European Commission. (2017b). *Proposal for a Directive of the European Parliament and of the Council amending Directive 2011/65/EU on the restriction of the use of certain hazardous substances in electrical and electronic equipment* (No. 2017/0013).

European Commission. (2017c). *Report from the Commission to the European Parliament, the Council, the European Economic and Social Committee and the Committee of the Regions on the implementation of the Circular Economy Action Plan* (No. COM (2017) 33). Brussels: European Commission.

European Commission. (2017d). *Roadmap Development of a Monitoring Framework for the Circular Economy*.

European Commission. (2018a). *Commission Staff Working Document. Measuring progress towards circular economy in the European Union – Key indicators for a monitoring framework. Accompanying the document Communication from the Commission to the European Parliament, the Council, the European Economic and Social Committee and the Committee of the Regions* (No. SWD (2018) 17).

European Commission. (2018b). *Communication from the Commission to the European Parliament, the Council, the European Economic and Social Committee and the Committee of the Regions. A European Strategy for Plastics in a Circular Economy* (SWD (2018) 16, No. COM (2018) 28).

European Commission. (2018c). *Communication from the Commission to the European Parliament, the Council, the European Economic and Social Committee and the Committee of the Regions on a monitoring framework for the circular economy* (SWD (2018) 17, No. COM (2018) 29).

Felt, U., Barben, D., Irwin, A., Joly, P.-B., Rip, A., Stirling, A., & Stöckelová, T. (2013). *Science in Society: Caring for Our Futures in Turbulent Times*. ESF Science Policy Briefing. Strasbourg: European Science Foundation.

Fujimura, J. (2003). Future imaginaries: Genome scientists as sociocultural entrepreneurs. In A. Goodman, D. Heath, & S. Lindee (Eds.), *Genetic Nature/Culture: Anthropology and science beyond the culture divide*. Berkeley: University of California Press.

Giddens, A. (1991). *Modernity and Self-Identity: Self and Society in the Late Modern Age*. Stanford: Stanford University Press.

Gieryn, T. (1983). Boundary-work and the demarcation of science from non-science: Strains and interests in professional ideologies of scientists. *American Sociological Review*, 48(6), 781–795.

Haas, W., Krausmann, F., Wiedenhofer, D., & Heinz, M. (2015). How circular is the global economy? An assessment of material flows, waste production and recycling in the European Union and the world in 2005. *Journal of Industrial Ecology*, 19(5), 765–777.

Harrington, A., Rose, N., & Singh, I. (2006). Editors' Introduction. *BioSocieties*, 1(1), 5. doi:10.1017/S1745855205050209

Hecht, G. (2001). Technology, Politics, and National Identity in France. In M. T. Allen & G. Hecht (Eds.), *Technologies of Power* (pp. 253–294). Cambridge, MA: MIT Press.

Hölscher, L. (1999). *Die Entdeckung der Zukunft*. Frankfurt am Main: Fischer (Taschenbuch Verlag).

Hopwood, B., Mellor, M., & O'Brien, G. (2005). Sustainable development: Mapping different approaches. *Sustainable Development*, 13, 38–52.

Hultman, J., & Corvellec, H. (2012). The European waste hierarchy: From the sociomateriality of waste to a politics of consumption. *Environment and Planning A: Economy and Space*, 44(10), 2413–2427. doi:10.1068/a44668

Jasanoff, S. (2001). Image and Imagination: The Formation of Global Environmental Consciousness. In C. A. Miller & P. N. Edwards (Eds.), *Changing the Atmosphere: Expert Knowledge and Environmental Governance* (pp. 309–337). Cambridge, MA: MIT Press.

Jasanoff, S., & Kim, S.-H. (2009). Containing the atom: Sociotechnical imaginaries and nuclear power in the U.S. and South Korea. *Minerva*, 47(2), 119–146.

Jasanoff, S., & Kim, S.-H. (2015). *Dreamscapes of Modernity: Sociotechnical Imaginaries and the Fabrication of Power*. Chicago, IL: University of Chicago Press.

Knorr Cetina, K. (2001). "Viskurse" der Physik. Konsensbildung und visuelle Darstellung. In B. Heintz & J. Huber (Eds.), *Mit dem Auge denken. Strategien der Sichtbarmachung in wissenschaftlichen und virtuellen Welten* (pp. 305–320). Wien: Springer.

Koselleck, R. (1979). *Vergangene Zukunft*. Frankfurt am Main: Suhrkamp.

Latour, B. (1993). *We Have Never Been Modern*. Cambridge, MA: Harvard University Press.

Latour, B., & Woolgar, S. (1986). *Laboratory Life. The Construction of Scientific Facts*. Princeton, NJ: Princeton University Press.

Leese, M., & Meisch, S. (2015). Securitising sustainability? Questioning the "water, energy and food nexus". *Water Alternatives*, 8(1), 695–709.

Lente, H. van, & Rip, A. (1998). The rise of membrane technology: From rhetorics to social reality. *Social Studies of Science*, 28(2), 221–254.

Luhmann, N. (1976). The future cannot begin: Temporal structures in modern society. *Social Research*, 130–152.

Lynch, M. (1998). The production of scientific images: Vision and re-vision in the history, philosophy, and sociology of science. *Communication & Cognition. Monographies*, 31(2–3), 213–228.

Lynch, M., & Woolgar, S. (1990). *Representation in Scientific Practice*. Cambridge, MA: MIT Press.

Marin, J., & De Meulder, B. (2018). Interpreting circularity. Circular city representations concealing transition drivers. *Sustainability (Switzerland)*, 10(5). doi:10.3390/su10051310

Michael, M. (2000). Futures of the Present. From Performativity to Prehension. In N. Brown, B. Rappert, & A. Webster (Eds.), *Contested futures. A Sociology of Prospective Techno-Science* (pp. 21–39). Aldershot: Ashgate.

Mol, A. (2008). *The Logic of Care: Health and the Problem of Patient Choice*. London: Routledge.

Mol, A., Moser, I., & Pols, J. (2015). *Care in Practice: On Tinkering in Clinics, Homes and Farms* (Vol. 8). Transcript Verlag.

Murray, A., Skene, K., Haynes, K., Murray, A., Skene, K., & Haynes, K. (2017). The circular economy: An interdisciplinary exploration of the concept and application in a global context. *Journal of Business Ethics*, 140(3), 369–380. doi:10.1007/s10551–10015–2693–2692

Mylan, J., Holmes, H., & Paddock, J. (2016). Re-introducing consumption to the "circular economy": A sociotechnical analysis of domestic food provisioning. *Sustainability*, 8(8). doi:10.3390/su8080794

Nerlich, B. (2008). Powered by imagination: Nanobots at the Science Photo Library. *Science as Culture*, 17(3), 269–292. doi:10.1080/09505430802280743

Nowotny, H. (1989). *Eigenzeit: Entstehung und Strukturierung eines Zeitgefühls*. Frankfurt Am Main: Suhrkamp.

Nowotny, H. (1994). *Time: The Modern and Postmodern Experience*. Cambridge, UK: Polity Press.

Pereira, Â. G., & Saltelli, A. (2017). Post-normal institutional identities: Quality assurance, reflexivity and ethos of care. *Futures*, 91, 53–61.

Pfotenhauer, S., & Jasanoff, S. (2017). Panacea or diagnosis? Imaginaries of innovation and the 'MIT model' in three political cultures. *Social Studies of Science*, 47(6), 783–810. doi:10.1177/0306312717706110

Porter, T. M. (1995). *Trust in Numbers. The Pursuit of Objectivity in Science and Public Life*. Princeton, NJ: Princeton University Press.

Puig de la Bellacasa, M. (2011). Matters of care in technoscience: Assembling neglected things. *Social Studies of Science*, 41(1), 85–106.

Rheinberger, H. J. (1997). *Toward a History of Epistemic Things: Synthesizing Proteins in the Test Tube*. Stanford, CA: Stanford University Press.

Robinson, J. (2004). Squaring the circle? Some thoughts on the idea of sustainable development. *Ecological Economics*, 48(4), 369–384. doi:10.1016/j.ecolecon.2003.10.017

Sauvé, S., Bernard, S., & Sloan, P. (2016). Environmental sciences, sustainable development and circular economy: Alternative concepts for trans-disciplinary research. *Environmental Development*, 17, 48–56. doi:10.1016/j.envdev.2015.09.002

Sorokin, P. A., & Merton, R. (1937). Social time: A methodological and functional analysis. *American Journal of Sociology*, 42(5), 615–629.

Strand, R., Saltelli, A., Giampietro, M., Rommetveit, K., & Funtowicz, S. (2016). New narratives for innovation. *Journal of Cleaner Production*. doi:10.1016/j.jclepro.2016.10.194

Taylor, C. (2002). Modern social imaginaries. *Public Culture*, 14(1), 91–124. doi:10.12816/0027573

Turnhout, E., Neves, K., & de Lijster, E. (2014). 'Measurementality'in biodiversity governance: Knowledge, transparency, and the Intergovernmental Science-Policy

Platform on Biodiversity and Ecosystem Services (IPBES). *Environment and Planning A*, 46(3), 581–597.

Vidal-Legaz, B., Mancini, L., Blengini, G., Pavel, C., Marmier, A., Blagoeva, D., … Nita, V. (2016). *EU Raw Materials Scoreboard*. Luxembourg: Publications Office of the European Union.

Wajcman, J. (2014). *Pressed for Time: The Acceleration of Life in Digital Capitalism*. Chicago, IL: University of Chicago Press.

Welch, D., Keller, M., & Mandich, G. (2017). Imagined futures of everyday life in the circular economy. *Interactions*, 24(2), 46–51.

Winner, L. (1986). *The Whale and the Reactor: A Search for Limits in an Age of High Technology*. Chicago, IL: University of Chicago Press.

Zerubavel, E. (1985). *Hidden Rhythms: Schedules and Calendars in Social Life*. London: University of California Press.

7 Measuring circularity

Indicator development in the circular economy

Now we have gained a first understanding of the imaginary that is guiding circular economy policy development, we focus on a particular site that we argue is central in the negotiation and imagination of circularity and for questions about circular economy policies: the indicators that are being developed for measuring progress towards a circular economy. Drawing on a rich literature from the field of science and technology studies on the role of quantification in governance and the politics of indicators this chapter explores how circularity becomes both a measurable and governable entity and how particular circularities (and realities) are enacted at the expense of others. The purpose of the critical analysis presented in this chapter is also, however, to go beyond deconstruction and direct attention to potential implications of measuring circularity in certain ways. This chapter thus presents a reading of indicator development inspired by STS literature that highlights the productivity of measurement in governance practices. As Esther Turnhout so poignantly stated: "only what is counted counts".

Introduction

In the previous chapter we argued that to understand why circular economy policy looks like it does, it is important to analyse the sociotechnical imaginary that is guiding this policy. In doing so we showed how, despite leading European Commission policy makers publicly praising the revolutionary potential of this new policy, circular economy policies actually mobilise a number of imaginative resources that rehearse themes and tropes that are quite common in European policy making and not at all very new. This concerns models of innovation that perpetuate a certain techno-optimism, to ideas about sustainability that remain closely tied to the ethos of economic growth.

One of the central tropes that is being rehearsed is the model of "evidence-based policy making" itself. This is a central ideal of the European Commission and thus it is not at all surprising to find it in these policy documents and in statements of officials. However, we don't want to stop at merely stating its existence. Instead we use this chapter to dive deeper into how exactly this idea of evidence-based policy making plays out in the case of the circular economy, by exploring the indicators that have been developed by the European Commission to measure progress towards a circular economy (European Commission, 2018b).

The progress towards a circular economy is monitored through a number of indicators. One can for example learn about the generation of municipal waste per capita or recycling rates as well as about recyclable raw material trade. Furthermore, the indicators let us know the number of people currently employed in circular economy jobs. In Austria for example currently 1.49% of all people employed work in circular economy related jobs. These indicators also provide knowledge about the development of the circular economy. EU-wide trade in recyclable raw materials is increasing as are exports into non-EU countries. This information and many more are provided on a dedicated Eurostat website and through various reporting mechanisms. These indicators, however, not only provide information about circularity; the particular set of indicators additionally implies a collectively stabilised understanding of what circularity is and how circular futures look like. In that sense we understand these indicators as part of the imaginary of circularity we outlined in the previous chapter. Building on the analysis of the previous chapter we ask: how does the particular selection of indicators stabilise or challenge the imaginary of circularity visible in circular economy policy development? Why were particular indicators chosen and not others? What are potential issues with this particular representation of circularity?

To address these questions, we will first situate the analysis within literature from the field of science and technology studies (STS) to gain a better understanding of the role of quantification in governance. In particular, we will focus on the politics of indicator development and use. One of the central insights from these literatures is that, while quantifications are mostly understood as more or less accurate representations or descriptions of the world, they are in fact creating the very objects or phenomena they pretend to be measuring. Thus, in this chapter we direct attention to the performativity or reactivity of indicators. The second part of this chapter then provides an empirical exploration of indicator development at the European Commission, analysing how they contribute to the imaginary described in the previous chapter and directing attention to some issues with the indicators currently in use.

Quantification in governance

Recently there has been an increasing interest in the idea of evidence-based policy-making related to debates about so-called "post-truth" and "fake news". The European Commission for example hosted an event entitled "EU4Facts" in 2017, which aimed at strengthening trust in science. Additionally, new possibilities related to computerisation and novel analytical techniques subsumed under the umbrella term "big data" (Kitchin, 2014a, 2014b; Rieder & Simon, 2016) have fed onto this renewed focus on evidence-based politics.

Evidence in these discussions is usually understood as quantified knowledge about the world. The role of quantified knowledge in governance and policy-making, however, is hardly a recent phenomenon. Much to the contrary it has long sparked interest of historians and philosophers of science. Why is it, they ask, that numbers seem so attractive to actors in governance and policy? Where does this "trust in numbers" (Porter, 1995) come from?

First of all, it is important to note that the recent hype around big data and automated decision-making can easily hide the fact that quantification in governance is by no means a recent phenomenon. Population counts and statistics are closely tied to the emergence of the modern nation state and to colonial history. This led to the development of official bureaus of statistics in the nineteenth century (Desrosieres, 1998). The introduction of statistics led to

> the establishment of general forms, of categories of equivalence, and ter-
> minologies that transcend the singularities of individual situations, either
> through the categories of law (the judicial point of view) or through norms
> and standards (the standpoint of economy of management and efficiency).
>
> (ibid., p. 8)

These link to processes of state-making, "when several states undertake – as is the case today with the European Union – to harmonise their fiscal, social, and economic legislation in order to permit the free circulation of people, goods, and capital" (ibid., p. 8f). Statistics entered governance in the form of censuses. As such, they were also used in the governance of colonies, even more so than in the governance of homelands. Methods for classification and accounting allowed for gaining control over the complexities of foreign societies (Hacking, 1990).

This process is historically also tied to the emergence of cultures of objectivity and particular ideas of science and its place in society. Whereas in the early days of science ideas of "truth" were closely tied to experiments conducted by trustworthy gentlemen and witnessed by an audience of equally trustworthy social status, so-called "gentlemen science" (Shapin, 1999; Shapin & Schaffer, 1985), ideas of objectivity of the scientific method subsequently took on to signify impartiality and disinterestedness. This then establishes an idea of science as neutral and far removed from subjective judgement. What is trusted then are particular methods, experimental settings or procedures – standardised methods and automated data gathering and processing through big data (Rieder & Simon, 2016, 2017) – and no longer the integrity of gentlemen scientists. In this way a particular "moral economy of science" (Daston, 1995) was established and quantified evidence gained the ability to lend its wielders a sense of authority and legitimacy. Historians of science Lorraine Daston and Peter Galison argue that this tendency to preferably trust in quantified knowledge in particular builds on a correspondence of numbers to an ideal of "mechanical objectivity" (Daston, 1995; Daston & Galison, 1992). Relying on quantified evidence is thus closely entwined with questions of trust and legitimacy and an idealised ethos of science, in particular when it comes to the use of numbers in policy making (Kovacic, 2018).

In a climate of mistrust and a sense of democratic crisis as currently experienced in Europe and beyond it is thus no surprise that numbers take on the role of a mechanism of defending the legitimacy of governance authority.

The widespread use and general popularity of quantification in governance processes is furthermore attributed to the ability of numbers to travel and thus to function as a technology that allows for governing and knowing at a distance (Latour, 1987; Scott, 1998) and has also been referred to as a "technology of distance" (Porter, 1995: ix). This implies both geographic and cognitive distance. Quantified knowledge, so to say, makes it possible to make decisions from afar without an intimate local knowledge and thus can be regarded as a precondition for governance.

The construction of numbers that are able to travel across distance, however, is far from being easy. It requires considerable work and relies on previously established and often costly infrastructures of knowing (Latour, 1999; Latour & Woolgar, 1986). This includes actual technical infrastructures and institutional environments, but also refers to the development of methods and the training of a skilled workforce. On the other hand, once such "machineries" (Edwards, 2010) are put in place, they become quite stable and "sticky" (Waylen, Blackstock, & Holstead, 2015).

Evidence-based governance has also been described as a particular mode of governance. This means that the increasing reliance on facts and evidence implies a shift in ideas of governance as such. Such a shift for example entails that evidence-based governance relies less on imposing sanctions, but on a "soft" form of governing through establishing standards and through assessments, reports and rankings.

This observation of course does not sit easy with the idea that quantified knowledge humbly describes a stable world independent of knowledge practices. In fact, this view has been challenged in a number of empirical studies. Numbers and the infrastructures to create them, so the argument goes, are reactive and intervene in social life in the sense that they provide (often monetary) incentives to meet certain targets and improve rankings for example: they lead to a form of incorporation and self-governance thus actively shaping the world rather than merely describing it. The creation of national surveys for example became instrumental for stabilising a sense of belonging together within the highly abstract construct of a nation (Porter, 1995); environmental metrics constitute particular natures and modes of environmental governance (Turnhout, Hisschemöller, & Eijsackers, 2007); and metrics for measuring the performance of law schools led school administrators to adapt their schools to the needs of the performance indicators and in doing so led to an unintended homogenisation of types of law schools and the programs they offer (Espeland & Sauder, 2007). In that sense standardised quantified knowledge can be understood as a technology of "disciplining" (Foucault, 1981) in the sense that it enables bureaucracies to "see" and thus create governable objects. This perspective directs attention to the ways in which governing bodies are able to "see" (Law, 2009; Scott, 1998) their objects and to questions of how quantitative evidence is interwoven with the particular institutional sites in which these discussions take place.

Circular economy policy relies on governance through a particular form of quantification. By creating a set of indicators that are supposed to measure progress towards a circular economy the broader imaginative resources we described in the previous chapter are translated (i.e. simplified) into indicators of circularity. Before we turn to these indicators in more detail, we will briefly focus on indicators as a technology of knowledge.

Indicator politics

In thinking about indicators, it seems useful to start with the basic meaning of the word. To indicate something can very basically be a gesture. A gesture to show where something is situated or point out the direction to go to a tourist, for example (as most of us have experienced, especially indications of the latter sort very rarely have anything to do with the actual route). Indicating something, therefore, in a first understanding, can be described as illustrating something that cannot be known in a direct way.

A famous example of indicators are canaries, which have been used to detect carbon monoxide and other toxic gases in coal mines before they could become dangerous for workers. Another indicator from the sphere of ornithology is the so-called honeyguide or honeybird, birds who are known for leading humans to bee colonies.

In a similar manner also a barometer functions as an indicator in that it gives a measure of air pressure, which then again functions as an indicator for weather. It's hard to predict weather changes without complex technological systems, therefore the use of a barometer can give some indication.

Through these examples we start to grasp some of the characteristics of indicators. Indicators provide information that is not directly accessible: miners had no means of assessing the toxicity levels in mines, so they used canaries. Furthermore, to make sense of indicators some more or less explicit theory about how indicators relate to the phenomenon to be observed needs to be applied. While the relation between barometers and air pressure is more straightforward, predicting the weather on the basis of air pressure requires some more advanced theoretical knowledge about weather phenomena (in the most minimalistic form this can be a statement of the form "air pressure falls rapidly = thunderstorm very likely").

So, two things: first, indicators allow to gain information about something that can for various reasons not be directly observed. This is important to keep in mind when talking about indicators: they exist because of the inability to measure a certain thing or phenomenon or as Porter puts it "[a] quantitative index or indicator typically cannot measure the very thing of interest, but in its place something whose movements show a consistent relationship to that thing" (Porter, 1995: 34). This is worth noting: the very reason for indicators to exist in the first place is an inability of measurement. Instead of the thing itself we have a relationship, meaning that indicators necessarily presume a theoretical conception of how different phenomena relate to each other. What follows, and this is the second point, is that in order to make sense of indicators a certain amount of theoretical knowledge is needed. This might be comparatively easy when it comes to weather, but when a highly conceptual phenomenon such as circularity in the economy needs to be captured by means of relations to something else – it is not hard to imagine that things get tricky. But more of that later.

Birds and barometers are comparatively simple indicators. At this point it makes sense to introduce a rough typology of different indicators. Engle Merry distinguishes between counts, ratios and composites (Merry, 2016). Counts describe the number of people, things or events. Basic census data or different kinds of surveys are examples for this. Already, for this simple form of indicators, Merry identifies a number of critical questions: What is considered important to count? By what characteristics are things or entities identified, categorised and aggregated? Already these simple questions show that there is a lot of interpretative work that goes into such a seemingly simple act as counting; and this does not even touch on the political and cultural biases in counting. As Merry notes: "Countries count what they care about" (ibid.: 14). Ratios then refer to a relation between numbers, the level of recycling per capita, for example. Again, there are a number of questions that point to the politics of indicators such as questions about baselines for comparison. Finally, there are composites, which refers to combinations of multiple counts and ratios. As you might imagine, this kind of indicator requires a significant amount of technical expertise, theoretical assumptions about the phenomena under scrutiny and, again, interpretative work and decision making (ibid.: 15).

Throughout modern history there have been a number of very successful indicators measuring a plethora of different phenomena. In fact, a global proliferation of indicators can be observed and indicators are used in a broad range of different fields from global finance to public health, criminal justice, public statistics and climate change by all sorts of institutions from governments to NGOs (Rottenburg, Merry, Park, & Mugler, 2015). There are a number of indicators that gained global prominence such as for example the Human Development Index (HDI) measuring the development of different countries beyond GDP, or Freedom House, which assesses the degree of freedom in the world. One of the most famous indicators of course is the Gross Domestic Product (GDP), which is widely accepted as a measure for the wealth of a country although it is embroiled in on-going controversy (Fleurbaey, 2009; Kovacic & Giampietro, 2015; Stiglitz, Sen, & Fitoussi, 2017). Once such indicators are established, they become accepted as accurate descriptions of the world (in a quite literal sense, since coloured world maps are commonly used to visualise indicators) and often also seem to stand in for the phenomenon they are supposed to measure: IQ for example has become synonymous with intelligence.

But what makes an indicator successful? Engle Merry describes a number of features shared by successful indicators (Merry, 2016). Usually, such indicators are the outcome of research, analysis and experiment; then they are usually backed by powerful institutions. Also, successful indicators embody a theory of social change, which it does not explicitly articulate or test. Furthermore, as Merry argues, indicators provide simplified representations of more complex phenomena and are therefore convenient tools for decision making. And finally, for indicators to be successful they need to be politically acceptable. So, indicators need a strong theoretical and empirical base to gain legitimacy, but also rely on political and institutional support.

Once this is achieved, indicators can become very "seductive" (Merry, 2016), a promise to stand above politics by providing accurate descriptions of a world out there and thus hold governments accountable through comparable information. As we showed in the introduction, circular economy indicators are used for comparing EU member states in regard to their circularity achievements and also in relation to targeted goals. Given these features, indicators are mostly employed "as a technology of governance in situations where lines of authority are unclear, law is soft rather than hard, jurisdiction is ambiguous, and governance requires negotiations among sovereign nation-states" (ibid.: 10). We can easily see how this applies to governance in the EU and especially when it comes to environmental policy-making.

On a technical level, indicator development focuses on issues of availability, reliability and validity. One of the biggest issues, especially with environmental indicators, is the availability of useful and comparable data, as Esther Turnhout and her colleagues have demonstrated for the case if biodiversity governance (Turnhout, Neves, & de Lijster, 2014). In addition, scientific validity also can become an issue, when indicators are not subjected to rigorous peer review. And on a more abstract level they direct attention to the fact that not all aspects of biodiversity are equally quantifiable. This, of course, can create biases.

Despite their aura of objectivity, indicators rely on practices of interpretation both in their creation and use: this applies for example to the choice of measurement approaches and data sets, or to the definition of categories. They rely on expert opinions and are stabilised through particular epistemic communities and administrative infrastructures for collecting and processing data (Rottenburg et al., 2015: 4). Indicators thus are deeply "political" in the sense that implicit assumptions, motivations and concerns are part of their creation, they "do not stand outside regimes of power and governance but exist within them, both in their creation and in their on-going functioning" (Merry, 2016: 21). It is thus important to keep in mind that

> measuring can never be a completely neutral activity. It involves the exercise of power in the sense that rendering an object of interest measurable or legible (Scott, 1998) involves critical choices about what to measure and how. The problem, therefore, is that the seemingly neutral

tasks of measuring and counting in order to achieve transparency actually provide the basis for centralised control, coordination, and exchange.

(Turnhout et al., 2014: 583)

And furthermore:

> The technical is always political because there is always interpretation and judgement in systems of classification, in the choice of things to measure, in the weighting of constitutive elements, and in decisions about which denominator to use for a ratio. The political hides behind the technical.

(Merry, 2016: 21)

So, while indicators are commonly understood as providing actionable knowledge about the world "out there", they build on particular assumptions about science and how it relates to governance, thus about knowledge production and use. Crucially it involves the production of an object as legible and governable in the sense that how and by which standards an entity is measured, which aspects and dimensions enter a set of indicators for example is never straightforward and self-evident, but rather a matter of very mundane things such as data availability, methodological preferences and skills. Indicators from this perspective can be used as a window into the cultural worlds in which they were created; or the imaginative resources that become manifest.

It thus comes as no surprise that there is a strand of the debate that takes a critical stance towards the production and use of indicators and directs attention to a number of issues. On a more technical level authors have pointed to problems with simplification through classification and categorisation. This process favours comparability of contextualisation. Local knowledges and experiential knowledge thus are systematically undervalued. Furthermore "expertise inertia" and "data inertia" haven been highlighted as problematic issues: experts have power in developing indicators, thus it is their knowledge and preferences in regard to methods that determine what is being measured and how. Indicator cultures in that sense closely relate to "cultures of objectivity" (Porter, 1995) in that they draw on a cultural repertoire that builds on ideas about technocratic expertise, rationality and a general legibility of the (natural and social) world. It is also worth noting that the actors responsible for indicator development usually are members of cosmopolitan elites, which leads to the fact that certain voices are underrepresented in the development of indicators. These power relations are then inscribed in how we represent the world. Additionally, available data determine what can be measured.

Besides not being neutral, indicators are furthermore not independent from particular modes of governance. The proliferation of indicators from the 1980ies onwards coincided with a "radical redefinition of the relations between democracy and market that implied a shift in the definitions of liberty and governance" (Rottenburg et al., 2015: 3).

In a similar manner environmental sociologist Esther Turnhout argues that the Intergovernmental Science-Policy Platform on Biodiversity and Ecosystem Services (IPBES) follows a logic of "measurementality", which she describes as

> an "art of neoliberal governance" that emerges from privileging scientific techniques for assessing and measuring the environment as a set of standardized units which are further expressed, reified, and sedimented in policy and discourse and which, in turn, render the environment fungible. Which, in other words, break down the environment into discrete units such that they become commensurable and exchangeable.
>
> (Turnhout et al., 2014: 583)

This highlights how the institutionalisation of particular counting, mapping and monitoring practices together with a utilitarian framing of "the ecosystem", stabilises an economic logic in thinking about biodiversity and also privileges certain kinds of knowledge over others. Furthermore, it nicely shows that this way of framing biodiversity governance rests on a particular model of how science relates to policy "that assumes a direct and somewhat deterministic relationship between the production and use of knowledge" (Turnhout, Waterton, Neves, & Buiser, 2013: 155). The challenge of conserving biodiversity then becomes a problem of generating ever more knowledge and distributing it more effectively. Indicators for environmental governance thus tend to rehearse technocratic, economic and managerial discourses (science based linear model, biodiversity as ecosystem services, optimisation of knowledge production and use) by talking about seemingly positive principles like effectiveness, efficiency and transparency.

> To extend and play with Foucault's notion of "governmentality" (Dean, 1999; Foucault, 1991), we propose the term "measurementality" to signify an "art of neoliberal governance" that emerges from privileging scientific techniques for assessing and measuring the environment as a set of standardized units which are further expressed, reified, and sedimented in policy and discourse and which, in turn, render the environment fungible. Which, in other words, break down the environment into discrete units such that they become commensurable and exchangeable. As the surveillance of humans and nonhumans generates not only knowledge but also power relations (Foucault, 1977), we suggest that measurementality is key to the production of transparency. We propose this term because we think it is helpful to underscore the crucial role of standardized knowledge in current neoliberal environmental governance and the various different managerial, commodified, or other shapes it takes in practice and open it up to critical scrutiny.
>
> (Turnhout et al., 2014: 583)

Indicators can even run counter their initially intended effect. In her work on "critical limits" or "critical loads" of nature in terms of pollution, Kristin Asdal (2008) shows how ideas of "nature" and "economy" are brought together in debates about potential economic effects of pollution for agriculture and thus a form of economic life. She traces how through increasing budgets for environmental research in "centres for calculation" distinct studies about particular rivers helped to set up the idea of an integrated "nature-whole" that could be quantified in terms of critical loads of nature. Nature had been made visible through a series of activities and transformations. Not using nature's capacity to withstand pollution up to certain critical loads was equalled with a waste of resources and thus economically irrational. It is thus important to note that the implementation of particular metrics and indicators alone might not achieve the desired goals. Additionally, it is necessary to change the very frames and imaginative resources that we have culturally available to make sense of the environment and its relation to economy, innovation, governance and policy making. The link between numbers and the legitimacy of certain policies is thus not as straightforward as one might naively assume (Asdal, 2011; Stehr, 2005).

These critiques do not propose to get rid of quantification altogether. What they do is directing attention to how a mode of environmental governance through quantification and indicators can render opaque the more fundamental questions about the relation between environmental protection, our modes of governance through quantified knowledge and our economic system. In particular, work on indicators shows how certain ways of rendering nature accountable or visible stabilise particular epistemic, political, moral and social orderings.

It is therefore important to look at indicator development for the circular economy through the lens of a sociology of quantification and zoom in on the indicator politics at work. What is quantified? What is left out? What might be the problems with the ways circularity is currently turned into a quantifiable and governable object?

As with any policy field characterised by issues and institutions that heavily rely on scientific and technical concepts and expertise, the study of how the circular economy makes worlds and enacts and shifts power therefore has to address the seemingly mundane activities of producing monitoring frameworks, evidence and indicators. Looking at the circular economy monitoring framework (European Commission, 2018b) through the lens of the literatures discussed so far allows us to ask how imaginaries of circularity are instrumental in the set-up of particular centres of calculation with the stated objective of "measuring progress towards a Circular Economy" while at the same time being reshaped in the process.

For the remainder of this chapter we will provide an exploratory analysis of indicator development and the indicators used for measuring progress towards a circular economy.

Measuring progress and quantifying circularity

The development of the circular economy policy brings together a number of European institutions with organisations on national level, their different epistemic commitments and ideas about desirable futures. To understand how these actors create and negotiate sociotechnical imaginaries of circularity, and thereby claim power by promoting their own knowledge and agency, it is useful to think of their activities in terms of creating a measurable object that is the circular economy in different "centres of calculation". In a study on carbon accounting at the Norwegian Ministry of Finance, Asdal describes centres of calculation as sites "through which all governmental proposals that involve budget expenses or have consequences for 'the economy' must pass. (…) The Ministry of Finance has been enacted, and continuously enacts itself, as the ministry that draws things (ie, the economy) together" (Asdal, 2014: 2113).

In the case of circular economy policy, as we have laid out in the previous chapters, the European Commission Directorates-General for Environment (DG ENV), Climate Action (DG CLIMA) and Growth (DG GROW) collaborate in an effort to establish more circularity as a legitimate policy objective. The same institutions also work together on developing of indicators for measuring progress towards a circular economy, supported by statistical and technical expertise in DG ESTAT and various groups in the Joint Research Centre (DG JRC). Additionally, experts from agencies (such as the European Environment Agency) are contributing to the debates around the development of these indicators. Furthermore, there is an academic debate and also a number of NGOs take part in the debate.

Indicators about the circular economy first appeared as part of a broader set of indicators in the Raw Materials Scoreboard in 2016 (Vidal-Legaz et al., 2016). It was also in this year that the European Environment Agency published a scoping report listing indicators that were either already available or needed to be developed, that could be used to monitor progress towards the circular economy. Additionally, data availability for each indicator was assessed (European Environment Agency, 2016). Building on these efforts, the European Commission started developing a "monitoring framework", which was published in January 2018 (European Commission, 2018b) with a set of indicators assembled to measure progress towards a circular economy. This monitoring framework refers back to the representation of the circular economy first published in 2014, which we already discussed in the previous chapter, and in doing so rehearses the ideal of a "closed loop". In this representation, primary raw material extraction has disappeared, and secondary raw materials are used to close the circle. This representation breaks from previous communications, which stressed that "Primary raw materials, including renewable materials, will continue to play an important role in production processes, even in a circular economy" (European Commission, 2015).

The figure above is a schematic representation of the circular economy indicators. The monitoring framework aims at monitoring progress at EU and

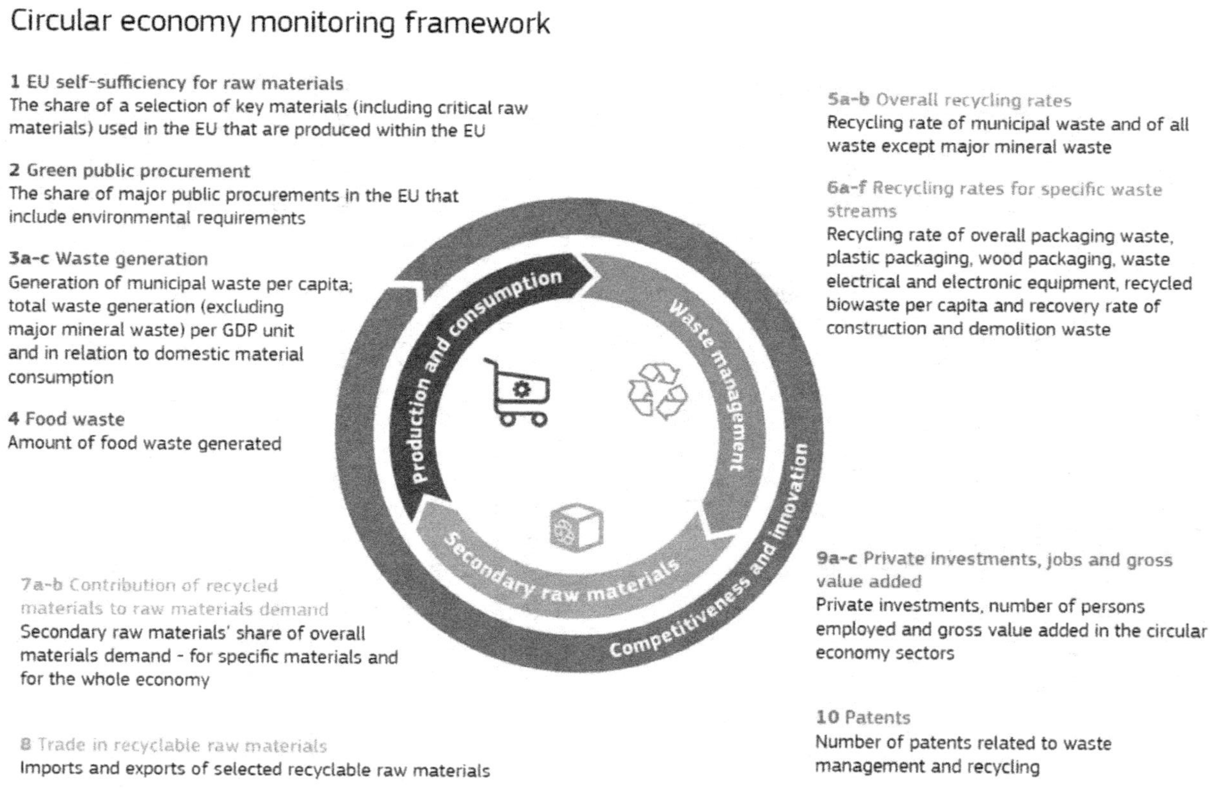
Circular economy monitoring framework
1 EU self-sufficiency for raw materials
The share of a selection of key materials (including critical raw materials) used in the EU that are produced within the EU
2 Green public procurement
The share of major public procurements in the EU that include environmental requirements
3a-c Waste generation
Generation of municipal waste per capita; total waste generation (excluding major mineral waste) per GDP unit and in relation to domestic material consumption
4 Food waste
Amount of food waste generated
5a-b Overall recycling rates
Recycling rate of municipal waste and of all waste except major mineral waste
6a-f Recycling rates for specific waste streams
Recycling rate of overall packaging waste, plastic packaging, wood packaging, waste electrical and electronic equipment, recycled biowaste per capita and recovery rate of construction and demolition waste
Production and consumption
Waste management
Secondary raw materials
Competitiveness and innovation
7a-b Contribution of recycled materials to raw materials demand
Secondary raw materials' share of overall materials demand - for specific materials and for the whole economy
8 Trade in recyclable raw materials
Imports and exports of selected recyclable raw materials
9a-c Private investments, jobs and gross value added
Private investments, number of persons employed and gross value added in the circular economy sectors
10 Patents
Number of patents related to waste management and recycling

Figure 7.1 Visual representation of the circular economy monitoring framework
Source: European Commission, 2018b

member state level, and is based on a set of ten indicators grouped into four policy domains of the circular economy. In this case, the focus is less on the phases or steps that need to be taken into account in the "life cycle" of a product. The representation references the set of competences, or knowledge areas, that are brought to bear in the regulation and monitoring of the circular economy.

The first group of indicators addresses the area of production and consumption. It includes indicators related on EU self-sufficiency for raw materials, green public procurement (under development) generation of municipal waste per capita, generation of waste per unit of GDP, generation of waste per unit of Domestic Material Consumption, and food waste (under development).

The second broader group assembles indicators on recycling rates: recycling rate of municipal waste, recycling rate of all waste excluding major mineral waste; recycling rate of packaging, recycling rate of plastic packaging, recycling rate of wooden packaging; recycling rate of electrical and electronic waste, recycling rate of biowaste, recovering rate of construction and demolition waste.

Secondary raw materials make up the third larger group of indicators for measuring progress towards a circular economy. These include end-of-life recycling of critical raw materials, circular material use rate (ratio of recycled waste material over the overall material demand), and trade in recyclable materials.

And finally, there are a number of indicators on the broader theme of competitiveness and innovation: gross investment in tangible goods in the recycling sector, number of persons employed in the circular economy sectors, gross value added in the circular economy sectors, number of patents related to recycling and secondary raw materials (see Table 7.1 for the complete list of indicators).

In order to better understand how choices are made, and accordingly how circular futures are imagined, it is first necessary to enter into some technical detail about waste management, reuse and recycling.

As we can see, a large part of the monitoring framework focuses on waste measurement. However, data regarding waste management tends to be rather fragmented and additionally there are various ways to count waste: waste can be accounted by stream, that is, plastic waste, electronic waste, food waste; it can be counted by source, that is, municipal solid waste, construction waste. Accounting both by stream (e.g. plastic packaging) and by source (e.g. municipal solid waste) may lead to double accounting. For this reason, it is not an easy task to aggregate different waste statistics and as a consequence, to get a good sense of how much waste is produced, how much can be recycled, and how much is being recycled. This is both a matter of data availability and a matter of comparability of the data that is available.

Then there is also an issue in regards to what is regarded to be a potential issue and thus what needs to be counted: this leads to a number of different questions that can be asked in relation to waste management: first, it is about the quantity of waste of course, but this is far from the only issue of waste

Table 7.1 Monitoring framework for the circular economy

"Production and consumption" indicators	- EU self-sufficiency for raw materials - green public procurement (under development) - generation of municipal waste per capita - generation of waste per unit of GDP - generation of waste per unit of Domestic Material Consumption - food waste (under development)
"Recycling rates" indicators	- recycling rate of municipal waste - recycling rate of all waste excluding major mineral waste - recycling rate of packaging - recycling rate of plastic packaging - recycling rate of wooden packaging - recycling rate of electrical and electronic waste - recycling rate of biowaste - recovering rate of construction and demolition waste
"Secondary raw materials" indicators	- end-of-life recycling of critical raw materials - circular material use rate - trade in recyclable materials
"Competitiveness and innovation" indicators	- gross investment in tangible goods in the recycling sector - number of persons employed in the circular economy sectors - gross value added in the circular economy sectors - number of patents related to recycling and secondary raw materials

generation. Waste generation also raises questions regarding hazardous substances present in waste, which may pose risks to recycling; or about the presence of rare earth elements, which may yield higher economic benefits from recycling.

In efforts to measure progress towards a circular economy specific attention is paid to the recycling of rare earth metals. This comes from a focus on self-sufficiency and a political interest in security of supply of critical raw materials. This interest is translated into a representation rooted in chemistry. In this representation recycling rates are reported through colour coding of the period table of elements (see Figure 7.2).

In regard to this table the European Commission states:

> In contrast to the indicators of the monitoring framework on waste management, which focus on collection or recycling rates of certain waste streams, this indicator measures recycling's contribution to materials demand per type of material for a selected subset of materials. In this sense this indicator provides complementary information on the recycling flow in the Sankey diagram on materials flows in the circular economy, i.e. a disaggregation per material of recycling's contribution to materials demand.
>
> (European Commission, 2018a)

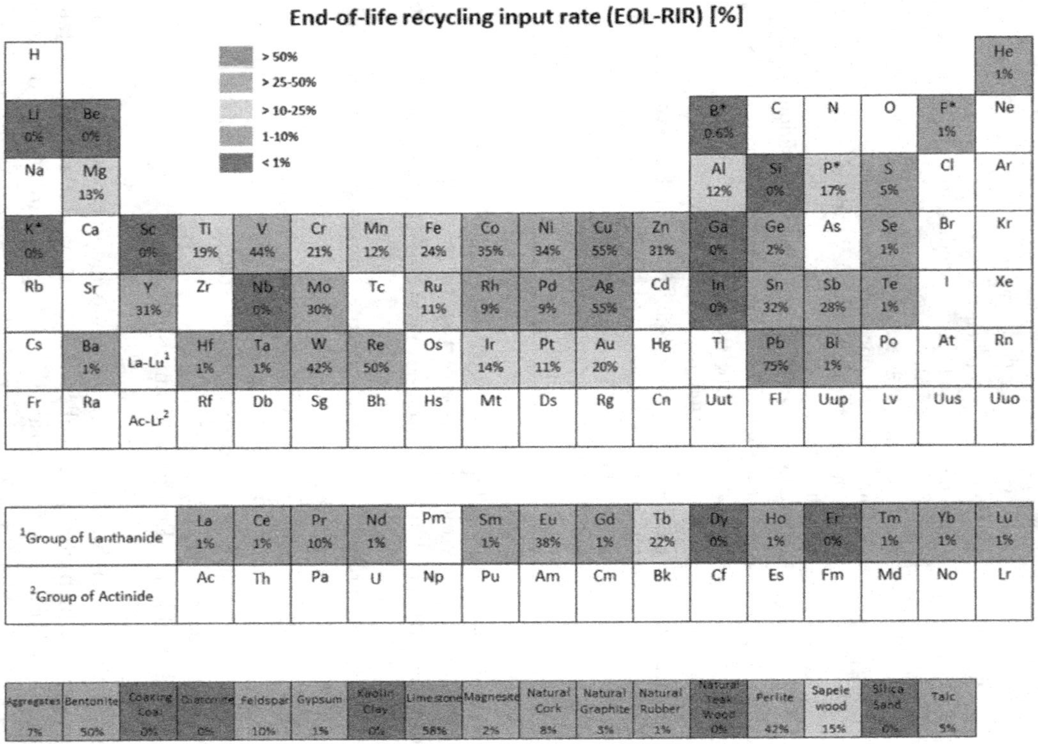

End-of-life recycling input rate (EOL-RIR) [%]

Legend:
- > 50%
- > 25-50%
- > 10-25%
- 1-10%
- < 1%

1	2	3	4	5	6	7	8	9	10	11	12	13	14	15	16	17	18
H																	He 1%
Li 0%	Be 0%											B* 0-<1	C	N	O	F* 1%	Ne
Na	Mg 13%											Al 12%	Si 0%	P* 17%	S 5%	Cl	Ar
K* 0%	Ca	Sc 0%	Ti 19%	V 44%	Cr 21%	Mn 12%	Fe 24%	Co 35%	Ni 34%	Cu 55%	Zn 31%	Ga 0%	Ge 2%	As	Se 1%	Br	Kr
Rb	Sr	Y 31%	Zr	Nb 0%	Mo 30%	Tc	Ru 11%	Rh 9%	Pd 9%	Ag 55%	Cd	In 0%	Sn 32%	Sb 28%	Te 1%	I	Xe
Cs	Ba 1%	La-Lu[1]	Hf 1%	Ta 1%	W 42%	Re 50%	Os	Ir 14%	Pt 11%	Au 20%	Hg	Tl	Pb 75%	Bi 1%	Po	At	Rn
Fr	Ra	Ac-Lr[2]	Rf	Db	Sg	Bh	Hs	Mt	Ds	Rg	Cn	Uut	Fl	Uup	Lv	Uus	Uuo

[1] Group of Lanthanide

La 1%	Ce 1%	Pr 10%	Nd 1%	Pm	Sm 1%	Eu 38%	Gd 1%	Tb 22%	Dy 0%	Ho 1%	Er 0%	Tm 1%	Yb 1%	Lu 1%

[2] Group of Actinide

Ac	Th	Pa	U	Np	Pu	Am	Cm	Bk	Cf	Es	Fm	Md	No	Lr

Aggregates	Bentonite	Coaking coa.	Diatomite	Feldspar	Gypsum	Kaolin/Clay	Limestone	Magnesit	Natural Cork	Natural Graphite	Natural Rubber	Natural Teak Wood	Perlite	Sapele wood	Silica sand	Talc
7%	50%	0%	0%	1.00%	1%	0%	58%	2%	8%	3%	1%	0%	42%	15%	0%	5%

* F = Fluorspar; P = Phosphate rock; K = Potash; Si = Silicon metal, B=Borates.

Figure 7.2 Representation of rare earth metals in recycled materials
Source: European Commission, 2018a

This quote brings us back to questions of counting and measurement, it is important to note that a recurrent challenge in waste generation and in waste management is to know how much waste is actually generated and, as a consequence, which are the main waste streams that need to be regulated. What sounds like a rather obvious statement, in practice becomes more complicated. Waste accounting is quite challenging, because not all waste is managed by public agencies and private companies do not report waste in the same way and therefore there are issues of commensurability. For instance, when companies sell their waste to other sectors or to other countries, they do not always report discarded materials as waste. If the accounting is done in monetary terms, companies report the revenues from the sale of discarded materials, not the quantities.

Furthermore, waste is measured by sector (e.g. construction waste, municipal solid waste) and by stream (e.g. plastics, electronic equipment, packaging), and there are important gaps in both cases. There are, for example, no statistics on waste produced by the agricultural and mining sectors and wastewater is generally not accounted for. While some of the indicators proposed by the monitoring framework aim to fill some of these knowledge gaps, such as the food waste indicator, there is no monitoring of the "overall picture". This means that it is impossible to know if the European Commission is monitoring a small or a large part of its waste production. Indeed, the technical argument can be made that it is difficult to know if the European Commission is monitoring 10% or 80% of its waste production.

As a consequence, measuring needs to be done through proxies and work-arounds. For this reason, many indicators refer to municipal solid waste, which is thought to represent about 10% of total waste in the European Union, and is a sector for which there are reliable data. The focus on municipal solid waste can be seen as a case of "data inertia" or, to use a more visual metaphor, of "lamp posting". Lamp posting refers to a practice, in which a lost key is searched near a lamp post, because that's where the light is. For the case of circular economy indicators, it means that the availability of data as well as of indicators drive policy goals.

In addition to these more practical concerns, there is also the more conceptual problem of how to actually measure waste: different pictures emerge when waste is measured by weight, by critical raw materials, or by hazardous materials. The monitoring framework focuses on the first two types of measurement, thus giving priority to the characterisation of waste flows and thus prioritising questions about how much waste is generated and how much is recycled, following a material flow analysis approach to circularity. Recycling is also difficult to measure. According to Stahel and Reday-Mulvey,

> it is impossible to make any precise statements concerning the recycling rate due to, for example, the diversity of nonindustrial recovery circuits or

the difficulty of distinguishing the parts of a car from the parts of an agricultural machine in a ton of scrap iron.

(1976: 71)

This reinforces a risk framing that highlights concerns about security and self-sufficiency in the provision and trade of critical raw materials. Framed in this way recycling in the context of a circular economy rehearses both a security narrative and a focus on economic concerns that shape how recycling and circularity can be thought of. There is a need for future research that dives more deeply into the actual discussions that led to the selection of this particular set of indicators and the justifications for the choices that were made.

After highlighting some more technical issues with the indicators that made it into the monitoring framework and thus into an institutionally stabilised idea of what the main characteristics and elements of a circular economy are, we also want to zoom in on a number of more theoretical concerns: first, we want to briefly explore the omissions and ask what is missing from this particular picture of the circular economy; and second, we want to indicate some of the effects, this set of indicators might have in the future.

Importantly, there are no indicators so far that reflect ideas about repair, reuse, sharing, product durability, and standardisation of designs which may help substitute parts rather than the whole product. The European Environment Agency report, which looked at policy objectives, related indicators and data availability, had suggestions for indicators on product durability and standardisation. Even though the circular economy is not just about waste, as the formulation of the policy progresses, the "more than waste" parts are so far omitted. This omission has already been criticised (Welch, Keller, & Mandich, 2016; 2017) and in addition current discussions also circle around question such as what actually is understood by the term "sharing economy" and how (and if) it fits into the concept of the circular economy. Our point here it is not to argue in favour of one set of indicators over others, but rather direct attention to the fact that these indicators (together with certain omissions) produce very particular trajectories and temporalities of Europe and other collectives in regard to where we come from and what desirable futures are.

In addition, there seems to be little attention paid to the question of how exactly the transition towards a circular economy is going to take place. Neither is there an allusion to transition models that go beyond an implicit techno-optimist innovation model that assumes that more circularity will be brought about by technological innovation, visible in indicators on patents and investments. Policy-makers in their discussions talk about both "substantial" and "evolutionary" change. There are reports, however, that argue that for moving towards more circularity more drastic socio-institutional changes in regard to modes of consumption and production will be needed; changes that go beyond what can be monitored through counting patents and eco-design achievements (Potting et al., 2017). When it comes to imagining the drivers of such a transition to a circular economy, however, the indicators show a clear emphasis on technological innovation. What is stabilised here is an "innovation imperative" (Pfotenhauer, Juhl, & Aarden, 2019) together with a traditional view of innovation advocating for technology-focused and expert-driven change (Funtowicz & Strand, 2007; Pfotenhauer & Jasanoff, 2017; Strand, Saltelli, Giampietro, Rommetveit, & Funtowicz, 2016). This becomes visible in the indicators under the heading "competitiveness and innovation", which measure private investments, jobs and gross value added together with number of new patents (*sic*), mainly patents on recycling technologies for different materials. Additionally, there are mentions of changing markets, which further points to the imagination of a producer-led transition towards a circular economy, and opens up the possibility for new actors to emerge, such as the "prosumer".

This general future orientation in describing the present is accompanied by particular spatio-temporalities when for example waste on a municipal level is described in particular time periods: "EU municipal waste generation per capita has dropped by 8% between 2006 and 2016 to an average of 480 kg per capita per year". In a similar manner the monitoring framework describes an increase in recycling rates for packaging waste between 2008 and 2015. The trajectories thus created are enforced by narrative framings like being a "steady improvement" or when the document states that trade with certain types of waste has "increased considerably between 2004 and 2016". These pasts, presents and futures that are created here are in a very literal sense plural as the time periods for measurement are rather arbitrary and depend on data availability.

Additionally, indicators create inner-European geographies of circularity by performing "comparability" between countries in terms of their achievements and potentials in regard to a progress towards a circular economy. In this sense, also the indicators stabilise the Euro-centric nature that has already been criticised for circular economy policy as a whole (Gregson, Crang, & Fuller, 2015); any discussion about how these European biophysical flows are embedded within global waste streams gets sidelined by a focus on European indicators and technical debates about measurement and data availability. Concerns about global environmental justice are accordingly systematically underrepresented. The focus on European industry ignores the fact that industrial production has been increasingly outsourced to emerging economies, and that the focus on "sharing", the shift from "consumption" to "lease", from production of goods to provision of services, may further accentuate the outsourcing of non-circular economic activities.

We may summarise that the indicators rehearse a collective European self-imagination that frames sustainability and environmental protection in terms of industrial activity and economic growth within Europe, a technology-centred idea of innovation, and a particular model of science-policy relations that promotes governing through monitoring, command and control.

Numbers, collective imagination and authority

In the first part of this chapter we developed, drawing on literature from science and technology studies, the argument that, although there has been a recent increase in attention to so-called evidence-based policy making, the use of statistics and quantitative forms of knowledge have a long history and are closely tied to the emergence of the modern nation state and to colonial history. This reliance on numbers corresponds to the emergence of "cultures of objectivity" (Porter, 1995) and to the ideal of "mechanical objectivity" (Daston & Galison, 1992; Porter, 1995), which describes an ethos of impartial and disinterested knowledge production. Relying on quantified evidence is thus closely entwined with questions of trust and legitimacy and a particular idealised ethos of science. This partially explains why in a climate of perceived mistrust and democratic crisis as currently experienced in Europe and beyond numbers take on the role of a mechanism of defending the legitimacy of governance authority.

Debates on quantification furthermore show, how numbers are not only means for describing reality, but a particular mode of governance. Representing nature and society through quantification practices is thus always intervention; numbers need to be scrutinised for their performative effects.

Thus, we argued that it is important to look at the politics of quantification and indicators (Asdal, 2008, 2011; Merry, 2016; Turnhout et al., 2007, 2014), in particular when it comes to the on-going development of circular economy policy and the construction of indicators for measuring progress towards more circularity. Looking at indicator politics means to explore the social practices of creating them and asking how in turn they shape policy making, governance and social practices.

After we laid the theoretical groundwork, we provided a first exploratory analysis of indicator politics in circular economy policy by looking at the indicators that are currently being developed.

The first important thing to note is that there are a range of European Commission DGs collaborating with other EU institutions such as the European Environment Agency. What is also noteworthy is that these are all institutions that are mainly concerned with environmental policy. Politically more powerful DGs like DG ENER or DG AGRI are more cautious in entering circular economy policy. As we have argued in previous chapters, the circular economy thus needs to be interpreted as an attempt to get environmental concerns on the table. This becomes consequential for the framings of circularity and the imaginative resources mobilised (and rehearsed) in the selection of indicators.

Looking at the set of indicators being developed we discussed the particular focus on waste management, problems with measurement and omissions. We showed how waste measurement with its focus on municipal solid waste can be seen as a case of "data inertia" or "lamp-posting". In addition, we directed attention to the question of how to measure waste: different pictures emerge when waste is, measured either by weight or by hazardous materials. The monitoring framework focuses on measurement by weight and critical raw materials thus giving priority to the characterisation of waste flows and thus highlight questions about how much waste is generated and how much is recycled, following a material flow analysis approach to circularity.

This reinforces a risk-framing that highlights concerns about security and self-sufficiency in the provision and trade of critical raw materials. This already shows that there is a clear relation to the imaginary of circularity we discussed in the previous chapter. What we see in the indicators is a particular framing of circularity in terms of (resource supply) security and innovation. Circular economy rehearses both a security narrative and a focus on economic concerns that shape how recycling and circularity can be thought of. Ideas regarding the transition towards more circularity relies on tropes about technological innovation.

This rehearsal of EU policy tropes is important for thinking about the potential impact of circular economy policy and environmental policy more generally. It is useful to go back to Asdal's work on framings of "nature" and "non-authority" (Asdal, 2011) in her study of environmental pollution in Norway. Norwegian pollution control agencies attempted to gather power and authority in their offices through various quantification practices. And while the numbers were not disputed, they failed to produce the desired effect. Asdal argues that numbers alone did not lend power and authority to the pollution agency. It was only when nature was more and more understood as vulnerable by relevant actors and thus more closely related to what is commonly understood as "environment" that environmental pollution was reframed as a site of societal interest. It was this reframing and change in collective imaginations together with practices of accounting that eventually had an impact on policy making.

This is important to keep in mind also in relation to collectively imagining circularity. As we have shown both in the policy papers and in indicators for measuring progress more traditional tropes and imaginative resources are mobilised that frame environmental concerns in terms of the economic interests. As long as there are no alternative imaginative resources and different framings of environmental policies, they are very likely to continue to fail. To develop a better understanding of this problem, the next chapter will situate the circular economy within current debates on environmental governance, in particular it will focus on the water-energy-food nexus and explore the circular economy as a policy objective.

References

Asdal, K. (2008). Enacting things through numbers: Taking nature into account/ing. *Geoforum*, 39(1), 123–132.

Asdal, K. (2011). The office: The weakness of numbers and the production of non-authority. DOI:doi:10.1016/j.aos.2011.01.001

Asdal, K. (2014). From climate issue to oil issue: offices of public administration, versions of economics, and the ordinary technologies of politics. *Environment and Planning A*, 46(9), 2110–2124.

Daston, L. (1995). The moral economy of science. *Osiris*, 10, 3–24. Retrieved from http://www.jstor.org/stable/301910

Daston, L., & Galison, P. (1992). The image of objectivity. *Representations*, 40(Fall), 81–128.

Dean, M. (1999). *Governmentality, Power and Rule in Modern Society*. London: Sage.

Desrosieres, A. (1998). *The Politics of Large Numbers: A History of Statistical Reasoning*. Cambridge, MA: Harvard University Press.

Edwards, P. N. (2010). *A Vast Machine: Computer Models, Climate Data, and the Politics of Global Warming*. Cambridge, MA: MIT Press.

Espeland, W. N., & Sauder, M. (2007). Rankings and reactivity: How public measures recreate social worlds. *American Journal of Sociology*, 113(1), 1–40. doi:10.1086/517897

European Commission. (2015). *Communication from the Commission to the European Parliament, the Council, the European Economic and Social Committee and the Committee of the Regions. Closing the loop – An EU action plan for the Circular Economy EN* (No. COM (2015) 614). Brussels: European Commission.

European Commission. (2018a). *Commission Staff Working Document. Measuring progress towards circular economy in the European Union – Key indicators for a monitoring framework. Accompanying the document Communication from the Commission to the European Parliament, the Council, the European Economic and Social Committee and the Committee of the Regions* (No. SWD (2018) 17).

European Commission. (2018b). *Communication from the Commission to the European Parliament, the Council, the European Economic and Social Committee and the Committee of the Regions on a monitoring framework for the circular economy* (SWD (2018) 17, No. COM (2018) 29).

European Environment Agency. (2016). *Circular Economy in Europe: Developing the Knowledge Base*. Luxembourg: European Commission.

Fleurbaey, M. (2009). Beyond GDP: The quest for a measure of social welfare. *Journal of Economic Literature*, 47(4), 1029–1075. doi:10.1257/jel.47.4.1029

Foucault, M. (1977). *Discipline and Punish: The Birth of the Prison*. London: Allen Lane.

Foucault, M. (1981). *Archäologie des Wissens*. Frankfurt am Main: Suhrkamp.

Foucault, M. (1991). Governmentality. In G. Burchell, C. Gordon, & P. Miller (Eds.), *The Foucault Effect: Studies in Governmentality* (pp. 87–105). Chicago, IL: University of Chicago Press.

Funtowicz, S., & Strand, R. (2007). Models of science and policy. In T. Traavik & L. C. Lim (Eds.), *Biosafety First: Holistic Approaches to Risk and Uncertainty in Genetic Engineering and Genetically Modified Organisms* (pp. 263–278). Trondheim: Tapir Academic Press.

Gregson, N., Crang, M., & Fuller, S. (2015). Interrogating the circular economy: the moral economy of resource recovery in the EU. *Economy and Society*, 44(2), 218–243. doi:10.1080/03085147.2015.1013353

Hacking, I. (1990). *The Taming of Chance*. Cambridge, UK: Cambridge University Press.

Kitchin, R. (2014a). Big Data, new epistemologies and paradigm shifts. *Big Data & Society*, 1(1), 1–12. doi:10.1177/2053951714528481

Kitchin, R. (2014b). *The Data Revolution: Big Data, Open Data, Data Infrastructures and their Consequences*. London: Sage.

Kovacic, Z. (2018). Conceptualizing numbers at the science–policy interface. *Science, Technology, & Human Values*, 43(6), 1039–1065.

Kovacic, Z., & Giampietro, M. (2015). Beyond "beyond GDP indicators:" The need for reflexivity in science for governance. *Ecological Complexity*, 21, 53–61.

Latour, B. (1987). *Science in Action. How to Follow Scientists and Engineers Through Society*. Cambridge, MA: Harvard University Press.

Latour, B. (1999). *Pandora's Hope. Essays on the Reality of Science Studies*. Cambridge, MA/London: Harvard University Press.

Latour, B., & Woolgar, S. (1986). *Laboratory Life. The Construction of Scientific Facts*. Princeton, NJ: Princeton University Press.

Law, J. (2009). Seeing like a survey. *Cultural Sociology*, 3(2), 239–256. Retrieved from http://cus.sagepub.com/content/3/2/239.abstract

Merry, S. E. (2016). *The Seductions of Quantification: Measuring Human Rights, Gender Violence, and Sex Trafficking*. Chicago, IL: University of Chicago Press.

Pfotenhauer, S., & Jasanoff, S. (2017). Panacea or diagnosis? Imaginaries of innovation and the 'MIT model' in three political cultures. *Social Studies of Science*, 47(6), 783–810. doi:10.1177/0306312717706110

Pfotenhauer, S. M., Juhl, J., & Aarden, E. (2019). Challenging the "deficit model" of innovation: Framing policy issues under the innovation imperative. *Research Policy*, 48(4), 895–904.

Porter, T. M. (1995). *Trust in Numbers: The Pursuit of Objectivity in Science and Public Life*. Princeton, NJ: Princeton University Press.

Potting, J., Nierhoff, N., Montevecchi, F., Antikainen, R., Colgan, S., Hauser, A., … Hanemaaijer, A. (2017). *Input to the European Commission from European EPAs about monitoring progress of the transition towards a circular economy in the European Union*.

Rieder, G., & Simon, J. (2016). Datatrust: Or, the political quest for numerical evidence and the epistemologies of Big Data. *Big Data & Society*, 3(1), 1–6.

Rieder, G., & Simon, J. (2017). Big Data: A New Empiricism and its Epistemic and Socio-Political Consequences. In *Berechenbarkeit der Welt?* (pp. 85–105). Dordrecht: Springer.

Rottenburg, R., Merry, S. E., Park, S.-J., & Mugler, J. (2015). *The World of Indicators: The Making of Governmental Knowledge through Quantification*. Cambridge, UK: Cambridge University Press.

Scott, J. C. (1998). *Seeing Like a State: How Certain Schemes to Improve the Human Condition Have Failed*. Cambridge, MA: Yale University Press.

Shapin, S. (1999). The House of Experiment in Seventeenth-Century England. In M. Biagioli (Ed.), *The Science Studies Reader* (pp. 479–504). New York/London: Routledge.

Shapin, S., & Schaffer, S. (1985). *Leviathan and the Air-Pump. Hobbes, Boyle and the Experimental Life*. Princeton, NJ: Princeton University Press.

Stahel, W. R., & Reday-Mulvey, G. (1976). *Jobs for Tomorrow: The Potential for Substituting Manpower for Energy*. Brussels: European Commission.

Stehr, N. (2005). *Knowledge Politics: Governing the Consequences of Science and Technology*. Boulder, CO: Paradigm Publishers.

Stiglitz, J. E., Sen, A., & Fitoussi, J. (2017). *Report by the Commission on the Measurement of Economic Performance and Social Progress*. Retrieved from www.stiglitz-sen-fitoussi.fr

Strand, R., Saltelli, A., Giampietro, M., Rommetveit, K., & Funtowicz, S. (2016). New narratives for innovation. *Journal of Cleaner Production*. doi:10.1016/j.jclepro.2016.10.194

Turnhout, E., Bloomfield, B., Hulme, M., Vogel, J., & Wynne, B. (2012). Conservation policy: Listen to the voices of experience. *Nature*, 488(7412), 454–455.

Turnhout, E., Hisschemöller, M., & Eijsackers, H. (2007). Ecological indicators: Between the two fires of science and policy. *Ecological Indicators*, 7(2), 215–228.

Turnhout, E., Neves, K., & de Lijster, E. (2014). "Measurementality" in biodiversity governance: knowledge, transparency, and the Intergovernmental Science-Policy Platform on Biodiversity and Ecosystem Services (IPBES). *Environment and Planning A*, 46(3), 581–597.

Turnhout, E., Waterton, C., Neves, K., & Buizer, M. (2013). Rethinking biodiversity: From goods and services to "living with". *Conservation Letters*, 6(3), 154–161.

Vidal-Legaz, B., Mancini, L., Blengini, G., Pavel, C., Marmier, A., Blagoeva, D., ... Nita, V. (2016). *EU Raw Materials Scoreboard*. Luxembourg: Publications Office of the European Union.

Waylen, K., Blackstock, K., & Holstead, K. (2015). How does legacy create sticking points for environmental management? Insights from challenges to implementation of the ecosystem approach. *Ecology and Society*, 20(2).

Welch, D., Keller, M., & Mandich, G. (2016). Imagined futures of the Circular Economy. In N. Spurling & L. Kuijer (Eds.), *Everyday Futures* (pp. 23–31). Lancaster: Institute for Social Futures.

Welch, D., Keller, M., & Mandich, G. (2017). Imagined futures of everyday life in the circular economy. *Interactions*, (March–April), 46–51.

8 Governing circularity

How to govern in the nexus

Summing up the second part of the book we will situate the critical discussion of circular economy policies within a broader debate of governance and current debates about the water-energy-food nexus. Key ingredients in the framing of the circular economy (win-win narratives, focus on synergies) are dictated by the necessity to work across multiple directorates and build alliances between epistemic networks. These results contribute to the study of the science-policy interface and shed light on the specificities of emerging nexus policies. While STS literatures focus on problematic aspects of quantification, power, and standardisation, the nexus debate adds another important layer, which is the need to work across policy domains and negotiate interests and discourses. New elements come into play in the study of the science-policy interface, crucially, the reduction of uncertainty to technical footnotes, and a loss of understanding of field-specific uncertainties in favour of cross-cutting benefits. The circular economy thus gathers consensus based on high-level and generic aspirations to do good by the environment. Good intentions are shielded from criticism and disagreement, creating an apparent consensus. As a result, the European Commission stated in 2019 that the circular economy action plan has been delivered, even though it is too early to see any changes in the level of circularity, as measured by the Commission itself.

Introduction

This chapter develops a critique of the circular economy from the observation of how science and policy interact. The circular economy is not a concept originated from science, which has been used to inform policy, but rather a concept mainstreamed for policy (see Chapter 3), for which science has been asked to provide evidence through, for example, indicators as discussed in Chapter 7. In this chapter we delve into the interactions and mutually constitutive practices in science and in policymaking that characterise the circular economy – as knowledge and as a policy.

We argue that the circular economy is a nexus policy. A nexus policy is a policy that aims at overcoming silos, that is, fragmented policies that try to govern one issue at the time. The circular economy is a nexus policy because it aims to reconcile economic interests and environmental concerns, by allegedly transforming the challenge of waste management into the opportunity to keep the value of resources for as long as possible in the economy. The term nexus describes the connections between different variables: in European policy, the nexus between water–energy–food–ecosystem (WEFE) has created interest, but the elements of the nexus vary from study to study. The International Atomic Energy Agency refers to the nexus between climate–land–energy–water (CLEW), and the German International Cooperation Agency (GIZ) promotes the water–energy–food nexus. In this chapter, we refer to the nexus between the economy and the environment, which are the policy areas of the circular economy. The nexus is a concept used to describe both the interrelations between things "out there", and the governance challenge of working across policy domains, to match the interconnectedness "out there" with interconnected policies.

The "nexus" is a popular term because it focuses on the possibility of forming policy alliances. Speaking of the nexus makes it possible to change the language from the discussion of "trade-offs", "constraints" and "limits" to the creation of "synergies", "opportunities" and "win-win" solutions. In the European context, this means that environmental concerns about the sustainable use of natural resources such as land, water and renewable energies are not cast in opposition to economic goals but rather as a means to meet those goals.

The need for policy and regulatory proposals to be cast in positive terms is not new; it can be traced back to the great statesmen of the Roman Empire if one so wishes. Closer to our time, Otto von Bismarck defined politics as the art of the possible. The contemporary need for nexus policies to be positive, however, stems in part from the need to recover from the financial crisis of 2009. Before the crisis, the European Commission was part of the "beyond GDP" debate (European Communities, 2009). Tellingly, the "nexus" makes its appearance in European policy in 2011, directly after the crisis, through a conference held in Bonn, Germany, called "The Water, Energy and Food Security Nexus – Solutions for the Green Economy", organised by the German Federal Government (Leese & Meisch, 2015). The circular economy is a further evolution of nexus thinking, which made its policy appearance in 2014, and which puts nexus thinking in practice, by transforming constraints into business opportunities, and waste into resources. Publications such as the 1972 report *The Limits to Growth*, published by the Club of Rome, spoke about environmental and economic priorities as incompatible. The circular economy recasts this debate in positive terms, positing the potential or even actual compatibility between environmental sustainability and economic growth.

In practice, however, there is contested knowledge (e.g. about the possibility and impossibility of circularity); scientific uncertainty (e.g. about the health effects of recycling materials that contain toxic chemicals); systemic complexity and unpredictability (e.g. about rebound effects of innovation, resource efficiency, and the creation of new services); conflicts of interest (e.g. about the desirability of sharing economy models such as Uber and Airbnb); and a variety of static and dynamic historical contingencies that induce institutional and political constraints on governance. Accordingly, policy-making and govern-ance in general cannot be described in terms of rational choice models but rather as an *art* of identifying, creating and making use of limited windows of opportunity. The circular economy is one of the multiple attempts, together with green growth and resource efficiency, to create a window of opportunity for environmental concerns to be heard in the aftermath of the 2009 financial and economic crisis, but at the cost of silencing uncertainties and converting environmental concerns into environmental opportunities. Previous policy ideas were not necessarily scrutinised about their uncertainties, but we argue that the concepts of "sustainable development" and "green growth" do not silence the tension between economic growth and sustainability. One could read these concepts as conditional: development as long as it is sustainable, growth provided that it is green. The circular economy, on the other hand, does not carry in its formulation any implicit nor explicit tension.

The epistemic network (Rommetveit, 2013) that gives rise to the idea of circular economy is policy-based. For this reason, the understanding of the worldview of the circular economy is necessarily situated in the study of the science-policy interface. In this chapter we will argue that the policy base of the circular economy has: i) epistemic implications, for the circular economy to be a win-win policy, uncertainties are silenced; ii) political implications, the circular economy is put in motion by depoliticising and deepening the tech-nocratic management of environmental resources; and iii) a credibility deficit, since the delivery of the circular economy has little to do with changes in the degree of circularity of the economy.

Theoretical lenses

This chapter develops a critique of the circular economy from the point of view of the science-policy interface, building mainly on two approaches: post normal science (Funtowicz & Ravetz, 1990, 1993; Pereira & Funtowicz, 2009) and techno-epistemic networks (Foss Ballo, 2015; Rommetveit, 2013). Post normal science analyses how scientific information is used for policy in the context of uncertainty, complexity, high stakes and urgent decisions. The concept of techno-epistemic networks builds on the work on epistemic communities (Haas, 1992), which identifies the actors and institutions that contribute to the creation of knowledge that is used to inform or legitimise policy. In Chapter 2, we gave an overview of the disciplines that gave rise to the circular economy. In this chapter, we take a step forward and argue that the circular economy creates its own knowledge base, by defining what constitutes evidence with regard to circularity.

"Post-normal science (PNS) is a critical concept originally developed to describe situations in which there are important or controversial policy pro-blems informed by an incomplete, uncertain or contested knowledge base" (Strand, 2018). Post-normal science questions the assumption that facts are certain, that facts and values can be separated, and that values can be aggregated to define social preferences that guide in decision-making. Post-normal science contextualises the dialogue between science and policy. In the ideal realm, policy makers seek scientific advice when faced with uncertainty (Haas, 1992), and science is supposed to reduce uncertainty. Funtowicz and Ravetz (1993) observe that the context that has often characterised environmental policy, is one in which stakes are high and decisions have to be made according to politically established timeframes. Urgent decisions may need to be taken before scientific research has reached any conclusions.

Of particular interest to our discussion is the post-normal science take on uncertainty. Funtowicz and Ravetz wrote extensively on the vagueness and ambiguity associated with numbers (Funtowicz & Ravetz, 1990), and argue that the quality of scientific information is not self-evident, but should be explicitly communicated. With regard to the science–policy interface, this means that science should communicate facts as well as uncertainty to policy. By acknowledging that there are limits to knowledge, post-normal science questions the concept of expertise. The line between experts and non-experts is blurred.

The definition of expert does not depend on the level of knowledge, but on belonging to epistemic communities. According to Haas, the experts are "cognitive baggage handlers" that carry ideas, and "gatekeepers governing the entry of new ideas into institutions" (1992: 27). Peter Haas famously attempted to capture the central features of expertise by his concept of "epistemic communities" (Haas, 1989; 1992):

> a network of professionals with recognized expertise and competence in a particular domain and an authoritative claim to policy-relevant knowledge within that domain or issue-area. Although an epistemic community may consist of professionals from a variety of disciplines and backgrounds, they have (1) a shared set of normative and principled beliefs, which provide a value-based rationale for the social action of community members; (2) shared causal beliefs, which are derived from their analysis of practices leading or contributing to a central set of problems in their domain and which then serve as the basis for elucidating the multiple linkages between possible policy actions and desired outcomes; (3) shared notions of validity- that is, inter-subjective, internally defined criteria for weighing and validating knowledge in the domain of their expertise; and (4) a common policy enterprise-that is, a set of common practices associated with a set of problems to which their professional competence is directed, presumably out of the conviction that human welfare will be enhanced as a consequence.
>
> (Haas, 1992: 3)

Epistemic communities are rarely stable entities. Rather, they emerge around certain issues or policies and bring together ideas about the public good, desirable futures, beliefs about how to get there, about the knowledge necessary for getting there, criteria for its validity and about the actors relevant in that endeavour. More recently and more closely related to the concept of socio-technical imaginaries Foss-Ballo (2015) in her work on Norwegian energy policy describes the 'techno-epistemic networks' – a term developed by Rommetveit (2013) – that are instrumental in the stabilisation and maintenance of a particular imaginary guiding energy policy. The concept of network is used to refer to a hybridity of roles and (professional) identities, introducing more heterogeneity than the concept of community. Epistemic networks are called techno-epistemic networks when they focus on technoscience, that is, the use of the scientific method to develop technology and the use of technology as a means to apply the scientific method.

Such networks also contribute to the assemblage and stabilisation of certain imaginations by embedding them in a particular institutional setting. These networks stabilise normative ideas about certain ways of knowing and acting in the world. These are ideas of which problems need to be solved, what the most promising means for solving these problems are, and importantly, how to measure and govern transitions to a circular economy.

Techno fixing policy

By joining environmental and economic policy goals, the circular economy joins different modes of interaction between science and policy. It should be noted that science may be used to inform as well as justify policy decisions, and that the rationale of policy decisions is often defined ex-post as a means of making sense of multiple interests, actions, negotiations and other engagements that allow for policies to come into being (Colebatch, 2005). Even though there are no set rules or habits in the use of science for policy, different science-policy models have emerged from different policy arenas. For instance, the precautionary principle was formulated in the 1992 United Nations conference in Rio de Janeiro (UNCED, 1992) in the context of environmental policy making.

Funtowicz and Strand (2007) identify different science-policy models, which can be used as heuristic tools to understand how different models are supported by different kinds of rationality. For instance, the modern model assumes a utilitarian rationality, whereby rational actors "choose those policy options that, according to the scientific evidence, best meet their preferences" (Funtowicz & Strand, 2007: 263). According to the precautionary model, if there are threats to human health or the environment, action should be taken even in the absence of full scientific certainty. The precautionary principle[1] was introduced as a supplement to the simple rational choice model, adding decision principles of precaution and preventive action to utilitarian rationality.

Different models of science-policy interfaces attribute different roles to evidence and uncertainty. Uncertainty as well as certainty may inform policy. The modern model emphasises the use of scientific evidence, while the precautionary model arises from the management of uncertainty. Evidence and uncertainty are not either-or conditions, that is, the presence of evidence does not exclude uncertainty. Scientific evidence is characterised by uncertainty, which can be expressed for instance as error margins and confidence intervals. Uncertainty, however, can also be used in a broader sense to discuss the limits of a particular problem framing. Framings act like blinders, by focusing attention on a limited set of variables and causal relationships, they leave out other sources of knowledge. The management of uncertainty in the latter sense can be understood as not restricting the problem definition to only one type of knowledge.

One example of how the uncertainty in problem framing can be communicated is given by Carnot, considered the father of thermodynamics. Carnot (1824), in the closing paragraphs of his book *Reflections on the Motive Power of Fire*, comments on the uncertainty created by focusing solely on the efficiency of engines, and on the need to take into account other factors. He writes:

> We should not expect ever to utilize in practice all the motive power of combustibles. The attempts made to attain this result would be far more harmful than useful if they caused other important considerations to be neglected. The economy of the combustible is only one of the conditions to be fulfilled in heat-engines. In many cases it is only secondary. It should often give precedence to safety, to strength, to the durability of the engine, to the small space which it must occupy, to small cost of installation, etc. To know how to appreciate in each case, at their true value, the considerations of convenience and economy which may present themselves; to know how to discern the more important of those which are only secondary; to balance them properly against each other; in order to attain the best results by the simplest means; such should be the leading characteristics of the man called to direct, to co-ordinate the labour of his fellow men, to make them co-operate towards a useful end, whatsoever it may be.
>
> (Carnot, 1824: 59)

This cautionary note is a means of expressing what is left out of the model. In the case of combustion engines, the model of fuel use does not take into account issues of safety, strength, durability, cost, and so on. Carnot warns that the variables that are left out are equally, if not more, important than efficiency of fuel use. Importantly, the knowledge of what is left out of the model is a prerogative of the modeller and for this reason has to be communicated by the modeller.

Knowledge about the relevance of factors such as safety, durability and cost cannot be deduced from the study of efficiency in fuel use. This type of knowledge may rather be associated with experience, with knowledge of the context of application of engines, knowledge about the needs that engines serve. Knowledge that comes from experience is referred to as tacit knowledge. Crucially, uncertainty is often part of the tacit knowledge and is not explicitly communicated. In the case of craftmanship, as the apprentice learns from the master through practice, knowledge about uncertainty is also acquired through practice. In the case of the circular economy, the "nexus" between different fields of expertise relies mainly on the explicit knowledge, the models, rather than the tacit knowledge. The challenge of the circular economy policy is not only that of combining different types of evidence, but also of conveying the tacit knowledge derived from experience and craftsmanship and the ability to deal with the expressed and implicit uncertainties linked to different types of evidence.

The discussion of what is left out of the model may happen within a scientific field and usually governed by what Haas (1992) calls inter-subjective notions of validity of knowledge. When different disciplines are put in dialogue, however, the internally defined criteria become background knowledge of the experts and practitioners of the field. Dialogue between disciplines is based on the contribution that each discipline makes, on the different perspectives that can be used to describe, understand and analyse an issue. The mixing of knowledge claims that is promoted by nexus thinking brings together different epistemic communities, and in so doing leaves out the internal discussions of what constitutes knowledge and uncertainty in each field.

The circular economy brings together disciplines that have been in dialogue multiple times, such as through the idea of sustainable development. In this case, however, we speak of a nexus policy to highlight how the economic and environmental components are joined through a win–win logic. The concept of the nexus was developed to thematise the challenges posed by the complexity of interactions in the socioeconomic and biophysical systems. However, speaking of "the nexus" may be interpreted in different ways: on one hand, the nexus can be an invitation to more holistic assessments of governance and of the issues to be governed, and on the other hand, the nexus may give a sense of concreteness to these complex interactions and make them manageable. In both cases, the nexus may invite reductionism. If used as a holistic concept, the challenge may become one of broadening the boundaries of the nexus (should it include also the eco-system, land use, climate, and waste?), rather than a recognition of the limited capacity of science and policy to describe and govern complex systems. If used as a managerial tool, the nexus creates boundaries for the complex web of interactions between, for instance, water, energy, and food. Stirling argues that "Ideas that there exist single technological 'solutions' to such massive, complex, pervasive and intensely interlinked societal challenges, are highly instrumental simplifications" (Stirling, 2015). The nexus as a pronoun in definite, singular form, reduces interdependencies to a well-defined concept, which gives the impression that complex interactions, interdependencies and feedback loops can be controlled, and therefore depoliticises governance.

Having discussed the epistemic implications of the win–win logic for the understanding of evidence and uncertainty in the circular economy, we go back to the question of the relationship between science and policy, and ask: Which type of policymaking does the nexus thinking of the circular economy enable? And at the same time, how does circular economy policy-making contribute to the definition of what constitutes evidence and what constitutes uncertainty?

Nexus policies are not just a means of signalling interactions between different policy domains, but are policies oriented towards consensus. The circular economy transforms uncertainties of waste management into opportunities for new business models, for the values of materials to be kept in the economy, for waste to become a (re-)source of materials and energy. The circular economy is different from the idea of sustainable development from this point of view. Sustainable development embodies a tension: development should be pursued but needs to be sustainable, economic growth is desirable if sustainable. The circular economy eliminates the "buts" and the "ifs". The tensions, risks and uncertainties in the circular economy proposal are downplayed, and the focus is on benefits and opportunities. The Ellen MacArthur Foundation argues that the circular economy reduces the risks of the linear economy, linked to price volatility, security of supply and political instability (Ellen MacArthur Foundation, 2013). Leese and Meisch (2015) argue that "The nexus is in fact conceived of as something that is very much manageable, even if planetary boundaries have already been crossed" (ibid.: 704). Knowledge about the nexus can be put to fruition, they add, to support economic growth and neoliberal policies.

Consensus is reached by silencing the uncertainties and reconciling different ideas about rationality and social preferences in policymaking. The win-win logic of the circular economy combines material accounting methods with eco-design and business models by downplaying the uncertainties and the cautionary notes. Materials appear both in economic accounts as an input in the production function and in environmental accounts as what is extracted from the environment. Both fields use accounting techniques, which are quantified in monetary terms or in terms of weight, embedded water, embedded energy, et cetera. By focusing on accounting techniques, the quantities of materials become the defining feature of the circular economy. The tacit knowledge about how many times materials such as paper and textiles can be recycled, becomes a side note, reported in Staff Working Documents rather than in Communications of the European Commission. The risks that hazardous substances pose to recycling are solved by referring to eco-design and the promise that through innovation, materials in the future will no longer contain hazardous substances (European Commission, 2018a). The threat of finite stocks of natural resources is replaced by the possibility of creating a new source of (secondary) resources within the economy (Ellen MacArthur Foundation, 2013). The issue that "linear economic activities" such as agriculture and manufacturing are outsourced to countries outside of the European Union, which may not be moving towards circularity, is not mentioned. The circular economy is a means to govern the economy-environment nexus by internalising the side-effects of natural resources extraction and of waste disposal. The hitherto ungovernable interlinkages between the economy and the ecosystem are rendered manageable by transferring the reservoirs of natural resources from the ecosystem to the economic system.

By downplaying the uncertainties, the precautionary model loses its raison d'être and the science policy interface is governed by utilitarian rationality. The circular economy should be pursued because it represents a business opportunity and a means of supporting economic growth and creating jobs (Stahel & Reday-Mulvey, 1976). Minimising costs in economic modelling becomes synonymous with minimising waste in environmental accounting. Hence, entrepreneurship and innovation become legitimate means of delivering sustainability. Sustainability is rendered technical through innovation, eco-design and technology. It is depoliticised by transferring agency from the government to corporate and social entrepreneurship.

An apparent consensus

The circular economy rehearses the practice of letting "Science speak Truth to Power" and then simply implementing the logical consequences of that Truth, based on clear values and preferences. We have discussed in the previous section how Truth is constructed by silencing uncertainties and rendering sustainability a technical issue. An additional criticism of the mantra of science speaking truth to power is that it simplifies the notion of power. Power is not a homogenous and well-defined institution, but rather an assembly of people, institutions, practices, traditions, political interests and so on. In the European context, power is negotiated among Directorates of the European Commission, satellite agencies that provide "in house" science advice to the Commission, the European Parliament and the Council of Europe. This multiplicity of agencies is part of the techno-epistemic network of the circular economy. As noted in Chapter 2, the circular economy emerges from policy rather than from academia.

In large bureaucratic institutions such as the European Commission, the nexus between policies may lead to a deepening of technocratic governance, through which open conflicts within institutions are avoided, but also the benefits of new insights that may arise from collaboration efforts are not enjoyed. The economy–environment nexus may become a box-ticking exercise, not because of lack of good will on the part of individuals working in the institutions involved, but because of the large time requirements, the difficulty of changing working culture in a daily reality of endless meetings and information overflow, and the difficulties in establishing dialogue across different institutional languages. The circular economy reflects the fragmented character of European policy making, by building an alliance between the political interests of different agencies, such as the Directorate-General for Environment and the Directorate-General for Internal Market, Industry, Entrepreneurship and SMEs" This alliance, however, is built by depoliticising environmental governance and reducing sustainability to technocratic management.

As the circular economy proposal is depoliticised, the concept appears to draw consensus. A policy officer argued that "no one would argue for less circularity" (workshop, May 2018). Blanket statements about the universal desirability of circularity appeal to ethics. On ethical grounds, no one would argue that more waste should be produced. By linking circularity to ethics, the issue that full circularity is not possible (as discussed in Chapter 5) can be acknowledged without losing legitimacy. Circularity should be pursued to the greatest extent possible, and a more circular economy is assumed to be better than a less circular economy independently of the (in)adequacy of the concept of circularity in describing the economic process.

The principles that no one would argue for less circularity and that "we are moving in the right direction" (workshop, May 2018) express two important features of epistemic networks, namely the shared set of normative and principled beliefs about what is desirable and what is "right", and a common commitment to policy that is inclusive of the environment. It should be noted that different opinions were expressed at the workshop, and that what we are characterising as an epistemic network is not a homogenous entity. Nevertheless, there seems to be a general commitment to making environmental protection part of governance. The use of rhetorical arguments such as "no one would argue for less circularity" and the reference to the right direction, invite a smiling consensus, and make it difficult to articulate criticisms. As a result, commitment to environmental values is given priority over the terms under which the mainstreaming of environmental policy happens. Members of the epistemic network recognise and are aware of the limits of circularity, yet value the symbolic role of the circular economy in mainstreaming environmental policy. The circular economy is depoliticised to fit multiple political agendas, decoupling the association of environmental protection with the political left.

By rendering the circular economy a "neutral" policy, the proposal is also de-contextualised. The ethical claims that support the circular economy reflect a Eurocentric vision of sustainability. The collective "we" behind the desirability of the circular economy is closely linked to European identity. Waste picking is an important source of income for the poorest strata of society in much of the developing world (Dias, 2016; Rutkowski & Rutkowski, 2015). The idea that waste can be turned into a resource is, from the point of view of

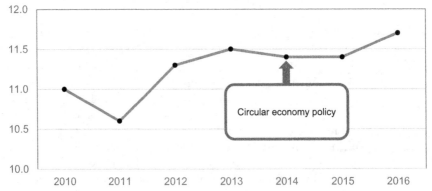

Figure 8.1 Circular material use rate
Source: Eurostat European Commission, 2019

waste pickers, far from new. In the European version of recycling, the "new" concept of circular economy serves to make the image of waste management and recycling more attractive.

The Eurocentric vision of sustainability is the result of the co-production of scientific practices and institutional arrangements. According to Rip (1997), modern science emerged from the purification of science starting in the second half of the eighteenth century. Purification was based on the cognitive separation between pure and applied sciences, and on institutional shifts towards the professionalisation of science and higher education. Due to this separation, pure science was tasked with the new challenge of proving its societal relevance. Sustainability as a concept is mobilised as an abstract sponsor to claim relevance. Relevance to sustainability has both a symbolic and financial value for professional science, which is supported by public funding. The apparent consensus around the circular economy is the result of the mutually reinforcing tendencies in: i) European research funding and science policy, which are more and more directed at solving "social challenges", and ii) the participation of the Directorates of the European Commission and EU Agencies in the epistemic networks that create knowledge about the circular economy, which have the institutional mandate of providing solutions. In other words, both research and policy about the circular economy have the requirement of providing solutions, and the space to voice concerns and articulate criticism is limited. The consensus about the desirability of a circular economy may well be more determined by circumstances than by convictions.

The circular economy has been delivered

In March 2019, the European Commission issued a press release stating that the "Commission delivers on Circular Economy Action Plan" (European Commission, 2019b). The press release refers to the fact that over 50 actions planned under the Circular Economy Action Plan have been delivered or are being implemented. At the same time, Eurostat, the statistical agency of the European Commission, warns that in spite of high rates of separate waste collection, only 12% of material resources come from recycled products in the European Union (Eurostat, 2019).

Statistics about circularity are only available up to the year 2016, making any statements about changes in levels of circularity since the onset of the circular economy policy (2014) premature. Considering a longer time span, in biophysical terms, the circularity of the European Union has increased from 11% in 2010 to 11.7% in 2016 (see Figure 8.1). The delivery of the circular economy package has nothing to do with the degree of circularity of the economy, which cannot be observed yet from the statistical data available. Policy efforts, however, have led to the proliferation of actions and measures under the Circular Economy Package. The circular economy Action Plan includes 54 actions (European Commission, 2019a). Because most actions are regulatory in nature, including for example amendments to existing directives, one could expect the effect of the Action Plan on the level of circularity of the European Union to increase in the future. Nevertheless, the present situation warns that there may be an important gap between the number of initiatives and the material effectiveness of this policy.

We argue that the premature claim of material effectiveness creates a credibility deficit that may erode public trust in science and policy. There is a correspondence between science and policy interests, because as much as €335 million have been devoted to research on the circular economy and because considerable resources and efforts have been directed to the creation of indicators for the circular economy. However, the policy has not yet materialised beyond the creation of new accounting protocols and the training of new technocrats responsible for "monitoring progress" (European Commission, 2018b). The European Union has organised stakeholder conferences in 2015, 2018 and 2019, and has created a stakeholder platform in 2017. These initiatives, however, have had mainly an informative character. As a result, the science-policy interface runs the risk of becoming a science-policy bubble, detached from society and the economy.

The apparent consensus around the circular economy and the consensus logic of nexus policies not only exclude controversy from the circular economy imaginary, but also annul the capacity to diagnose policy ineffectiveness, and possibly failure. In the epistemic network composed of technocrats and scientists that develop the accounting methods used to measure circularity, an echo chamber is created. The shared normative commitment to include environmental concerns in policymaking means that the terms under which the environment is included are of secondary importance. Inclusion in any form is seen as "moving in the right direction". In practice, the right direction may end up being no direction at all.

Note

1 The sustainable development summit of 1992 in Rio de Janeiro gave rise to the precautionary principle. Principle 15 of the Rio declaration states that "In order to protect the environment, the precautionary approach shall be widely applied by States according to their capabilities. Where there are threats of serious or irreversible damage, lack of full scientific certainty shall not be used as a reason for postponing cost-effective measures to prevent environmental degradation" (UNCED, 1992).

References

Carnot, S. (1824). *Reflections on the Motive Power of Fire, and on Machines Fitted to Develop that Power*. Paris: Bachelier.

Colebatch, H. K. (2005). Policy analysis, policy practice and political science. *Australian Journal of Public Administration*, 64(3), 14–23. doi:10.1111/j.1467-8500.2005.00448.x

Dias, S. M. (2016). Waste pickers and cities. *Environment and Urbanization*, 28(2), 375–390. doi:10.1177/0956247816657302

Ellen MacArthur Foundation. (2013). *Towards the Circular Economy*. Retrieved from www.ellenmacarthurfoundation.org/assets/downloads/publications/Ellen-MacArthur-Foundation-Towards-the-Circular-Economy-vol.1.pdf

European Commission. (2018a). *Commission Staff Working Document accompanying the document Communication from the Commission to the European Parliament, the Council, the European Economic and Social Committee and the Committee of the Regions on the implementation of the circular economy* (No. 20 final).

European Commission. (2018b). *Commission Staff Working Document. Measuring progress towards circular economy in the European Union – Key indicators for a monitoring framework. Accompanying the document Communication from the Commission to the European Parliament, the Council, the European Economic and Social Committee and the Committee of the Regions* (No. SWD (2018) 17).

European Commission. (2019a). *Commission Staff Working Document. Accompanying the document Report from the Commission to the European Parliament, the Council, the European Economic and Social Committee and the Committee of the Regions on the implementation of the Circular Economy Action Plan*. Brussels: European Commission.

European Commission. (2019b, March). *Closing the loop: Commission delivers on Circular Economy Action Plan*. Press Release, pp. 2019–2021.

European Communities. (2009). *Beyond GDP. Measuring Progress, True Wealth and Well-Being*. Luxembourg: Publication offices of the European Commission.

Eurostat. (2019, March). *Record recycling rates and use of recycled materials in the EU*. News Release.

Eurostat European Commission. (2019). *Circular Material Use Rate*. Brussels: Eurostat European Commission.

Foss Ballo, I. (2015). Imagining energy futures: Sociotechnical imaginaries of the future Smart Grid in Norway. *Energy Research & Social Science*. doi:10.1016/j.erss.2015.08.015

Funtowicz, S. O., & Ravetz, J. R. (1990). *Uncertainty and Quality in Science for Policy* (Vol. 6). Dordrecht: Kluwer Academic Publishers. doi:10.1016/0921–8009(92)90014-J

Funtowicz, S. O., & Ravetz, J. R. (1993). Science for the post-normal age. *Futures*, (September), 739–755. doi:0016–3287/93/07739–17

Funtowicz, S. O., & Strand, R. (2007). Models of science and policy. In T. Traavik (Ed.) *Biosafety First-Holistic Approaches to Risk and Uncertainty in Genetic Engineering and Genetically Modified Organisms* (pp. 263–278). Trondheim, Norway: Tapir Academic Press.

Haas, P. M. (1989). Do regimes matter? Epistemic communities and Mediterranean pollution control. *International Organization*, 43(3), 377–403.

Haas, P. M. (1992). Introduction: Epistemic communities and international policy coordination. *International Organization*, 46. doi:10.1017/S0020818300001442

Leese, M., & Meisch, S. (2015). Securitising sustainability? Questioning the "Water, Energy and Food Nexus". *Water Alternatives*, 8(1), 695–709.

Pereira, A. G., & Funtowicz, S. O. (Eds.) (2009). *Science for Policy*. Oxford: Oxford University Press.

Rip, A. (1997). A cognitive approach to relevance of science. *Social Science Information*, 36(4), 615–640.

Rommetveit, K. (2013). *Working Paper on the Concept of Epistemic Networks* (No. Deliverable D1.1). Bergen: University of Bergen.

Rutkowski, J. E., & Rutkowski, E. W. (2015). Expanding worldwide urban solid waste recycling: The Brazilian social technology in waste pickers inclusion. *Waste Management and Research*, 33(12), 1084–1093. doi:10.1177/0734242X15607424

Stahel, W. R., & Reday-Mulvey, G. (1976). *Jobs for Tomorrow: The Potential for Sub-stituting Manpower for Energy*. Brussels: European Commission.

Stirling, A. (2015). *Developing "Nexus Capabilities": Towards Transdisciplinary Methodologies*. Brighton: University of Sussex.

Strand, R. (2018). Post-Normal Science. In C. Spash (Ed.), *Routledge Handbook of Ecological Economics* (pp. 288–297). London and New York: Routledge.

UNCED. (1992). *The Rio Declaration on Environment and Development*. doi:10.1017/S037689290003157X

Part III

The future of change

9 Narratives of stop and go

This chapter places the circular economy in a broader analysis of two grand narratives that have competed for political attention since the final decades of the twentieth century: the "Bios" narrative of technoscience, innovation and growth and the "Geos" narrative of limits to growth. The circular economy can be seen as yet another attempt within the Bios narrative to meet a concern raised in the Geos narrative and the system sciences that inform it. In that translation from Geos to Bios, however, the original concerns are lost out of sight. Hence, the circular economy may be a success even if biodiversity is lost, wilderness is lost, biophysical funds are compromised, and the climate is changing for worse.

From the Geos perspective, the failure might be explained in terms of power differentials between the industry and finance lobbies representing the Bios on one hand, and the NGOs that speak for Geos on the other. We argue that the problem runs deeper and is connected to an asymmetry between Bios and Geos with respect to what actions they can suggest and legitimise. Geos is a narrative of "Stop!" while Bios is a narrative of "Go!", continue and accelerate. Geos says "Stop somehow and do something else", but it does not say what. For instance, calls for cutting climate emissions may sound concrete but are not in themselves actionable. "Cut" as in cutting emissions means "do something in order to induce a change that ultimately result in 50% lower emissions".

Antonio Gramsci famously wrote: "The crisis consists precisely in the fact that the old is dying and the new cannot be born; in this interregnum morbid phenomena of the most varied kind come to pass". The chapter ends with a discussion of the circular economy as a possibly morbid phenomenon. The old that is dying is the current economic system characterised by accelerating throughput and destruction of funds in the biosphere. There are limits to growth, and humanity is approaching them. The new that apparently cannot be born yet, is a type of human civilisation that manages to live in less tension with the rest of the biosphere. The Geos narrative offers glimpses of the new but it does not say what to do. Something is done, but unfortunately it does not retain the original purpose because it is appropriated and conditioned by a different meta-narrative, follows a different institutional logic and is legitimised by a different order of worth. The European Union, originally a trade union for coal and steel, hence appears as an *ancien régime* that seems readier to sacrifice long-term environmental sustainability than the prospects of economic growth and an affluent capitalist economy.

Introduction: going beyond unfair criticisms of the proponents of the circular economy

So far in this book, we have not only presented but also severely criticised the EU policy initiatives for the circular economy. Chapters 2 and 5 argued that ecological economics shows that the economy cannot be circular. The policies are the result of political negotiation and sociotechnical imagination that only to a very small degree is founded in sound science or real evidence. The economy will not become circular and these policies are not likely to be particularly conducive to sustainable development.

Against this backdrop, it would be easy to fall into the trap of discrediting or even ridiculing circular economy proponents in the policy world. We believe that would be a serious mistake for two reasons. First, we have no reason to question the sincere intentions of governmental as well as non-governmental actors who have worked to conceive of, develop or support these policies. In text, conversations and formal interviews all of them have expressed a strong commitment to the need for change towards sustainability and a greater care for the environment. Nobody holds the ultimate blueprint for how to achieve such change and nobody should be ridiculed for trying to devise a way forward.

Second, critics of official environmental policy and governance may ignore the depth of the challenge of implementing strong policies for sustainability within the existing institutions of governance. The challenge is deeper than overcoming power structures and political economies. First of all, we are reminded of Otto von Bismarck's famous definition of politics as the art of the possible. Political institutions are designed for the creation of compromises among a multiplicity of interests, of which sustainability is but one. Moreover, the challenge is fundamentally an epistemological issue, a matter of what kind of knowledge can justify what kind of action. This chapter is devoted to unfolding some of these issues, placing the circular economy in a broader analysis of two grand narratives that have competed for political attention since the final decades of the twentieth century: the "Bios" narrative of technoscience, innovation and growth and the "Geos" narrative of limits to growth.

We have already mentioned how the circular economy is the most recent in a series of attempts to reconcile the goals of growth and sustainability, following the tradition from Brundtland's "sustainable development". In the previous chapter, we placed the circular economy as a "nexus policy", which tries to resolve conflicts between policy areas by avoiding trade-offs and constructing so-called win-win solutions. A statement by one of our informants – "No-one would argue for less circularity" – brilliantly illustrates the teleological element in this type of policy work. In order to gain support for a policy, one needs to show that it is *good,* that it puts forward a desirable goal, preferably one that is universally desirable. In a Norwegian research project, Jill Loga (2004) coined the term *"godhetsmakt"*, which may be translated into "goodness power", for the type of political power that can be mobilised by being able to display (and define) what is 'Good'. One of her main points is exactly that it is politically impossible to argue against the 'Good':

> It becomes impossible to oppose [...] goodness because one would appear as evil, cynical or selfish. If one appropriates and speaks from the position of goodness, one becomes unimpeachable, immunized against criticism. Goodness only needs to be stated to become a conclusion.
>
> (323, our translation)

This type of power will be well-known within some religious communities. Indeed, goodness power runs well with dogmatic orthodoxies, wishful thinking and lip-serving hierarchies, and it is not irrelevant to ask whether this is not also part of the reality of the European Commission services and other large bureaucracies. Among those of us who have tried to deliver bad news as part of science for policy – such as the fact that the economy cannot be circular – the bitter joke by Upton Sinclair is not without traction: "It is difficult to get a man to understand something, when his salary depends on his not understanding it".

The Upton Sinclair quote is cynical and insinuates bad faith on the individual level. The "man", the individual, could be able to understand but does not want to because of self-interest. In our formal and informal interactions with policy-makers we hardly ever encountered such individuals. A better description, placing explanatory power in the cognitive dimension and on the institutional level, was suggested by Steve Rayner (2012) who developed Ravetz' concept of usable ignorance (Ravetz, 1987) into that of "socially constructed ignorance":

> To make sense of the complexity of the world so that they can act, individuals and institutions need to develop simplified, self-consistent versions of that world. The process of doing so means that much of what is known about the world needs to be excluded from those versions, and in particular that knowledge which is in tension or outright contradiction with those versions must be expunged. This is "uncomfortable knowledge".
>
> (Rayner 2012: 107)

One of the most elementary principles of ethics is that ought implies can: One cannot hold against someone that they do not act in a certain way if they cannot act in that way.

Acts, action and activity are at the very heart of this matter. Uncomfortable knowledge, in Rayner's analysis, is not primarily characterised by creating affects and emotions of discomfort. It is uncomfortable in the sense that it is experienced as not actionable or even worse: Its presence and implications destroy the justification for action. Those of us who have delivered uncomfortable knowledge, may have experienced the response not so much of downright denial but more of resignation: "What do you want us to do then? You are just criticising, you are not providing a positive message with suggestions for what to do".

Modern societies, modern institutions and Western thought may all be said to have a preference for activity over passivity. Michael Bar-Eli and colleagues were able to give a striking illustration in their studies of football goalkeepers (Bar-eli & Azar, 2009; Bar-eli, Azar, Ritov, Keidar-levin, & Schein, 2007). When trying to save a penalty kick, goalkeepers almost always (94%) jump to the left or the right, and they even have to decide on the direction before the ball moves in order not to be late. However, video analysis shows that they would have saved a lot more goals if they simply remained still. Almost a third of penalty kicks go towards the centre, and a standing goalkeeper has a good probability of saving it at all heights. Bar-Eli and his team discuss this in terms of *action bias*. From interviews, they learned that goalkeepers believe that they would be severely criticised if there is a goal and they stood still and "did nothing". Their belief may very well be justified, not the least as football spectators are concerned. Action bias/intervention bias has also been discussed in the context of over-diagnostics and over-treatment in medicine (Foy & Filippone, 2013).

Later, we shall briefly return to the issue of Western and modern action bias and its possible alternatives in non-Western, non-modern thought. For what follows, however, we shall assume that modern institutions such as environmental governance and economic policy-making do have the call for action inscribed into them. Their purpose is to act and to facilitate action. Furthermore, the challenges that, say, a Directorate-General for Environment is confronted with, are of a different nature and order of magnitude than football. Indeed, the challenges of climate change, pollution, loss of biodiversity are all posed as impending disasters unless action is taken.

Bios and Geos: two competing grand narratives

What kind of action can at all be indicated in a Western, modern, science-based culture? Rommetveit, Strand, Fjelland, Funtowicz, & Saltelli (2013) performed a broad analysis of science-based policy discourse and identified two underlying narratives behind the myriad of individual instances of policy initiative and science advice. Rommetveit et al. called them "two tales of the present". We will follow Jean-François Lyotard (1979) and refer to them as "grand narratives", that is, narratives behind the narratives, that define the preconditions for how knowledge and experience is ordered and explained in the discourse. The two were called "Bios" and "Geos", respectively.

Bios is the grand narrative emblematically represented and justified by the success of biotechnology, genetic engineering and the molecular life sciences. It is:

the one of the necessary and sufficient role of innovation, growth, adaptation, evolution, and the centrality of new and emerging sciences and technologies such as life science and biotechnology.

(Rommetveit et al. 2013: 58–59)

Bios expresses a strong belief in progress and what a philosopher of technology would recognise as technological optimism and determinism. Progress is defined in scientific, technological and economic terms, and it is above all biotechnology and information and communication technologies that deliver the progress in all three dimensions. Progress is not only desirable but necessary. The necessity of progress is explained in several ways. First, there is a fear, grounded in neoclassical economics, that stagnation is dangerous to the economic system, globally and definitely regionally as this would make the country or region lose competitive advantage and lag behind other countries and regions. Second, progress is needed to meet various social problems. Following the financial crisis at the turn of the twentieth century, such social problems became increasingly framed as "grand challenges", in part also to cast them in positive terms, to "capture political and public imagination" (ERA Expert Group, 2008: 8) and keep the support for extensive public funding of research and innovation.

The knowledge base drawn upon in Bios is constituted by technoscience – molecular life science, biotechnology, material science, informatics and gradually nanotechnology, systems biology, material science – but also cognitive science, neoclassical economics and evolutionary theory. These are sciences of progress, activity and achievement: the knowledge drawn upon by Bios expresses how to construct certain things or systems and what they can achieve; or how to change, manipulate or control something; or otherwise how to make some kind of progress. Bios is a narrative of progress, evolution and acceleration. Change is ubiquitous, necessary, and desirable. Change has taken place, is taking place, and it is accelerating. The video talks of the late Swedish medical researcher and public speaker Hans Rosling can be invoked as an illustration of the positivity of Bios: the world is generally changing for the better and those who say otherwise are ill-informed or speaking in bad faith. And, by far, the key factor for progress is science. In this way, Bios is in line with a longer tradition of Enlightenment. The focus of attention in this type of Enlightenment, however, is the marriage between human utopia for all and business opportunities in a world of fierce competition. This strange marriage has been studied also under other labels, such as the sociology of expectations in science and technology (Borup, Brown, Konrad, & Van Lente, 2006) and political economies of hope (Novas, 2006).

We believe that any reader familiar with richer societies at the time of writing – the year of 2019 and more generally the first part of the twenty-first century – can confirm that the grand narrative of Bios still is pervasive, to an astonishing level, we would say. Blunt, unqualified statements about progress and innovation for growth, the bioeconomy, information society,

	BIOS	**GEOS**
Main symbol	 Double helix	 Gaia
Grand narrative	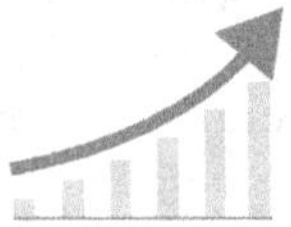 Growth	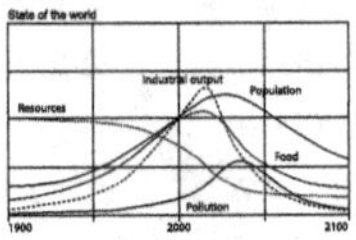 Limits
Main sciences and technologies	Evolutionary theory, molecular biology, ICTs, cognitive science, nanoscience, converging technologies, neo-classical economics, etc.	Earth system science, ecology, geosciences, climatology, Big History, ecological economics, etc.
Institutions	Nation state	Post-national

Figure 9.1 Bios and Geos
Source: Adapted from Rommetveit et al., 2013

the need for disruptive innovation et cetera, are constantly delivered by entrepreneurs, investors, politicians and scientists. They fill research policy documents, public statements and "networking" arenas for these so-called elites, from Davos to Dubai, from Singapore to Silicon Valley. Being a grand narrative, Bios shapes the discourse for so many actors that there are realms in business, science, politics and government in which it is not even visible anymore as a set of claims to be evaluated and contested. Those who contest are either disregarded, silenced or simply not there. Part of the readership of this book – ecologists, sociologists, environmentalists – might confirm the pervasiveness of Bios and still note that they do not frequent too many arenas in which Bios is dominant. Sometimes, one is reminded of this world of opportunity and positivity when picking up a flight magazine in an aeroplane, or scrolling through the bestsellers for businessmen at the airport bookstore. It is as if they belong to a different world.

An interesting anecdote in this regard, of the segregation of public discourses, is how the appearance of a 15-year-old Swedish climate activist, Greta Thunberg, caused sensation and scandal in the public sphere on an international level in 2018–2019. Greta Thunberg started in 2018 to skip school every Friday and strike in front of the Swedish Parliament, demanding that action be taken against climate change. Her initiative was publicised by mass media and social media, and soon inspired school strikes in several other European countries. "Fridays for Future" is unique because of the large mobilisation of teenagers it created. In July 2019, OPEC Secretary General Mohammad Barkindo was reported by the news agency AFP to have called Thunberg and her peers "perhaps the greatest threat" to oil industry and complained that her "unscientific" attacks on the industry were misleading society to, quote, "believe oil is the cause of climate change". We interpret this incident as a sign of the degree of insulation inside the Bios narrative, after three decades of climate policies. The Intergovernmental Panel on Climate Change being established in 1988. It is a UN body with 195 country members, including Nigeria, whose technical delegation in UN climate negotiations was headed by the same Mohammad Barkindo since 1991. Yet, the OPEC Secretary General was taken aback by the teenage climate activist.

What Thunberg does so effectively is to express through words and actions the key features of Geos. It should be noted, however, that the great approval raised by Fridays for Future among the political and financial sectors, as well as from scientists, is based largely on ambiguity: the agreement on the problem definition does not generate an agreement about the possible solution (De Marchi & Funtowicz, 2019). The grand narrative of Geos is also rooted in Enlightenment and a strong belief in Science but the sciences are different ones. They include ecology and environmental science, geoscience, climate science and ecological economics and other system sciences that focus on the Earth as a planet limited in space, materially closed and with limited resources and biological, meteorological and biophysical systems that are more or less perturbed and at risk due to human activity. In the figure above, Bios is symbolised by the double helix of DNA. The achievement of the double helix invokes the Baconian idea of Man's control over Nature (using the new science to penetrate her more secret and remote parts, to stay within Francis Bacon's idiom (Bacon, 1620)). The icon of Geos, on the other hand, is the picture of Earth taken from the moon rockets: finite, beautiful, vulnerable and fragile (Rommetveit et al. 2013). With historical precursors both in Malthus and nature conservation, Geos found its shape as a grand narrative from the moon travels but more notably the "discovery" of environmental pollution with Rachel Carson's book *Silent Spring* and James Lovelock's Gaia hypothesis that considered Planet Earth as almost a kind of organism. The advancements in system sciences led to debates in economics such as those reviewed in Chapter 3 but also in ecology, from *Limits to Growth* and onwards, and the huge development and upscaling of climate science from the 1990s. In 2000, Crutzen and Stoermer (2000) proposed that the planet is moving into a new geological era characterised by the implications of human activity, the anthropocene. Simultaneously, political causes and organisations have been co-produced, including the whole field of environmental activism, Greenpeace and other NGOs, green parties and degrowth/post-growth movements. Environmental governance also developed as a sector of policy and public administration, the Norwegian Ministry of the Environment being established in 1972 as the first of its kind, soon to be followed by many other countries.

Narratives of stop and go

Still, it seems that the two tales underlie decisive perplexities of the present, where "science" seems to be supporting differing political projects. Put briefly:

listening to dominant voices in science today, one (Geos) tells us to Stop!; another (Bios) urges us to speed up.

(Rommetveit et al. 2013: 71)

The Post-Modern Condition by Lyotard (1979) did not so much construct an alternative position to the Grand Narrative of Modernity and Enlightenment; in that sense it was not postmodernist. Rather, it tried to argue as a matter of fact that late twentieth century societies were becoming incredulous to meta-narratives as such, that is, that these societies were entering into a post-modern condition. Part of Lyotard's argument was that developments in science and its social contract were conducive to the post-modern condition, for example the development of ICTs, chaos theory, et cetera. While the argument may appear as less than convincing – Lyotard himself later criticised his work for being ill-informed – the general diagnosis of the book, a transition towards incredulity towards one grand narrative and towards multiculturalism, polyphony and fragmentation of the public sphere, seemed to resonate with a larger audience towards the end of the twentieth century.

When we speak of Bios and Geos as grand narratives, they are accordingly not grand in the ultimate, monolithic or totalitarian sense. Rather, they coexist in a larger universe of meta-narratives. Unlike Bios and Geos, some of these other meta-narratives are explicitly critical of (Western and masculine conceptions of) the Enlightenment tradition or simply more distant from it, developing alternative worldviews based in new or old sources of spirituality. Notwithstanding their differences, Bios and Geos are both narratives that aspire for power within the institutions of modern states, in politics, science and business. They have also both been successful in that regard, each in its own way.

Yet, even by their own tales, the nature and degree of success is vastly different. The Bios narrative is by its own structure self-confirming and self-vindicating: Examples of achievements confirm the positive outlook on opportunity and change, while failures only suggest that we try again. Not even the financial crisis of 2007–2008 changed the direction of policies. In general, the recipe was more of the same, at higher speed. There is always a new opportunity, think positive! The Geos narrative, on the other hand, is informed by system variables, which tell us how many animal and plant species have become extinct, how many ecosystems are collapsing and how much ice has melted. In general, the system sciences have been showing that things are not going well: Biodiversity is lost, wilderness is lost, biophysical funds are compromised, and the climate is changing for worse. Geos does not only say that Earth is finite but also that time is running out.

Climate change is particularly interesting as this issue has been receiving considerable political attention since the 1990s. Still, in spite of national policies and international agreements, climate gas emissions have not decreased, except during the financial crisis when low economic activity in some countries also implied lower emissions. What has not been seen during the first three decades of climate change as a main political issue, are large scale changes in sectors and infrastructures of production and consumption that actually already reduced emissions. What has been observed, in addition to a lot of talk about the climate, is mainly the development of a new type of trade, that is, carbon emission trading.

We shall not discuss the rationale and effectiveness of carbon emission trading. What is evident, though, is that it is a type of practice that belongs with the grand narrative of Bios, of producing progress and solving a grand challenge by applying neoclassical economics and creating new business opportunities. This type of strategy is not new. Two decades ago, it was called ecological modernisation (Hajer, 1997). Its justification and support lie in the success stories of achievements and opportunities. From Bios-centred governmental perspectives within as outside of the EU, carbon emission trading is not falsified by the lack of emission reductions. Carbon emission trading and the circular economy are two crystal clear examples of attempts to address a concern from Geos and solve it within Bios. From the perspective of Geos, this approach runs the risk of confusing ends and means and ultimately focusing on economic opportunity at the expense of the original goal of environmental sustainability. We have seen this in Chapters 6 and 7: a Bios-inspired, optimistic theory of change is taken for granted and built into the policy indicators, and in the end something like the increasing number of eco-patents is taken as evidence that the environment has been saved. From the Geos perspective, in science as in NGOs, there is constant reason for disappointment as environmental goals are translated into what is perceived as superficial and sometimes perverse political action.

The analysis of what causes the disappointing state of affairs runs the risk of becoming equally superficial, akin to what we described in the introduction of this chapter. There is of course a power differential between the industry and finance lobbies representing the Bios on one hand, and the NGOs that speak for Geos on the other, and we are not arguing that there is never any hypocrisy, bad faith or wilful ignorance. However, the problem runs deeper and is connected to an asymmetry between Bios and Geos with respect to what actions they can suggest and legitimise. Geos is a narrative of "Stop!" while Bios is a narrative of "Go!".

The Bios meta-narrative is an endless source of empowering motivational speech. It creates the conditions for encouragements to create, build, trade, prosper, try and fail, and most fundamentally, act. While Bios embraces the new, the novel, the innovation, it actually tells us that we can continue to do what we are good at doing, inside the existing economic system and model of production and consumption. Furthermore, as noted above, the actor may himself evaluate his own achievement by his own success criteria. If policy has introduced carbon emission trading as a good thing, the entrepreneurial spirit may be confident that he can do the right thing by whole-heartedly unleashing his creative energies on making money and trading emissions well. We say "he" rather than "he and she" because the Bios world is primarily a man's world.

Geos has almost the opposite structure. It tells us that time is running out and that action is urgent, but it does not say what should be done. At the first glance it may seem to prescribe action: "Cut emissions by 50%!". The problem, however, is that "cutting emissions by 50%" is not an act like, say, cutting a rope in two. "Cut" as in "cutting emissions" is a metaphor. The literal meaning of "cut" in this expression is "do something in order to induce a change that ultimately result in 50% lower emissions as measured by science". It does not by itself give direction as to what concretely is to be done. It does not state a theory of change that the action is to be grounded upon. And finally, it does not even allow the actor to trust or even evaluate his or her own achievement. The success is to be decided upon by system science, in this case climate research. Geos says "Stop somehow and do something else", but it does not say what. The theory of change is not really much addressed by the underlying scientific basis for the narrative. If the world of Bios is Aldous Huxley's *Brave New World*, the world of Geos is that of Franz Kafka.

This is why the problem runs deeper than the asymmetry between optimism and pessimism, which arguably also is part of the picture. The French sociologists Luc Boltansky and Laurent Thévenot (2006) claimed that there are six ways of arguing for legitimacy in modern societies, or six "orders of worth", as they called them. For instance, one order of worth is that of passion, inspiration and strong emotion; another is that of the market and profitability; a third is that of industry, efficiency, productivity and rationality. Bruno Latour pointed out early that the problem of political ecology, and we would add, Geos in general, is that it does not fit well in any of the orders of worth (Latour, 1998). This is why green parties struggle to become big, in Latour's analysis. A narrative of Stop does not appeal to the market and industry orders of worth, and rarely has it been able to appeal to inspiration and emotion. The Greta Thunberg story is interesting because it might be the beginning of a change in this regard. Still, the problem of action is highly visible also in this case. We stated above that Thunberg effectively expresses through words and actions the key features of Geos. What are these actions? They are school strikes, protests to urge others – the adults – to find out what to do in order to solve the problem.

Carbon emission trading and the circular economy are actionable. They devise concrete actions or ensure actors such as eco-innovators or waste managers that they are justified in doing what they do. By having been appropriated by the grand narrative of Bios, they appeal to the market and industry orders of worth and so they can be rendered with legitimacy in modern societies. A pure message from climate science, on the other hand, is mainly a call for Stop! without much instruction about how to proceed. There are of course serious attempts at developing a positive programme of alternative non-Bios cultures, lifestyles and economies, such as in the Degrowth movement or perhaps better, *Buen Vivir*. It is too early to know if they could appeal to other orders of worth – of tradition, of inspiration and above all of the civic world. Neither do we think that Boltansky, Thevenot or Latour said the final word on societal legitimacy. Part of the Geos narrative is that a different social world is called for than the one analysed by contemporary sociologists. In their analysis of climate policy development, however, Rommetveit et al. (2010) warned against the imbalance between the strength and urgency of the narrative of Stop, and the relative weakness of the alternative action programme. If action is perceived as highly urgent but the institutions find little way forward, this may build up a policy vacuum that can lead to rash and dangerous actions as well as poor leadership.

Crisis

In his prison notebooks, Italian marxist Antonio Gramsci wrote in 1930:

> The crisis consists precisely in the fact that the old is dying and the new cannot be born; in this interregnum morbid phenomena of the most varied kind come to pass.
>
> (Gramsci, 2011: 32–33.)

In 2019, at the time of writing of this book, Gramsci's famous quote on the crisis was gaining popularity among the authors and our colleagues; we already used in Chapter 4. The book was written during the presidency of Donald Trump in the United States of America and the upsurge of right-wing nationalist populism in several European countries. It was completed while the political establishment of the United Kingdom was disintegrating over how to try to leave the European Union. Every day there was a piece of news, about political utterances and decisions that would have been unthinkable only ten years ago. Crisis had become a word of everyday discourse.

On this background, the policies of the circular economy may appear as rational and orderly. Yet, we have found it useful to reflect on the circular economy in light of the Gramsci quote. For those who support our analysis in previous chapters and agree that i) the economy cannot be circular and ii) the circular economy policies are not necessarily conducive to sustainability by protecting or regenerating biophysical funds, the circular economy can indeed be seen as a morbid phenomenon. The old that is dying is the current economic system characterised by accelerating throughput and destruction of funds in the biosphere. There are limits to growth, and humanity is approaching them. The new that apparently cannot be born yet, is a type of human civilisation that manages to live in less tension with the rest of the biosphere. Through the Geos narrative one can see glimpses of the new that has to be born but they are not actionable. So, they become appropriated by other narratives and logics. Something has to be done, something is done, but unfortunately it does not retain the original purpose because it is conditioned by a different meta-narrative, follows a different institutional logic and is legitimised by a different order of worth. These are the morbid symptoms.

What was too early to know at the time of writing, was the possible connection between these orderly morbid symptoms of strange policies and socially constructed ignorance within old bureaucracies, and the morbid symptoms of old political parties in disintegration and a White House in apparent chaos. We suspect that there may be such connections and that this might be part of the wider processes of fragmentation alluded to by Lyotard already in 1979. Geos and right-wing populism have that in common with post-colonial and feminist critiques that they all in their ways have ceased to respect and subdue to the older, monolithic grand narrative of Modernity. Most European governments and EU institutions are still (in 2019) led by old political, financial, and scientific elites but these elites are trying their best somehow to accommodate the pressures from critics and devise policies of ecological modernisation *à la* circular economy to please the environmentalists and accommodate advice from systems sciences; and install strict immigration policies to please right-wing populists. The problem – or luck, depending on the perspective and the issue – is that the room for reform is quite limited within the institutional logic, actually strictly limited by design in order for the institutions not to be destroyed by mood swings in the citizenry. In the case of immigration, it might be that most of the readers of this book will agree with the authors, in favour of a conservative stance, notably towards upholding human rights and UN conventions and against xenophobe practices. In the case of environmental sustainability, we might be the radicals and see the conservative nature of the institutions as an existential threat. The European Union, originally a trade union for coal and steel, seems readier to sacrifice long-term environmental sustainability than the prospects of economic growth and an affluent capitalist economy.

References

Bacon, F. (1620/2019). *Novum Organum*. Dumfries & Galloway: Anodos Books.

Bar-eli, M., & Azar, O. H. (2009). Penalty kicks in soccer: An empirical analysis of shooting strategies and goalkeepers' preferences. *Soccer & Society*, 10(2), 183–191.

Bar-eli, M., Azar, O. H., Ritov, I., Keidar-levin, Y., & Schein, G. (2007). Action bias among elite soccer goalkeepers: The case of penalty kicks. *Journal of Economic Psychology*, 28(5), 606–621.

Boltanski, L., & Thévenot, L. (2006). *On Justification: Economies of Worth*. Princeton, NJ: Princeton University Press.

Borup, M., Brown, N., Konrad, K., & Van Lente, H. (2006). The sociology of expectations in science and technology. *Technology Analysis and Strategic Management*, 18(3–4), 285–298. doi:10.1080/09537320600777002

Crutzen, P. J., & Stoermer, E. F. (2000). The "Anthropocene". *Global Change Newsletter*, 41, 17–18.

De Marchi, B., & Funtowicz, S. O. (2019). Comunicare tra fatti alternativi. Tutti dalla parte di Greta? *Epidemiologia e Prevenzione*, 43(2–3), 201–202.

ERA Expert Group. (2008). Challenging Europe's research: Rationales for the European Research Area (ERA). doi:10.2777/39044

Foy, A. J., & Filippone, E. J. (2013). The case for intervention bias in the practice of medicine. *Yale Journal of Biology and Medicine*, 86(2), 271–280.

Gramsci, A. (2011). *Antonio Gramsci Prison Notebooks*. New York: Columbia University Press.

Hajer, M. (1997). *The Politics of Environmental Discourse: Ecological Modernization and the Policy Process*. Oxford: Clarendon Press. doi:10.1093/019829333X.001.0001

Latour, B. (1998). To modernize or to ecologize? That's the question. In B. Braun & N. Castree (Eds.), *Remaking Reality: Nature at the Millenium* (pp. 221–242). London: Routledge.

Loga, J. M. (2004). *Godhetsmakt*. Bergen: University of Bergen.

Lyotard, J.-F. (1979). *The Postmodern Condition: A Report on Knowledge*. Manchester: Manchester University Press.

Novas, C. (2006). The political economy of hope: Patients' organizations, science and biovalue. *BioSocieties*, 1(3), 289–305. doi:10.1017/s1745855206003024

Ravetz, J. R. (1987). Usable knowledge, usable ignorance: Incomplete science with policy implications. *Knowledge: Creation, Diffusion, Utilization*, 9(1), 87–116. doi:10.1177/107554708700900104

Rayner, S. (2012). Uncomfortable knowledge: the social construction of ignorance in science and environmental policy discourses. *Economy and Society*, 41(October), 107–125. doi:10.1080/03085147.2011.637335

Rommetveit, K., Funtowicz, S., & Strand, R. (2010). Knowledge, democracy and action in response to climate change. In R. Bhaskar, C. Frank, K. G. Høyer, P. Næss, & J. Parker (Eds.), *Interdisciplinarity and Climate Change: Transforming Knowledge and Practice for Our Global Future* (pp. 149–163). London and New York: Routledge. doi:10.4324/9780203855317

Rommetveit, K., Strand, R., Fjelland, R., Funtowicz, S., & Saltelli, A. (2013). *What can history teach us about the prospects of a European Research Area?* European Commission. doi:10.2788/1057

10 What kind of science is needed in a changing world?

In Chapter 10, we return to one of the starting points of science and technology studies, namely that science and technology not only produce both opportunities and risks for society, but also change society and the environment. We thus ask what kind of knowledge would be useful for governance of change towards sustainability – or more precisely: for governance in and not of complexity, to draw on Arie Rip's distinction. We take a brief detour on different theories of complexity and argue that the circular economy may fall into reductionist complexity. As an alternative, we argue that what is needed is an epistemology of complexity to navigate the multiple non-equivalent representations of the economy and its relationship with the environment, rather than a description of what complexity is. This approach develops a "quantitative story-telling" for governance in complexity. Quantitative story-telling combines STS/social research that identifies policy narratives and imaginaries with quantitative methods to explore their biophysical feasibility and economic viability. Rather than trying (in vain) to speak Truth to Power, this type of science aims to improve political and democratic dialogue by exploring and clarifying the implications of different policy options. This could be one strategy to possibly utilise the knowledge from the sciences mentioned in Chapter 9 as those studying Earth as a finite and limited system without necessarily falling into the narratives of Stop.

Introduction

In the previous chapter, we compared two important grand narratives in debates about sustainability, and governance towards sustainability. The Bios narrative is the narrative of success and prosperity through technoscience, innovation and growth, and it recommends that we continue current trends and accelerate them. It embraces innovation-driven change, but at the same time it asks us to go on as before. The Geos narrative is the narrative of limits to growth, and it recommends us to stop – stop growing, stop emitting, stop degrading and destroying the biosphere. In Chapter 9, we noted how the circular economy is yet an instance of what happens when concerns originating in

Geos struggle to find their implementation in policy and end up being refor-mulated in the Bios narrative. Consequently, the circular economy becomes an ambition for growth.

We also noted how Bios and Geos are similar. They are both meta-narratives driven by scientific worldviews, albeit from very different sciences. Each in their own way, they embody the idea of science speaking Truth to Power and the idea that science can facilitate the proper governance *of* complex states of affairs. In Chapter 8 we discussed the circular economy as a case of nexus governance and argued why one cannot govern complexity. Humans are not the Demon from Laplace's famous thought experiment, sitting outside the universe and getting a full objective view of the system from the point of nowhere. There is no Archimedean point from which "we", as governing bodies, scientists or societies, can have total power and full control. What can be done, is to govern within the system, govern *in* complexity. Bios and Geos both fall subject to this critique. They are meta-narratives with implicit goals of the governance *of* complexity.

The primary norm of the mindset of governance *in* complexity is that of reflexivity, that is, to be willing and able to critical introspection and to study one's own role and identity within the system and one's own strengths and limitations. In Chapter 8 we introduced the concept of post-normal science (PNS). PNS can be seen as one example to develop what Ulrich Beck called reflexive modernisation, that is, practices and worldviews that do not break with modernity and modern institutions such as science, bureaucracy and democracy but rather try to develop them to incorporate self-criticism and reflexivity. This is exactly what Bios and Geos do not do: They do not accommodate storylines of "what if we are wrong?" Reflexive insights become uncomfortable in Bios and Geos, or simple invisible or illegitimate within the social construct of ignorance that these meta-narratives facilitate.

Most of this book has been devoted to critical analysis, hopefully with the academic rigour called for in such exercises, although we have not been afraid of entering into philosophising. In the two final chapters we aim to be more constructive and suggest a way forward, as an alternative to the features of the circular economy policies that we have criticised. This also means that we will have to enter into more speculative territory. The ambition of this chapter is to indicate the type of scientific knowledge needed for better governance in complexity. The short answer is that it would have to be more reflexive and more robust in use. In order to be so, it would have to better manage uncer-tainty and ambiguity. It would constitute a way of knowing with more humi-lity (Jasanoff, 2003).

For scientists, the first step towards humility is to understand that science not only solves but also creates social problems (Ravetz, 1971). Science and tech-nology deliver both benefits and risks for society and the natural environment. The case of nuclear power is emblematic of this change. The use of nuclear bombs in World War II contributed to the perception that technologies can be used both for the advancement of society and for its destruction. The possibility of misuse of science and technology meant that science is something that needs to be governed, and that does not automatically lead to progress. The threat of mutual assured destruction from a nuclear war led Ulrich Beck (1992) to develop the concept of risk society.

Normal accidents

The case of nuclear energy also advanced thinking about the consequences of the increasing complexity of technology and the interconnectedness of science and technology. In his book *Normal Accidents*, Charles Perrow (1984) argues that multiple and unexpected failures are built into complex systems that are tightly coupled. As a consequence, nuclear accidents are unavoidable, that is, normal. According to Perrow, normal accidents cannot be designed out. This insight indicates the limits of scientific knowledge in the context of complexity. More research and better technology will not solve the problem of accidents because the high number of processes and the high interdependence between processes makes complex systems hard to control.

Through technological innovation and the development of large-scale projects, science has become big science, and has become increasingly interwoven with technology. As a consequence, the governance of science and technology involves not only the assessment of benefits and risks, but it requires also understanding how techno-science changes and its context. As Strand puts it, "Scientific discovery and technological innovation produces benefits but also risks and hazards for society and the environment, and more fundamentally it changes *society*, the environment and the human condition" (2013: 112). Science produces maps of the world but to an ever-larger degree it also facilitates the change of the terrain. Boulding and Daly talked of the planet as a spaceship, as a full world. Science has been a key factor in that change from the empty to the full world.

There are many examples of technologies and innovations that have changed society and the environment: computers were supposed to make computing faster and have completely changed the way people work; the internet has revolutionised communication, trade and interpersonal relationships; modern agriculture based on industrial machinery has changed land use, with impacts on global climate; the use of chlorofluorocarbons (CFC) for refrigeration has impacted the ozone layer, et cetera.

The circular economy explicitly aims at changing the economic system and its relationship to the environment, and in some definitions also society by promoting sharing and repair cultures, and changes in consumption habits. Imaginaries of the circular economy, however, are based on an idea of governing that treats complex systems as if they could be controlled. Circular economy definitions do not include uncertainties, risks, or unintended consequences. We have seen in Chapter 5 that an unintended effect of real circularity in the biophysical sense would be to slow down the economic process. Rather than being limited merely by the rate of extraction of ready-made resources from stocks, production in a biophysically circular economy would need to adapt to the pace at which the system can recycle and regenerate resources. The radical openness of modern economies, in which both primary and secondary inputs and waste are traded, adds considerable uncertainty to the plausibility of circularity, both because of definitional and monitoring difficulties.

The increasing interpenetration of science and technology and the ambition to make systemic changes imply a challenge for governance. The challenge is not one of governance of technology and innovation, but governance in the new context created by the introduction of new technologies and innovation. As new challenges arise with the introduction of new technologies or new uses of technology, new measures need to be introduced, as for example, the General Data Protection Regulation for the use of personal data, the ban and regulation of substances such as CFCs and DDT. Governance in a changing world means that the boat needs to be built while at sea, or that the control room of the spaceship would need to be rebuilt during flight, to stay with Boulding's metaphor.

In that kind of context, what type of knowledge would be needed?

Knowledge for a changing world

The discussion of normal accidents raises the issue of complexity and of the limits of knowledge in governing risk. Complexity is often invoked as a criticism of reductionism, with important contributions from the fields of ecology (Holling, 1973), biology (Rosen, 1991) and thermodynamics (Nicolis & Prigogine, 1977). The environment, society, the economy, are not as simple as reductionist models describe them to be. Hence, governance that relies on the accuracy of simplified models is doomed to fail. Reductionism is necessary for action: a full description of the world would be messy and unmanageable, leading to paralysis rather than to action. The problem is that simplified descriptions are reified: instead of keeping in mind that a description is a partial representation of the whole, the knowledge gained through descriptions is given privilege. Sandra Mitchell (2009) explains that compositional materialism is conflated with descriptive fundamentalism. Compositional materialism refers to the observation that there is one kind of substance from which all things are made: atoms. Fundamentalism arises when the description of atoms is privileged, and is assumed to be a complete description of the world.

Governance through reductionism becomes governance of descriptions; of signs and not the referents of the signs. As Steve Rayner (2012) puts it, "an object or activity, such as a computer model, designed to inform management of a real-world phenomenon actually becomes the object of management". This is the case of the circular economy, in which implementation has focused mainly on the production of indicators of circularity and the recompilation of statistics. When the European Commission stated that the circular economy had been delivered in 2019, no improvements in the degree of circularity of the concrete, biophysical economic system had yet materialised. In this situation, governance of descriptions (in this case, statistics of circularity) may substitute the governance of the material circularity of the economy.

But what is complexity? Complexity is often explained as a situation in which the whole is more than the sum of the parts. The whole is more than the sum of the parts because the parts interact with each other in non-linear ways, leading to the emergence of properties at the level of the whole that cannot be observed in the parts. An example of complex system is a water molecule: wetness is a property of the whole that cannot be observed, nor deduced from the observation of the parts (hydrogen and oxygen). This definition says both something about the system, and about how the system is analysed. A useful starting point, therefore, is to distinguish between complexity as a property of the system (ontic definition) and complexity as a challenge of producing knowledge that is not reductionist (epistemic definition). An overview of existing definitions can be found in Mitchell (2009) and Salthe (1993).

Ontic complexity is understood as a property of the system, something that can be measured and objectively observed. The object of the study of complexity is generally "a system", that is, a whole made up of parts. The analysis of complexity describes the system in terms of: i) emergence, whereby the whole is more than the sum of the parts, ii) non-linearity, because causes and effects do not follow a one-to-one mapping but may be amplified by positive feedbacks or reduced through negative feedbacks, and iii) sensitivity to initial conditions, when the first changes of a system create a path dependence that progressively reduces the number of options available. The concept of complex adaptive systems is used to introduce the element of self-organisation, which entails that complex systems organise around attractors, and differentiates complex from random.

Strand (2002) refers to ontic complexity as thin complexity, and Geyer (2012) speaks of reductionist complexity. What complexity does in this case is to enlarge the scope of what is observed, from one (set of) aspect(s) to many (sets of) aspects. This approach does not escape reductionism. It may, at best, lead to reflexive reductionism in which choices of what to observe and how are made explicit. An example of this type of reductionism is the "holistic" interpretation of the nexus (discussed in Chapter 8), which aims at describing the whole by including more and more variables and modelling more and more interconnections. Another example of reductionist complexity may be cubism. Picasso represents faces from several different angles all at once. It is an attempt to approach the reality of faces in their totality. The real face has both a profile and full face, so Picasso presents both at the same time in one image that captures the reality of the face. The reductionism of holistic descriptions can be explained by the observation that the sum of the parts is greater than the whole (Allen et al., 2017), because the whole constrains the parts and limits their functions to interactions with each other and with the whole. Independent parts may express more functions than parts in a whole.

Returning to the question of what type of knowledge is needed in a changing world, ontic complexity may produce better descriptions of the "changing world" but does not solve the challenge of building the boat while at sea. Governing complex systems is not just about governing more things, nor about combining more representations through multi-, inter- or transdisciplinarity. In the context of emerging properties, irreversibility, non-linearity, etc. multiple descriptions entail contradictions, inconsistencies and require coming to terms with uncertainty. For this reason, complexity in the context of governance is most usefully understood in epistemic terms.

Epistemic complexity refers to the implications of complexity for knowledge. What does it mean to observe the whole rather than the parts? How can one reconcile the non-equivalent descriptions of the whole and the parts? In this case, the contribution of complexity theory is not a richer description of the system to be observed, but of the relationship between observer and the observable. Epistemic complexity focuses on hierarchies (Salthe, 2012), scales of analysis (Allen, 1987), non-equivalent representations (Rosen, 1991; 1985). Ahl & Allen (1996) speak of hierarchy theory as the theory of the role of the observer. The object of study in this case is not a material system, but the relationship between the system (which may be a social, political, biophysical, or information system) and the observer. Epistemic complexity does not study "systems" but rather "the holon", a concept introduced by Arthur Koestler (1968) and further developed by Allen & Starr (1982) to describe the process through which representations, interpretation and action constitute each other through a semiotic process. The holon (whole-part duality) makes it clear that parts and wholes do not exist "out there" but are observer-defined units of analysis. When postmodern Andy Warhol presents multiple images of Marilyn Monroe, he is not interested in the true image of the movie star, rather he is investigating the process of copying in multiple experiences. The point of epistemic complexity is not to combine all the multiple representations of Marilyn Monroe into one true representation, but to investigate the observer-observation duality.

The epistemic definition resonates with some of the challenges of governing the circular economy. The knowledge that is needed changes at different scales: the knowledge of how to recycle at the level of industrial processes is not a guide for societal transitions. The plurality of representations of circularity is evident in the high variety of indicators produced by European agencies, in which measures of waste by stream (plastic, organic, electronic, etc.) do not map onto measures of waste by source (municipal, construction, agricultural, etc.), nor onto measures related to the context of waste (hazardous, rare earth elements, etc.).

The important effort undertaken by the European Commission to measure circularity, therefore, does not necessarily provide a clear picture of how much waste is produced overall, how much of the separate waste collection goes into recycling and how much is exported. We argue that the circular economy is based on a sixteenth century map not because of lack of statistics, but because of complexity. As a consequence, the sixteenth century map is not a temporary state of uncertainty that can be overcome with more research, but a result of the inconsistencies and contradictions that emerge with complexity. More research may increase the number of multiple non-equivalent descriptions of the holon, which contributes to the knowledge base but also increases ambiguity.

Ambiguity

Ambiguity is generally thought to be a problem for decision making, because it is associated to vagueness and to a lack of clarity in indicating which option to pursue. We argue that in the case of multiple non-equivalent representations, vagueness is not due to lack of precision but to the fact that precision is spurious in the context of complexity. Different options refer to different representations.

Kovacic & Di Felice (2019) define ambiguity as the uncertainty created by the existence of multiple non-equivalent representations of the same issue. Ambiguity is not just a matter of different opinions, as may be the case of contrasting perceptions about the rise in the price of oil (perceived as beneficial by oil producers and problematic by oil importers). Stirling (2007; 1993) speaks of ambiguity as a type of uncertainty, which is caused not by lack of knowledge (the outcomes are known) but by the impossibility of defining probabilities, or otherwise ranking the different outcomes. This is why we speak of non-equivalent representations: equivalence allows ranking, while, for instance, temperature and length cannot be ranked as better or worse descriptions. In linking ambiguity to complexity, we argue that it is important to acknowledge the existence of incommensurability in the knowledge base. That is, although a lot of information can be produced about, for instance, the circular economy, there is no univocal way to combine these representations. Ambiguity emerges as the result of contradictions and inconsistencies between non-equivalent scientific representations, which cannot be scientifically solved. We stress the term scientific to signal that we are not arguing for relativism, or for an everything goes definition of ambiguity. One can analyse the quality of different knowledge claims, as is done by Quantitative Story-Telling described below. Quality, however, is not linked to truth, but it is rather defined as fitness for purpose (Funtowicz & Ravetz, 1993).

The purpose of circular representations of the economy may be to show how the outputs of one industry are used as inputs of another industry. The purpose of entropic representations is to show that materials are degraded through use. Circular representations are useful in the study of industrial symbiosis. Entropic representations are useful in the study of how many times one can recycle materials such as paper and textiles, or to point out the impossibility of recycling food and energy. Ambiguity emerges when ideas of industrial symbiosis are used to inform policy not only about the industrial sector, but about the economy as a whole, as in the circular economy.

The role of ambiguity in policy has been widely analysed in the literature (Funtowicz & Ravetz, 1990; Matland, 1995; Smith & Stirling, 2007; Stirling, 1993; Zahariadis, 2008). Matland (1995) distinguishes between ambiguity of goals, which is necessary to limit conflict, and ambiguity of means, which helps define policy when there is uncertainty over the technology needed or over the role that various organisations are to play in the implementation process. With reference to the EU, Zahariadis (2008) explains that ambiguity is an integral part of the policy-making process in contexts where there is a plurality of, often contrasting, interests, a multiplicity and high turnover of actors, and highly bureaucratic systems that lead to a fragmentation of the policy process. The position of the circular economy as a nexus policy that aims to build a bridge between environmental and economic policy, enhances the multiplicity of actors, the bureaucratic requirements and the plurality of interests.

Understanding the function of ambiguity in the policy process has important consequences for the interface between science and policy. Matland (1995) warns against the dysfunctional effects of clarity in policy implementation. The success of the circular economy imaginary may be better explained as the result of the alliances it allows because of the knowledge gaps and multiple interpretations that the concept allows. Although the Ellen MacArthur Foundation argues that an "exact account of the complete economic benefits" (2013: 6) would be more desirable to guide policy for the circular economy, it may be that it is precisely the ambiguity of a sixteenth century map that gathers support for the circular economy.

Governance in complexity

Complexity decouples truth from action, determinism from prediction, and rationality from certainty. Local rules can be described in deterministic terms, and can be rational, but at the level of the whole, that does not make the system easy to steer. Change, introduced by science and technology, poses a problem of uncertainty – both for science and for governance.

Uncertainty is not just a problem of missing data (which could be collected with more time, money, technology), not just a problem of models (which could be improved, refined, integrated, made interdisciplinary), not just a problem of ignorance (which could be reduced with more research, with the involvement of different people, cultures, practices). Uncertainty is also due to an object of study that changes as one studies it, and because one studies it. This is a problem that is well known in macroeconomics, for example in the mutually reinforcing interactions between inflation and expectations.

Complexity generates irreducible uncertainty for scientific research through radical openness. Radical openness is a situation in which the model of a system is embedded in a larger system, so that the boundaries of the representation can be expanded indefinitely until one produces a global model (Chu et al., 2003). This is the case of the circular economy. The system boundaries within which circularity should be measured are difficult to define: should one take into account only industry, or also agriculture and the energy sector? Should one take into account imports and exports or only what is extracted and discarded within national borders? If one expands the system boundaries to include imports and exports of inputs and waste, circularity needs to be defined at the level of the global economy, as for example done by Haas et al. (2015). The global economy, however, relies on the terrestrial ecosystem for the recycling of some resources, such as water and soil, which are processes that occur over hundreds of years, a scale at which economic cycles are irrelevant. Moreover, the earth relies on solar radiation for the water cycle, and at that scale, the very existence of humans may be irrelevant. The circulation of material resources is a case of radical openness, which leads to irreducible uncertainty.

The challenge for governance becomes one of: i) defining at which scale one should intervene, and ii) at which scale one should monitor results. Increasing the circularity of the European Union economies may lead to a relocation of "linear economic activities" to countries outside of the European Union, which in turn would lead to very different policy outcomes depending on whether results are measured at the European level or at the global level.

A second challenge is given by the fact that complex systems are adaptable. Governance occurs in a changing world, not a static world that can be observed from afar. One's actions and observations impact what is being observed and acted upon, and one is changed by observing and acting. In epistemic terms, this is referred to as contextuality. Chu et al. (2003) define contextuality as a situation in which multiple representations can be made of the same system, and in which although different representations share some system elements, these elements are linked to different causal explanations in different models. In the circular economy, this is the case of innovation. On one hand, innovation can improve product durability, thereby reducing the turnover of material resources and waste. On the other hand, innovating production processes and products means substituting current products and machinery for more circular products and machinery, thereby increasing the requirement of material resources needed for the restructuring of the production processes involved – and increasing waste by disposing of the less circular products and machinery. The causality between innovation and material throughput changes depending on the context.

Adaptability is not an argument against the adoption of innovations, rather it flags that innovation changes its context and its agents. For this reason, we argue that one is changed by observing and acting. In terms of governance, adaptability does not mean that actions will not have their intended effects, but that these effects may take place in a changing context and in a changing governance regime. For example, people's careers are rarely linear paths, in which one decides which profession to have, acquires professional education and training for that profession, and then works in the sector one envisioned when one first chose what to study. More often, while acquiring the education and training people redefine what their interests are; when they enter the job market, they adapt to the opportunities available and end up using the skills acquired in ways that they did not envision when they first chose what to study. The education and training acquired are useful, complexity does not mean that actions are ineffective. However, effects cannot be predicted and can only partially be steered.

We describe this situation as governance *in* complexity rather than governance *of* complexity, following Rip (2006). According to Rip, governance *of* complexity aims at governing systems "out there". Governance *in* complexity means that "in its non-modernist version, the governance actor recognises that being part of the evolving patterns, s/he can at best modulate them" (ibid.: 83). Governance *in* complexity is, therefore, a step back from grand challenges and the ambition to steer systemic economy-wide change, in favour of smaller and more localised interventions, which are updated and adapted to context while being implemented. Complexity does not need to lead to paralysis, but it does reduce the ambition of the circular economy.

Governance *in* complexity is based on the humility to recognise knowledge and its limits, and on the modesty to give prudent, rather than authoritative, advice to policy. Governance in the context of complexity entails letting go of predictability and control, letting go of precise science and allowing for uncertainty to be part of the information that science produces. That is, governance *in* complexity could be seen as a shift from treating uncertainty as a temporary issue, as something that more research and more funds can fix, into something that is unavoidably part of science and of policy making.

Scientific advice to policy

What type of advice can science give to policy in the context of uncertainty and complexity? We argue that in complexity, quantitative evidence becomes a form of "quantitative story-telling" about the governance of these systems. Quantitative story-telling is an approach developed in the research project MAGIC, which combines social research of policy narratives and imaginaries with quantitative methods of integrated assessment to explore the biophysical feasibility and economic viability of narratives (Ripa & Giampietro, 2017; Saltelli & Giampietro, 2017). Rather than trying (in vain) to speak Truth to Power, this type of analysis aims to improve political and democratic dialogue by exploring and clarifying the implications of policy options in relation to different purposes. Quantitative story-telling takes up the idea of knowledge quality assessment, and assesses the quality (in terms of fitness for purpose) of quantitative evidence, rather than its precision, accuracy, or truthfulness.

Returning to the example of circular and entropic representations of the economy, it becomes clear that quality is a relational concept. As opposed to truth, which can be defined in absolute terms, there is no absolute "best" representation in terms of quality. The circular representation is better for industrial process design, but may be worse in terms of climate change policy. If one focuses on the possible strategies for circularity of energy flows, such as the improvement of waste-to-energy processes, one may neglect the fact that energy use is always entropic, and always produces CO_2 emissions, therefore a circular economy may be as bad for climate as a linear economy. With regard to emissions, it is not the circularity of energy sources that counts, but the absolute consumption of energy. In addition, recycling processes are often energy intensive, and the climate impact of the circular sector of the economy should be analysed before embracing the circular economy as a win–win solution.

Quantitative story-telling consists of translating the plurality of world-views into a plurality of non-equivalent quantifications to compare and contrast different problem definitions. The application of Quantitative Story-Telling consists of using numbers to assess the quality story-tellings by using multiple scales of analysis to identify alternative narratives describing the same issue. Instead of looking for precise quantitative measurements formalised in a given scale and dimensions of analysis, the goal is to provide a richer characterisation of the system under study as a remedy against "hypocognition" (Lakoff, 2010), the limited understanding of problems due to the framing chosen, which implies a filtering on alternative explanations and on the definition of relevant aspects. The definition of what is relevant is brought to the fore, rather than buried in modelling practices, and is subject to debate.

Quantitative Story-Telling uses quantification to identify different narratives. Quantification is not merely the numerical expression of an observation but is the consequence of a series of pre-analytical choices made by a story-teller when choosing *what* to observe and *how*. Circularity can be operationalised by observing waste materials or chemical components in waste – and waste materials can be measured by weight, by volume, or by calorific value, while chemical components may be measured by toxicity or economic value. What is quantified depends on the choices of the observer. For this reason, instead of referring to the analyst as observer, the concept of story-teller is preferred. Story-telling implies agency: the choice of narrative and the consequent observation depend on the goals of the analysis, and are not a view from nowhere.

As Rittel and Webber point out, the information used to represent a problem "depends on one's idea for solving it" (1973: 161). In this context, numbers are not seen as conveying information but rather as representing a given perception. The insistence on the story-teller makes it possible to analyse apparent inconsistencies between different quantitative representations as the result of differences in purpose. Quantitative story-telling reconciles pluralism with quantification by treating numbers as a simplified representation of complex systems.

Quantitative Story-Telling emphasises how the use of quantification does not necessarily lead to closure, agreement or consistency. As a consequence, the act of quantification can co-exist with non-quantification (Callon & Law, 2005), without establishing a hierarchy of evidence. In the case of the circular economy, this means that the quantification of material flows in the economy is not necessarily of higher quality than a theoretical discussion of the effects of circularity on the pace of economic growth.

Some problems may not have a solution

Complexity informs decision-making about the trade-offs, the lack of control, and the contradictions, but is not necessarily conducive to action and solutions. One of the recurrent concepts of complexity is non-linearity. In the realm of policy, non-linearity means that policy measures might not achieve the expected outcomes. If there is no control of the system, actions and reactions are only loosely coupled. The fear is accordingly that awareness of complexity may lead to policy paralysis. In the MAGIC research project, the

> EC policy stakeholders who discussed the societal metabolism analyses were not necessarily convinced by our findings. This reluctance is unsurprising given the unconventional nature of the societal metabolism analysis; and that the results challenge existing policy without providing ready-to-implement solutions.
>
> (Matthews et al., 2017)

It does not come easy to policy-makers, nor their scientific advisors, to admit that one does not know what to do. It is close to a taboo in the political culture of the modern state, indeed of any state. If those in charge do not know what to do, is there even the need for a government? In this respect, the linear model of science speaking Truth to Power plays an important role in justifying the existence of government in the modern, secular state, equivalent to the legitimacy provided by religious authority in many pre-modern states. The linear model assumes that truth consists of clear yes and no instructions about well-defined problems. Power acts rationally and does what science reveals is the right action towards the desired outcomes. The science of well-defined problems is reductionist science.

High level of complexity means that there may not be easy solutions, and, in some cases, that some problems do not have a solution at all. This consideration does not inform decision making but absolves a very important function: that of taking a step back and asking, does it make sense for policy to be solution oriented? Is policy only necessary when there is "a problem" that needs to be "solved"? Complexity science does not speak towards what should be done but towards the quality of the process. Quantification does not preclude responsibility in the interpretation of evidence and of uncertainty.

We argue that the role of complexity-informed analyses is not that of offering solutions to policy problems, but that of facilitating change in institutional culture, to improve the quality of engagements between science and policy, rather than relying solely on the contested notions of truth and rationality for decision making.

With regard to the circular economy, complexity appears in the creation of feedback loops that slow down the economic process, in the openness of the system that renders material flows unaccountable, etc. From a theoretical point of view, the circular economy is an impossibility. In terms of policy process, however, the circular economy has the potential to introduce some changes. Waste management has changed its reputation: from an unpalatable subject that is rendered as an engineering problem of estimating the caloric content of waste for incinerators, the velocity of stirring probes in sludge treatment, and the speed of anaerobic digestion of organic waste, to something valuable that should be kept in the economy for as long as possible. Waste has gained status both in environmental concerns and as an economic opportunity. The potential of waste management to generate cultural change in institutions, however, is hindered by the technocratisation of the circular economy – which becomes about measuring circularity and producing indicators, rather than advancing knowledge about the yin and yang of economic processes, the fact that growth cannot happen without waste, and that negentropy cannot be decoupled from entropy.

For this reason, the critique of existing narratives is only partially aimed at improving the robustness of scientific evidence used to inform policy. Another important aim is that of contributing to the process of governance. In this respect, the message that there are no easy solutions is aimed at opening a reflection about the plausibility of solution-oriented policies. An alternative could be more prudent policies, increased awareness of the pros and cons of different policy measures, and a better understanding of uncertainty and complexity.

Less ambitious, more sensible policies

The circular economy in Europe is being put into action by mobilising accounting technologies and producing statistics and indicators about circularity. As argued in Chapter 7, indicators both measure and shape circularity. In this chapter, we add that accounting technologies restrict the circular economy to a technical issue and create a knowledge base for circular economy policy based on reductionism. The circular economy, however, is both radically open and characterised by contextuality, two challenges of complexity. As a result, reductionist policies are bound to fail to increase circularity in the biophysical sense.

As an alternative, we argue that a complexity informed policy should be less ambitious, more modest and prudent with respect to uncertainty. Rather than insisting on making the economy as a whole more circular, while recognising that the economy cannot be 100% circular, higher quality policy should tackle specific challenges, such as improving waste management, and increasing product durability, because of their own merits in complying with the waste hierarchy.

Ravetz (1971) introduced the essentially Aristotelian distinction between technical and practical problems into philosophy of science and its role(s) in society. "Technical" and "practical" in this context stand in a relation to each other in much the same way as "how" and "why", alluding to the Greek philosophical concepts of *techné* and *praxis*. Practical problems are about purposes, human, societal, and environmental needs. As such they can only be formulated and negotiated in the social world and cannot avoid having a political dimension. Technical problems are problems whose solutions are given by technical specifications. In Ravetz' analysis, perhaps the most harmful type of reductionism is the excessive belief in the success of applying science (and we would add bureaucracy) to reduce practical problems to technical problems.

What we are proposing in this chapter, is that the circular economy can live better if it avoids reduction to a merely technical problem, defined by measurements and indicators. Circular economy policies would be a success even though the economy cannot be circular, if they could inspire and stimulate creativity and entrepreneurship in civil society to develop and prepare stepping stones and building blocks towards a type of civilisation that destroys less of the biosphere. While this idea does not conform at all with current ideas about effective governance in large bureaucracies, we would not be surprised if politicians agree. What we propose, is less technocracy, more politics and more agency in civil society.

References

Ahl, V., & Allen, T. F. H. (1996). *Hierarchy Theory: A Vision, Vocabulary, and Epistemology*. New York: Columbia University Press.

Allen, T. F. H. (1987). Hierarchical complexity in ecology: a nonEuclidean conception of the data space. In I. C. Prentice, & E. van der Maarel, (Eds.), *Theory and Models in Vegetation Science* (pp. 17–25). Dordrecht: Springer Netherlands. doi:10.1007/978-94-009-4061-1

Allen, T. F. H., Austin, P., Giampietro, M., Kovacic, Z., Ramly, E., & Tainter, J. (2017). Mapping degrees of complexity, complicatedness, and emergent complexity. *Ecological Complexity*. doi:10.1016/j.ecocom.2017.05.004

Allen, T. F. H., & Starr, T. B. (1982). *Hierarchy Perspectives for Ecological Complexity*. Chicago, IL: University of Chicago Press.

Beck, U. (1992). *Risk Society: Towards a New Modernity*. London: Sage.

Callon, M., & Law, J. (2005). On qualculation, agency, and otherness. *Environmental Planning D: Society and Space*, 23, 717–733. doi:10.1068/d343t

Chu, D., Strand, R., & Fjelland, R. (2003). Theories of complexity: Common denominators of complex systems. *Complexity*, 8, 19–30. doi:10.1002/cplx.10059

Ellen MacArthur Foundation. (2013). *Towards the Circular Economy*. Retrieved from www.ellenmacarthurfoundation.org/assets/downloads/publications/Ellen-MacArthur-Foundation-Towards-the-Circular-Economy-vol.1.pdf

Funtowicz, S. O., & Ravetz, J. R. (1990). *Uncertainty and quality in science for policy*. Dordrecht: Kluwer Academic Publishers. doi:10.1016/0921–8009(92)90014-J

Funtowicz, S. O., & Ravetz, J. R. (1993). Science for the post-normal age. *Futures*, 739–755. doi:0016–3287/93/07739–17

Geyer, R. (2012). Can complexity move UK policy beyond "evidence-based policy making" and the "audit culture"? Applying a "complexity cascade" to education and health policy. *Polit. Stud.*, 60, 20–43. doi:10.1111/j.1467–9248.2011.00903.x

Haas, W., Krausmann, F., Wiedenhofer, D., & Heinz, M. (2015). How circular is the global economy? An assessment of material flows, waste production and recycling in the European Union and the world in 2005. *J. Ind. Ecol.*, 19, 765–777.

Holling, C. S. (1973). Resilience and stability of ecological systems. *Annual Review of Ecology and Systematics*, 4, 1–24.

Jasanoff, S. (2003). Technologies of humility: citizen participation in. *Minerva*, 41, 223–244.

Koestler, A. (1968). *The Ghost in the Machine*. London: Hutchinson.

Kovacic, Z., & Di Felice, L. J., 2019). Complexity, uncertainty and ambiguity: implications for European Union energy governance. *Energy Res. Soc. Sci.*, 53, 159–169.

Lakoff, G. (2010). Why it matters how we frame the environment. *Environmental Communication: A Journal of Nature and Culture*, 4, 70–81. doi:10.1080/17524030903529749

Matland, R. E. (1995). Synthesizing the implementation literature: The ambiguity-conflict model of policy implementation. *Journal of Public Administration Research and Theory*, 5, 145–174. doi:10.1093/oxfordjournals.jpart.a037242

Matthews, K. B., Blackstock, K. L., Rivington, M., Waylen, K. A., Miller, D. G., Wardell-Johnson, D., Kovacic, Z., Renner, A., Ripa, M., & Giampietro, M. (2017). Delivering more than the "Sum of the Parts": using quantitative storytelling to address the challenges of conducting science for policy in the EU land, water and energy nexus. 22nd Int. Congr. Model. Simul.

Mitchell, M. (2009). *Complexity: A Guided Tour*. Oxford: Oxford University Press.

Mitchell, S. D. (2009). *Unsimple Truths: Science, Complexity and Policy*. Chicago, IL: University of Chicago Press.

Nicolis, G., & Prigogine, I. (1977). *Self-Organization in Non-Equilibrium Structures*. New York: Wiley.

Perrow, C. (1984). *Normal Accidents: Living with High Risk Technologies*. New York: Basic Books.

Ravetz, J. R. (1971). *Scientific Knowledge and its Social Problems*. Oxford: Oxford University Press.

Rayner, S., 2012). Uncomfortable knowledge: the social construction of ignorance in science and environmental policy discourses. *Economy and Society*, 41, 107–125. doi:10.1080/03085147.2011.637335

Rip, A. (2006). A co-evolutionary approach to reflexive governance and its ironies. In J. P. Voss, D. Bauknecht, & R. Kemp (Eds.), *Reflexive Governance for Sustainable Development*. Cheltenham: Edward Elgar.

Ripa, M., & Giampietro, M. (2017). *Report on nexus security using Quantitative Story-Telling MAGIC* (H2020-GA 689669) Project Deliverable 4.1. Barcelona.

Rittel, H. W., & Webber, M. M. (1973). Dilemmas in a general theory of planning. *Policy Sciences*, 4, 155–169.

Rosen, R. (1991). *Life Itself: A Comprehensive Inquiry into the Nature, Origin, and Fabrication of Life*. New York: Columbia University Press.

Rosen, R. (1985). *Anticipatory Systems*. Oxford: Pergamon Press.

Saltelli, A., & Giampietro, M. (2017). What is wrong with evidence based policy, and how can it be improved? *Futures*, 91, 62–71.

Salthe, S. N. (2012. Hierarchical structures. *Axiomathes*, 22, 355–383. doi:10.1017/CBO9781107415324.004

Salthe, S. N. (1993). *Development and Evolution: Complexity and Change in Biology*. Boston: MIT Press.

Smith, A., & Stirling, A. (2007). Moving outside or inside? Objectification and reflexivity in the governance of socio-technical systems. *Journal of Environmental Policy Planning*, 9, 351–373. doi:10.1080/15239080701622873

Stirling, A. (1993). Keep it complex. *Nature*, 468, 1029–1031.

Stirling, A. (2007). Risk, precaution and science: towards a more constructive policy debate. *EMBO Rep.*, 8, 309–315.

Strand, R. (2002). Complexity, ideology and governance. *Emergence*, 4, 164–183.

Strand, R. (2013). Science, utopia and the human condition. *International Journal of Foresight and Innovation Policy*, 9, 110–124. doi:10.1504/ijfip.2013.058614

Zahariadis, N. (2008). Ambiguity and choice in European public policy. *Journal of European Public Policy*, 15, 514–530.

11 From the sixteenth to the twenty-first century

We conclude our journey through the concepts and politics of the circular economy with a forward outlook. Building on the discussion in Chapter 10, we suggest ways in which insights from complexity theory could be used to move from sixteenth century maps to twenty-first century modes of science-policy interfacing. We take inspiration from Annemarie Mol in distinguishing between logics of care and logics of choice in science-policy engagements. The logic of choice is based on the understanding of the science-policy interface as one-off engagements in which scientific information is passed on to decision-makers. Logics of care acknowledge the non-linear nature of policy-making as well as the contingencies and uncertainties involved. Taking seriously this view of the relationship between knowledge and policy making we argue for continuous engagement between a multiplicity of actors, with purposes that may go beyond decision-making and include social learning. This chapter explores ways in which indicators and "maps" could be constructed for the circular economy in a way that takes into account a plurality of social actors, beyond policy-makers and experts, and that faces the challenge of interfacing different stakes and values away from a confrontation between "Stop" and "Go" narratives and towards a care-based engagement. We conclude by looking at Eastern philosophy for inspiration: we resist the urge to provide a list of policy recommendations for the economy, and prefer to reflect on the way in which environmental, economic and social questions are governed.

Coming to terms with incomplete knowledge

As we discussed in Chapter 8, the circular economy is characterised by uncertainty. It is difficult to know how much waste is produced and how much is recycled, there are different accounting methods for the waste leading to problems of double accounting and data gaps, different countries collect statistics on material use in different ways and data are not always comparable, et cetera. Innovation plays an important role in the circular economy, as new products are supposed to be invented that are more durable, new processes are required to recycle and remanufacture products, new business models are needed to provide sharing opportunities and repair services. We argue that some of these uncertainties are irreducible: that is, more research will not lead to complete knowledge. As some questions are answered, new questions emerge. Platforms such as Airbnb and Uber may be one possible answer to business models for the sharing economy, but also raise new questions of quality, safety and health regulation, taxation, real estate speculation, creation of more precarious jobs and erosion of the welfare state, et cetera.

In this context, we argue that a different relationship between science and policy is required. The metaphor of the sixteenth century map suggests that gaps can be filled and that imaginaries can be turned into realities, in a trajectory towards a state in which science can be able to speak truth to power. We argue that the change that is needed is not from little evidence to more evidence in support of circular economy policies, but from the illusion of certainty to making sense of science under conditions of irreducible uncertainty. The twenty-first century map is not the exact map, it is a map of how to use the knowledge one has, recognise its limits, and make decisions under uncertainty. Science needs to speak both about the possibilities and the uncertainties to policy.

Communicating uncertainty is not just a matter of adding spread and probability distributions to data and indicators. Just like it is unfair to criticise policy officers for failing to live up to the aspiration of making European society more sustainable, when there are no clear pathways to follow, we also argue that it is unfair to add uncertainty analysis to the evidence that is presented to policy officers, and criticise them for their poor understanding of probability, when there is no complete knowledge. Communicating uncertainty is not just a matter of sharing the details of calculations, it is a means of recognising the fallibility and limits of scientific knowledge. Communicating uncertainty is a reflexive exercise that invites scientists to recognise that they do not know what to do either. The science-policy interface thus changes from a matter of communication to a collaboration, a shared responsibility, that is less about facts and more about humility. We argue that *how* science speaks to policy matters.

Logic of choice and logic of care

Governance in complexity is not about shifting responsibility. It is not about taking responsibility away from science and letting the policy-maker deal with uncertainty. A fruitful parallel can be made with health care: a doctor that informs the patient or the patient's family about their options with regard to a risky surgery does not make the decision any easier. Informing corresponds to a logic of choice: you know what the options are, now choose. The problem of complexity and uncertainty is not that it is difficult to communicate, but that in communicating uncertainty one shifts the burden of making an impossible choice to policy-makers. An alternative to that would be thinking of the science policy interface through the logic of care (Mol, 2008): difficult decisions are difficult to make.

Several scholars in the field of Science and Technology Studies have directed attention to the issue of "care" in technoscience (Felt et al., 2013; Mol, 2008; Puig de la Bellacasa, 2011). As an alternative to logics of choice that focus on one-time engagements for the sake of decision making based on sound scientific evidence, care-oriented approaches emphasise the need for continuous long-term engagement between heterogeneous actors thus taking into account the temporal dimension of technoscientific innovation. The shift from a logic of choice to a logic of care is especially important when acknowledging the complexity of contemporary problems and the uncertainty of scientific knowledge claims in situations in which there are no clear-cut options to choose from (Funtowicz & Strand, 2007).

The logic of care is not about being pessimistic and focusing on what cannot be done. Admitting the limits of knowledge does not mean that no policy advice can be given by science other than focusing on the environmental disasters that need to be stopped, or on unintended consequences. However, whereas the idea of unintended consequences subtly suggests that it is not possible (and thus not necessary) to think about all the problems that may arise from novel technologies, the logic of care invites dialogue, openness, humility. It invites relationships that are protracted in time. Humility means letting go of the idea of infallibility, without tossing science out with the famous bath water. While scientific knowledge cannot be used to predict the exact height that a child will grow up to, it can be used to say that certainly one will not grow to five metres in height. Biological laws hold even if they do not produce precise predictions. As scientists, we have to be able to say that we don't know, or that we did not get the result we expected, without losing funding. Care and humility thus invite reflection on the limits of science. In doing so they shift the focus away from a mere choice between scientifically pre-determined options back to the political practice of negotiation and decision-making. This then might counteract an ongoing 'de-politicisation' of policy-making. De-politicisation as a term has been used to direct attention the exactly this overly optimistic view of the potential of science to close controversies in policy-making and governance. This is the view that science will be able to exactly state for example tolerable exposures to certain chemicals, limits to environmental pollution or the what counts as hazardous substances in recycled materials. As such, authoritative scientific knowledge becomes a means for enabling the ideal of management and control in situations of uncertainty and ambiguity. The danger in this is that relying on science in situations of uncertainty might lead to a pre-emptive and misleading closure of necessary political debates. Thinking about the actors who should legitimately participate in such debates is one avenue of politicisation, considering different modes of participation is another one. This is, what thinking in terms of care directs attention to as Maria Puig de la Bellacasa points out:

> This version of caring for technology carries well the double significance of care as an everyday labour of maintenance that is also an ethical

obligation: we must take care of things in order to remain responsible for their becomings.

(Puig de la Bellacasa, 2011: 90)

One-off decisions are replaced by ideas of maintenance and staying responsible for the becoming of things. This means that the relation between science and policy needs to be re-thought and new modes of engagement need to be devised. It also entails letting go of the idea that there might be easy fixes for contemporary challenges. Crucially this would also bring with it a shift in accountability relations and potentially pose difficult questions about who is to blame if something goes wrong. This is also described in the work of Megan K. Halpern and her colleagues in their STS inspired reading of Mary Shelley's Frankenstein – a literary figure that has been used as a metaphor for scientific overreach and risky technologies. In their view, this is not a novel about the dangers of technology, but rather a reminder that it is evidently important not to abandon our creations to the world, but instead to participate "in the discourse and deliberation about how it is taken up and integrated into its social contexts" (Halpern, Sadowski, Eschrich, Finn, & Guston, 2016).

Care thus requires a cultural shift, that moves beyond and rejects easy-fix mentality. The silver bullets may be rare, but there may be long term improvements that require a lot of work and effort. A more responsible approach to the use of scientific information in policy would be understanding what science can contribute, where its strengths lie, and where its limits lie. The logic of care means building trust and respect for the knowledge of others, interest in understanding policy processes, the challenges that policy makers face, the multiple needs they have to attend to. Building respect and trust means that the effect of policies may not be predictable, but that does not automatically have to lead to crisis of trust in science and in political institutions.

We ended the previous chapter with a call for more agency in the public and in civil society. One strategy to deal with uncertainty and complexity, is to extend participation and create spaces for collective experimentation. Post-normal science, for example, refers to "extended peer communities" (Funtowicz & Ravetz, 1993) as a means of blurring the distinction between experts and lay people and extending the peer community of science. In the words of Ulrich Beck,

> In the fields of politics (and sub-politics) there is neither a single nor a 'best' solution, but always several solutions. As a consequence, political decision-making processes, no matter on what level they occur, can no longer be understood as the enforcement or implementation of a model determined in advance by some wise man or leader, whose rationality is not open to discussion and must be enforced even against the will and 'irrational resistance' of subordinated agencies, interests and citizens' groups. Both the formulation of the program and the decision-making process, as well as the enforcing of those decisions, must rather be

> understood as a process of *collective action* (Crozier and Friedberg 1979), and that means, even in the best case, collective learning and collective creation.
>
> (Beck, 1992: 191)

We argue that experimentation is a key concept in the context of uncertainty and complexity. Complexity can be paralysing, because every action may have a rebound effect, trade-offs, and other long-term aspects that are yet unknown. With our criticisms of the circular economy we do not suggest that nothing should be done, as in the "Stop" narrative. We rather sympathise with efforts to address problems of environmental degradation but argue that policy actions should not be implemented as solutions, but as experiments that may go wrong and may need to be corrected. Because experiments may go wrong, we speak of *collective* experimentation, to avoid that policies are tried out at the expense of those who cannot oppose them and cannot complain if things go wrong. The success of experiments such as participatory budgeting, first developed in the city of Porto Alegre in Brazil (de Souza Santos, 1998; Novy & Leubolt, 2005), lies precisely in the fact that the experiment involved the population at large, without exclusion of the poorer neighbourhoods, both in the design and evaluation of the project.

Extended participation also aims at opening up problem framings. By allowing a diverse set of actors to contribute to the discussions about the problems that need to be tackled, participatory science might be able to create "objects of care" (Halpern et al., 2016) and direct attention to "matters of concern" (Latour, 2004), as opposed to matters of fact. This is a means to distinguish, as discussed in Chapter 9, the legitimate concerns of policy makers who support the circular economy, from the sometimes illegitimate knowledge claims that are made about the potential of the circular economy. When it comes to matters of concern, the authors of this book share the concern for the unsustainability of the current economic system, for consumption patterns that privilege consumption over the quality of the experience. But we are also concerned about the authoritative use of scientific arguments that ignore decades of debates about the economic process, about the seemingly uncontroversial use of the circular economy imaginary that leaves little space for critical thinking. This points to the fact that "scientific and political authority are intertwined in culturally specific ways" (Brown, 2009: 212). When science stops to reflect its limits and potentially blind spots it runs the risk of becoming part of the problem in technocratic modes of evidence-based governance. Without critical thinking, can the circular economy have a scientific basis?

The twenty-first century map

Is the circular economy a good idea? Could anyone in his or her right mind seriously argue for less circularity? What is needed is not a yes or no answer to this question, but an understanding of what it means to answer one way or another. We have argued that policy should be based on a twenty-first century map, which is not a map that indicates where to go, but a map that helps to make sense of the uncertainties and complexities in science and in policy. In this section, we explore some of the debates that need to be taken into account with regard to the circular economy, in order to improve literacy of uncertainty and complexity.

One matter of concern central to the circular economy is sustainability. The sustainability debate raises a number of questions about how to care for the environment. Is it best to stop all human activity and stop interfering with the ecosystem? Is it possible to identify boundaries for human activity, within which it is environmentally safe to continue business as usual? What would it mean to cross those boundaries? Is the future of the environment at stake or is it the future of homo sapiens? Different images of the environment and different understandings of the relationship between humans and the environment come into play. Should there be areas of pristine environment, free from human intervention? Is human activity incompatible with the environment or are humans part of the ecosystem? These questions find different answers, some may support the creation of natural parks free of human activity, while others argue that indigenous peoples have been part of, for example, the rainforest ecosystem for thousands of years.

The sustainability debate is often framed as a matter of intergenerational justice. Which generation should take care of the environment? One possible reflection in this debate is to think not only of future generations, but also of past generations. From the eighteenth to the nineteenth centuries, forests in Central Europe had been decimated, to the point that contemporary reports spoke of desert-like landscapes. The advent of mechanisation in agriculture, which makes it harder to use marginal lands where tractors cannot be run, and the use of fossil fuels such as coal and gas for heating, have decreased demand for wood and contributed to the recovery of forested areas. The generations of the twentieth century could be said to have paid the "forested area" debt inherited from previous generations, but they have also caused new problems with the widespread use of fossil fuels. Which type of environment should one care for? The almost desert Europe of the past or the reforested Europe of the present? Is the fossil society worse for the environment than the wood-intensive society?

The circular economy side-steps these debates, by focusing on the economy. The environment is seldom part of the representations of the circular economy, except as an invisible source of raw materials or an equally invisible sink of waste and pollutants. The ecosystem is part of the imaginary of the Ellen MacArthur Foundation only as an idealised and stylised source of inspiration for industrial processes. We argue that these vague or almost absent notions of the environment fail to respond to the questions about sustainability of what, for whom and for how long (O'Connor, 2006). If sustainability is to be a matter of concern for the circular economy, the benefits of circularity need to be measured against the sustainability debate.

A second matter of concern is the question of habits and life style. The circular economy is about a change from the linear take-use-dispose model to circular re-use. Several criticisms have been raised, both towards circular products (Valenzuela & Böhm, 2017) and towards initiatives such as fair trade (Roy, Negrón-Gonzales, Opoku-Agyemang, & Talwalker, 2016) for failing to question the "more is better" assumption that underlies microeconomic models. By making consumption sustainable, for instance through circularity, people can continue to buy new things while feeling ethical about it. Circularity would then be a palliative to greater change, including changes in consumption patterns. This is a debate about life style and care for people. This criticism can include questions of equity: Whose consumption and whose life style are to be improved? The idea that people may lower their consumption makes sense in the Global North but is insulting in the slums of the Global South.

The idea of a sharing economy can be read both as an opportunity to re-think life styles and as an unquestioning reproduction of unequal patterns of consumption. Car sharing, for example, can be seen as an alternative to car ownership, or as an additional service that people use to travel long distance (as in the case of Bla-BlaCar, see www.blablacar.com) on top of owning a car for daily commuting. Can ideas of sharing economy lead to a deeper reflection about who needs to own what? Or is the sharing economy an elitist fantasy that ignores the fact that most of the world's poor don't even own a house, let alone a car? One may also ask who is supposed to share what. Sharing platforms are very popular with tourists seeking to rent a vacation home in Southern Europe, but no sharing platform exists that gives people access to the welfare state of Scandinavian countries.

The circular economy is associated with the need to raise awareness among "consumers" about the need to reduce waste and increase recycling. However, to care for people, it would be more important to take the issues that people care about seriously. Questions of equity, quality, life style, safety, et cetera. are central to this debate, to move away from superficial considerations of what people need to be informed about or convinced of. Care in this context means moving away from treating people as consumers, or as cyborgs that will respond rationally to a new influx of information, and engaging with people as beings capable of defining their own identity.

A third matter of concern raised in our discussion of the science-policy interface is how to care for the policy process. If the circular economy stems from the good intentions of policy makers to include environmental concerns in policy and if there is no clear solution to environmental degradation because of the complexity of the system, it is unfair to criticise policy makers for trying to do something. The care for the policy process involves two different debates: on one hand, the recognition of the very difficult job that policy makers have in the context of uncertainty and complexity, and on the other hand, the concern for the viability and desirability of the policy.

Recognising the value of good intentions is tricky. In Chapter 9, we pointed out the action bias both of the Bios and Geos meta-narratives. In first aid courses, one of the most important lessons is that moving an injured person around may do more harm than doing nothing. No matter the good intention to help, one should call emergency services and wait. In more general terms, having good intentions does not absolve people from taking responsibility for their actions if things go wrong. We speak of the good intentions of many policy officers as a way of recognising that bad policies are not necessarily the result of corrupt policy makers, nor lack of interest. When we criticise circular economy policies, we are not criticising the people who support this policy, and we recognise how difficult it is to govern in the context of uncertainty and complexity. Nevertheless, good intentions do not mean that the policy itself should not be criticised.

A fair criticism of the circular economy entails not only identifying the uncertainties, but also opening the debate about who should make decisions in the context of uncertainty. Who should make value judgements, when facts are not available? Who takes the blame if things go wrong? We argue that the "goodness power" of nexus policies and of the circular economy is not conducive to debates about uncertainty and responsibility. The logic of care should not be confused with apparent consensus. We turn again to Ulrich Beck to argue that in the context of uncertainty these debates need to be taken to society at large, and not be solved within the confined boundaries of the science-policy interface.

> Politics is no longer the only or even the central place where decisions are made on the arrangement of the political future. What is at stake in elections and campaigns is not the election of a 'leader of the nation' who then holds the reins of power and is to be held responsible for everything good and bad that happens during his term of office. If this were so, we would be living in a dictatorship that elects its dictator, but not in a democracy. One can go so far as to say that all notions of centralisation in politics are inversely proportional to the degree of democratisation of a society. It is so important to recognise this because the compulsion to operate with the fiction of centralised state power creates the background of expectations against which the reality of political interdependence appears as a weakness, a failure, which can only be corrected by a 'strong hand', even though it is the exact opposite, a sign of universalised citizen rebelliousness in the sense of active cooperation and opposition.
>
> (Beck, 1992: 233)

Non-violence and non-action: ancient oriental perspectives on governance

The French anthropologist and STS scholar Bruno Latour (Latour, 1998) used the Shakespearean formula when discussing the dilemma of sustainability: "To ecologize or to modernize, that's the question" (Latour 1998). What is this confusing, patchwork map of the circular economy in the twenty-first century indicated in the passages above? Is it at all something to consider in a modern society?

We will end this book with two replies to that question. One reply is the modern one: Yes, the acknowledgement of uncertainty and ambiguity, of the need for praxis and for piecemeal contributions to governance in complexity is indeed modern but not the type of modernity that was unreflexively embracing its grand narrative of progress. Rather, it would be a case of Ulrich Beck's reflexive modernisation whereby modern institutions try to implement the insight that they are not in control and that they do not only produce benefits but also unforeseen consequences, risk, uncertainty and ambiguous change.

At the same time, quoting the same Latour, "We have never been modern" (Latour, 1993). Modernity was never the clean cut between science and politics, nature and culture, and humanity and the non-humans as was proposed. On the contrary, these dichotomies resulted from a particular type of work at a particular stage of history. Latour called it a work of purification, an intellectual and ideological type of work to provide legitimacy to expanding human civilisation and technology into what Herman Daly called a full world. What should humanity do now that it is slowly realising that this was ideology even in its derogatory sense of false consciousness, and that this ideology was instrumental in arriving at a point where our own technology, knowledge and civilisation have become our largest threat to long-term survival?

Latour was right in pointing out that also political ecology were victims of what we bluntly choose to call false consciousness: They always talked as if they wanted to leave Nature alone but in actual practice, environmentalist action invariably was interventionist both in society and nature, regulating, moving and changing things (Latour, 1998). Geos suffers from the same action bias as Bios.

From an Occidental (and predominantly masculine) perspective that goes much further back in time than modernity, there is basically only one type of alternative to action and activity, namely passivity, nihilism, and surrender. The action bias resonates with and aggravates a sense of urgency: Environmental crises are impending (or even here). We have to act now, take control and fix the problem. What this book has argued, throughout all its chapters, is that the sense of urgency leads to bad choices and dysfunctional governance. Would it be possible to let go of the sense of urgency without denying the gravity of the situation or giving in to despair?

There are several directions to look for such possibilities. Ecofeminism is one such direction that we will not pursue in this volume. Another alternative is to make an intellectual travel to the East, to the Indian and yogic virtue of non-violence or *ahimsa,* of creating no harm or injury. When dealing with the challenge of governance in complexity, however, we have found it inspiring to go even further East, to the ancient Chinese concept of *wu wei* or non-action that emerged in Confucian thought almost three thousand years ago. The concept was further developed and refined in the Daoist philosophy, especially in the tradition of Zhuangzi, whose ways of explaining non-action make it quite different from passivity and surrender. Zhuangzi was a Chinese philosopher who is thought to have lived from the fourth to the third century BC. Works attributed to him have been translated in (Zhuangzi, 2003).

Dao (often written Tao) is a Chinese word that can be translated as "way". In Daoist philosophy it first of all refers to Nature, that is, Nature's Way or in more modern terms, the nature and workings of the Universe. Humans can also have their Dao. The Dao of a person is how that individual came to live her or his life in terms of practices and virtues. For instance, the "do" in martial arts such as ju-do, ken-do and aiki-do is the Japanese equivalent of the Chinese word Dao. "Do" signifies that the martial artist is anything but a technician or a trickster but has chosen a way of life. It is much more than a set of skills. Essentially it means that the person lives by a code of conduct and devotes her or himself to practice the martial art and thereby improve oneself in terms of virtue.

The fundamental insight from which all Daoist thought flows is that we should not confuse or conflate Nature or the Universe itself with our human concepts and descriptions of it. The first line of Laozi's *Tao Te Ching* states this in the most concise form: The Dao that is named is not the real Dao (Lao-Tzu, 1993). The name and the thing are not the same. Nature is more complex than our understanding and evades full description, and whenever humans forget this, they lead themselves into error. Two thousand years later a quite similar insight was elaborated in Western philosophy by Immanuel Kant: we have to distinguish between the world in itself, which we cannot observe, and the world as it appears to us with our particular sensory and cognitive apparatus, including our science.

Daoist understandings of *wu wei* and the Dao are radical and provocative to a Western modern mind who wants to take control and maximise utility. In its least provocative form, a Daoist perspective on the current environmental problems would advise against all forms of futile action. Nature is more powerful than man, and we do not solve problems in the long run by working against nature. Metaphorically speaking, water has to flow down the river and it is futile to spend a lot of energy on pushing water upwards the river. In ecological economics, the concept of the Dao has been applied by Mario Giampietro and colleagues (Giampietro, Mayumi, & Sorman, 2012) to highlight how and why reductionist approaches to environmental science and governance tend to fail. For instance, if humans are to stay on this planet we would have to respect the fact that water and nutrient cycles in the biosphere are not under our control and will never be. Accordingly, modern industrial societies need to stop disrupting them. Daoist classics were written in times of political if not environmental chaos in China. If we consider Daoism a philosophy of freedom, it is not a philosophy of how to free the world from suffering. Rather, it is a philosophy of how humans should free themselves, emotionally and spiritually, from the world and its necessities.

Doctrines of *wu wei* differ. In some later traditions in China, they are almost instrumentalist: One can effectively achieve one's goal by pushing less and steering the people in the right direction by silent, subtle and inconspicuous moves. Chinese thought knew of "nudging" millennia before it became fashionable in the West. Laozi's and Zhuangzi's *wu wei* is something different, however. Both these philosophical texts emphasise that the problems of unwise life and unwise governance begin with excessive ego, self-consciousness and desire. Wise governance in society as well as the wise way of living as a human being is characterised by overcoming conventional values, the ego and the pursuit of fame, power and utility. One step towards that goal is to overcome the desire to evaluate and classify everything as positive or negative, useful or useless, good or evil. What appears useless to humans, with our particular knowledge, timeframe, and cognitive apparatus, may indeed be useful in ways we do not appreciate – its description may indicate that a certain thing or state of affairs is useless or bad, but we should not make the mistake of conflating the description with the thing itself. Descriptions and concepts are something we use to pursue our desires; in order to overcome desires, we have to realise that concepts and desires are two sides of the same coin. Anachronistically we can also add, they are both connected to solutionism and will to power. Wisdom is therefore something quite different from knowledge and power. To the extent that language can convey or help grow wisdom, it will have to employ other strategies than describing states of affair. Indeed, Laozi is written as poetry, while Zhuangzi is a mixture of poetic fables to inspire wisdom and philosophical *reductio ad absurdum* to display the limitations of logic and rational argument. Zen Buddhism inherited this style with their paradoxes and *koans*.

Overcoming desires in turn overcomes the sense of urgency. The Dao will do what it will do. This does not mean that we should remain passive, because we are indeed part of the Dao, but it means that the wise person will plan less, because things are not going to go according to the will of the planner, but according to the will of the river. He or she will be less afraid of the result because we are often not capable of assessing correctly what is good and bad anyway, especially not in the long run. This means, of course, that one will have to prepare to accept losses, pain and ultimately death as part of the Dao. Indeed, the wise person will let go of the fear of pain and death. In the Western history of ideas, the same type of thought developed above all in Stoic philosophy.

The concept of a logic of care emerged out of care ethics, a brand of virtue ethics. The Daoist perspective resonates well with virtue ethics. Consequences of action will not be the evaluation criterion because consequences are neither under our control nor for us to assess, at least not in the short term. Laozi has been interpreted as suggesting that we look for our virtues in Nature – that the Dao of the Universe can inspire us to define our Dao, an idea that actually can be recognised in the butterfly diagram of the Ellen MacArthur Foundation. The same is true of biomimicry as a design concept for sustainable innovation. Zhuangzi does not seem to argue in that way; in that sense he predates Jean-Paul Sartre and philosophical existentialism by 2300 years by insisting that the free will of humans is part of the Dao, implying that we cannot avoid our own life choices. Humanity can choose to continue with our current economic system and refine that as our Dao. There is nothing wrong with this except that we are likely to destroy the very conditions of our existence and, with time, experience the collapse of biophysical funds and the collapse of human civilisation, perhaps even our extinction. The most consequent Stoic or Daoist might agree that this is a sad prospect but would add that this sadness is just ours. It is just the expression of a desire that we might want to let go of.

Zhuangzi would probably not conclude with such a level of Stoic indifference. Rather, he might ask what virtue that human Dao of consumption, growth and capitalism holds. Is this 'Way' the way we really want to live by? Funtowicz and Strand (2011) arrived at a similar conclusion in a piece on governance in uncertainty, complexity and change, via a reflection on Hannah Arendt's concept of praxis:

> Barring and bracketing the environmentalist talk – which also has been an important part of our own talk – of planetary dangers, we would like to propose that the planet is indeed not the object at risk. The object at risk is we ourselves as a collective (present and future) subjectivity and agency: the human right behind the human rights: that of personhood and hope. With personhood and hope in focus, the challenge is not the usual of what to do but, more importantly, how to do it as certain avenues of action are now deemed unacceptable.
>
> (ibid.: 1002)

The logic and ethics of care also lead to the necessity of politicisation, of bringing the questions of what to sustain, for whom, why and when, into the public sphere. With Arendt, one can render visible issues at stake that are graver than climate change: It is not obvious that an eco-totalitarian state *à la* Hitler, Stalin or Pol Pot is to be preferred to human extinction, however sustainable. With Zhuangzi, we are reminded that our own individual existence is limited to living now, however much we plan for the future. Chapter 10 ended with our constructive suggestion for the circular economy:

> Circular economy policies would be a success even though the economy cannot be circular, if they could inspire and stimulate creativity and entrepreneurship in civil society to develop and prepare stepping stones and building blocks towards a type of civilisation that destroys less of the biosphere.

We commented that this vision might even be palatable for politicians and citizens. Perhaps, though, that would depend on what implicit theory of change they would hold – perhaps they would tend to believe that such action is likely to ensure sustainability and secure livelihoods and wellbeing.

We do not hold such a belief. From the Daoist perspective we do not believe that humans can decide and control their future. At the time of writing, the year of 2019, the human population on Earth counted almost 8 billion individuals. It is wholly imaginable that the combination of such a large population, the current type of economic system and technosphere, and the already existing destructions of funds already is too much for a collapse to be avoided. Perhaps Earth can only absorb less than a billion humans with a relatively modest consumption and use of natural resources for any great length of time. If so, it is difficult to imagine that the transition from eight to one billion is going to be anything like the likeable imaginaries of the EU or the UN for that matter. It may also be the case that any effort now to avoid or soften that transition will have no impact on it, or perhaps even a paradoxical impact.

Still, from the Daoist perspective we would commit to the constructive programme, destroying less, improving waste management, paying respect to nature and other living beings, "going circular". If the economy requires more recycling, remanufacturing, repair and maintenance, these are economic sectors that need to be expanded and that need resources (energy, labour). This means a reallocation of resources from high value-added economic sectors to "background" or "infrastructural" economic sectors. This would change the economy from the (acceleration of) production of flows, to the maintenance of funds. Such changes would be profound and still they cannot guarantee that the future will be bright and that environmental disasters will be kept at bay. Overcoming solutionism and action bias means that one would have to let go of the insistence that the future must be bright, of the need of reaching Millennium Development Goals, Sustainable Development Goals and other such fantasies, and that there must be progress. Humans cannot decide what the world must be. We would commit to these changes because it would be a virtuous thing to do – it would be a good way for humans to live while on this planet, one of many possible good ways. Where it leads, nobody can know; but we do not have to know.

References

Beck, U. (1992). *Risk Society: Towards a New Modernity*. London: Sage.
Brown, J. (2009). Democracy, sustainability and dialogic accounting technologies: Taking pluralism seriously. *Critical Perspectives on Accounting*, 20, 313–342.
de Souza Santos, B. (1998). Participatory budgeting in Porto Alegre: Toward a redistributive democracy. *Politics & Society*, 26(4), 461–510.
Felt, U., Barben, D., Irwin, A., Joly, P.-B., Rip, A., Stirling, A., & Stockelová, T. (2013). *Science in Society: Caring for our Future in Turbulent Times*. Strasbourg: European Science Foundation.
Funtowicz, S. O., & Ravetz, J. R. (1993). Science for the post-normal age. *Futures*, (September), 739–755. doi:0016-3287/93/07739–17
Funtowicz, S. O., & Strand, R. (2007). Models of science and policy. In T. Traavik (Ed.) *Biosafety First-Holistic Approaches to Risk and Uncertainty in Genetic Engineering and Genetically Modified Organisms* (pp. 263–278). Trondheim, Norway: Tapir Academic Press.
Funtowicz, S., & Strand, R. (2011). Change and commitment: Beyond risk and responsibility. *Journal of Risk Research*, 14(8), 995–1003. doi:10.1080/13669877.2011.571784

Giampietro, M., Mayumi, K., & Sorman, A. H. (2012). *The Metabolic Pattern of Societies: Where Economists Fall Short*. London and New York: Routledge.

Halpern, M. K., Sadowski, J., Eschrich, J., Finn, E., & Guston, D. H. (2016). Stitching together creativity and responsibility. *Bulletin of Science, Technology & Society*, 36(1), 49–57. doi:10.1177/0270467616646637

Lao-Tzu. (1993). *Tao Te Ching*. New York: Hackett Publishing Company.

Latour, B. (1993). *We Have Never Been Modern*. Cambridge, MA: Harvard University Press.

Latour, B. (1998). To modernize or to ecologize? That's the question. In B. Braun, & N. Castree (Eds.), *Remaking Reality: Nature at the Millenium* (pp. 221–242). London: Routledge.

Latour, B. (2004). Why has critique run out of steam? From matters of fact to matters of concern. *Critical Inquiry*, 30(2), 225–248. doi:10.2307/1344358

Mol, A. (2008). *The Logic of Care: Health and the Problem of Patient Choice*. Oxon and New York: Routledge.

Novy, A., & Leubolt, B. (2005). Participatory budgeting in Porto Alegre: Social innovation and the dialectical relationship of state and civil society. *Urban Studies*, 42(11), 2023–2036. doi:10.1080/00420980500279828

O'Connor, M. (2006). The "four spheres" framework for sustainability. *Ecological Complexity*, 3(4), 285–292. doi:10.1016/j.ecocom.2007.02.002

Puig de la Bellacasa, M. (2011). Matters of care in technoscience: Assembling neglected things. *Social Studies of Science*, 41(1), 85–106. doi: 10.1177/0306312710380301

Roy, A., Negrón-Gonzales, G., Opoku-Agyemang, K., & Talwalker, C. (2016). *Encountering Poverty*. Oakland: University of California Press.

Valenzuela, F., & Böhm, S. (2017). Against wasted politics: A critique of the circular economy. *Ephemera Journal*, 17(7), 23–60.

Zhuangzi, Z. (2003). *Basic Writings*. New York: Columbia University Press.

Index

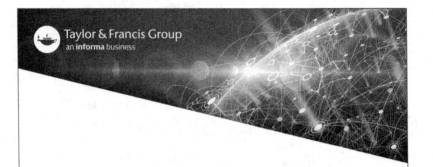

Printed in the United States
by Baker & Taylor Publisher Services